Mothers of
All Children

Mothers of All Children

*Women Reformers
and the
Rise of Juvenile Courts
in Progressive Era America*

Elizabeth J. Clapp

The Pennsylvania State University Press
University Park, Pennsylvania

Library of Congress Cataloging-in-Publication Data

Clapp, Elizabeth J. (Elizabeth Jane), 1960–
    Mothers of all children : women reformers and the rise of juvenile
courts in progressive-era America / Elizabeth J. Clapp.

        p.   cm.
    Includes bibliographical references and index.
    ISBN 0-271-01777-5 (cloth : alk. paper)
    ISBN 0-271-01778-3 (pbk. : alk. paper)
    1. Juvenile courts—United States—History.   2. Women social
reformers—United States—History.   3. United States—Social
conditions—1865–1918.   I. Title.
    KF9794.C58   1998
    345.73'081'09—dc21   97-49129
                                                                          CIP

Copyright © 1998 The Pennsylvania State University
All rights reserved
Printed in the United States of America
Published by The Pennsylvania State University Press
University Park, PA 16802-1003

It is the policy of The Pennsylvania State University Press to use acid-free paper for
the first printing of all clothbound books. Publications on uncoated stock satisfy
the minimum requirements of American National Standard for Information Sciences—Permanence of Paper for Printed Library Materials, ANSI Z39.48-1992.

Contents

For my parents, Richard and Susan Clapp

Acknowledgments

This book has been several years in gestation and during that time has undergone a large number of changes. As it has progressed, I have accumulated a vast number of debts both academic and personal. It is with great pleasure that I can at last acknowledge them.

My greatest debt is to Melvyn Stokes, an exemplary Ph.D. supervisor who indefatigably read and reread the manuscript at its various stages of development. His sharp eye for detail, encouragement, and good humor have been absolutely invaluable, and his influence is apparent even in the final manuscript. The year I spent as a graduate exchange student in the history department at the University of Illinois at Urbana-Champaign opened my mind to new aspects of American history and allowed me to pursue my research in a library possessing a collection of resources undreamed of on this side of the Atlantic. The faculty and graduate students of the history department provided an intellectual community that inspired me then and have continued to do so. Special thanks go to Jim Barrett as well as to Mark Leff, who introduced me to women's history. I also wish to thank Debra Allen, Terri Kaminski, and Elizabeth Dunn, for whose friendship and endless hours of discussion I am particularly grateful. Their families, too, have always been welcoming and generous.

I have been fortunate in the American History community in Britain, whose enthusiasm and scholarship have been a source of strength. Those attending seminars and conferences at which I have given papers have provided helpful criticism and suggestions for the improvement of the manuscript in various forms. The comments I received on the paper I gave at the Commonwealth Fund Conference on "Welfare, Women and the State," held at University College London in January 1993, helped especially to focus my ideas more clearly at a time when I was expanding my thesis into the manuscript for this book.

A number of people have read part or all of the manuscript at various stages. I would like to thank particularly Christine Bolt and Peter Parish, the examiners of my thesis, as well as Vivien Hart and several anonymous readers who commented on sections that have since been published as articles. Sonya Michel and another anonymous reader offered helpful comments and advice on how to revise the final manuscript. They all took time out of busy schedules, and I am grateful for their suggestions. I wish also to thank Peter Potter, my editor at the Pennsylvania State University Press, and his editorial team, who guided this manuscript through its various stages to publication with great patience and encouragement.

Sections of this book have previously appeared in *Mid-America and the Journal of American Studies*. I am grateful to the editors of these journals for permission to reuse some of the main arguments from my earlier articles.

In the course of my research both for the thesis and this book I have visited a number of libraries and archives on both sides of the Atlantic. Staff members at these facilities have impressed me with their professionalism and willingness to help. I extend my thanks particularly to Alison Cowden at the University of London Library; the archivists at the Chicago Historical Society Manuscripts Department; Mary Ann Bamberger and her colleagues at the Special Collections, University of Illinois at Chicago; Joan Surrey at the Rockford College Archives, Rockford, Illinois; the archivists in the Manuscript Division of the Library of Congress; and Cynthia Swanson, the Director of the Women's History and Resource Center of the General Federation of Women's Clubs in Washington, D.C.

In the course of my research for this book, I have received funding from a number of sources: University College London, which provided me a graduate exchange studentship at the University of Illinois at Urbana-Champaign; the Bellot Fund at University College London; the research fund of the Department of Economic and Social History, University of Birmingham; and the Arts Faculty Budget Centre Research Committee of the University of Leicester, which supplied a Grant in Aid of Research. I am very grateful to each of these bodies for their generous assistance.

I am fortunate in the support I have received from my colleagues in the history department at the University of Leicester, particularly Professor Bill Brock and Professor Richard Bonney, my senior colleagues, and Graham Smith, who has helped immeasurably in sorting out gremlins in the computer system.

Friends and family members have been unstinting in their support throughout this project. Susan-Mary Grant has shared with me the problems of being a female historian of the United States in the very male world of British academia. My brothers have provided both moral support and encouragement, as well as an unfailing ability to bring me back down to earth. My parents, Richard and Susan Clapp, have done more than I have any right to expect. Their love, interest, and assistance—both practical and moral—have always been without measure. This book is dedicated to them. Finally, I address my husband, David Wykes, who has never ceased to amaze me with his love, good humor, and sound practical editorial advice. Thank you.

Introduction

Unfortunate childhood must suffer unless women recognize that a larger motherhood is required of them than to care only for their own children. Until they give to every subject affecting childhood the mother thought and care, we shall see the same old system which has marred thousands of lives and made criminals of children who might just have easily have been made into good citizens.

—Mrs. Hannah Schoff, 1904

Although today the juvenile court movement is usually associated with Judge Ben Lindsey and the Denver Juvenile Court,[1] the first and probably most influential juvenile court was established in Chicago in July 1899. Women there were clearly the dominant influence in pushing for reform, and the juvenile courts established in many other cities and towns over the next decade were very often the result of initiatives by women reformers influenced by the Chicago model. By 1904 the pioneering role women had played in promoting the welfare of children was recognized by Mrs. Hannah Schoff in her contribution to a report on the development of the juvenile courts.[2] She noted especially that women had an important part to play in helping those children in trouble with the law. Mrs. Schoff believed that the best way to deal with these problem children was to secure a juvenile court in every state. She was clearly not alone, either in demanding that women take a central part in campaigning for such a reform or in articulating it in terms of woman's maternal duty. Many other women voiced similar beliefs, and women played a key role in campaigns for social welfare re-

1. This is the case in many general histories, but specialized histories of the juvenile court movement are more circumspect. For examples of the former, see Harold U. Faulkner, *The Quest for Social Justice, 1898–1914* (New York, 1931); Eric F. Goldman, *Rendezvous with Destiny: A History of Modern American Reform* (New York, 1952); Arthur A. Ekirch Jr., *Progressivism in America: A Study of the Era from Theodore Roosevelt to Woodrow Wilson* (New York, 1974); Samuel E. Morison, Henry S. Commager, and William E. Leuchtenberg, *A Concise History of the American Republic* (New York, 1977).

2. Hannah Kent Schoff, "A Campaign for Childhood," in Samuel J. Barrows, ed., *Children's Courts in the United States: Their Origins, Development and Results* (Washington D.C., 1904), 136.

form during the Progressive Era, especially those campaigns that focused on children. Nor was Mrs. Schoff the first woman to articulate these ideas, for the female reformers in Chicago had earlier framed their demand for a juvenile court in the name of their duty as mothers.

In examining the origins of the juvenile courts, this study focuses on the role of women reformers in the movement and the importance of gender consciousness in influencing the particular shape the reform took. Clearly, male reformers were also involved, but by placing this examination of the juvenile court movement within the context of recent scholarship by historians of women, it has become necessary to challenge previously held assumptions that men were the central and dominating force behind the movement.[3] In many respects, the juvenile court movement is illustrative of the concerns of gender historians. Until recently, the involvement of women in many Progressive Era social welfare reforms has been hidden, and historians have assumed that male reformers dominated.[4] This book contributes to the scholarship in this area by suggesting that women reformers played a pivotal role in one of the earliest of these social welfare reforms—the establishment of juvenile courts.

The establishment of juvenile courts in cities across the United States was one of the earliest social welfare reforms of the Progressive Era and represented a major change in the way in which the law dealt with wayward children. The first juvenile court law was passed in Illinois in 1899. Within a decade, twenty-two other states had passed similar laws, based on the Illinois example. The speed at which juvenile court laws were adopted across the United States reflects the extent to which they met a clearly felt need among reformers for new ways of dealing with dependent and delinquent

3. The most useful earlier works on the establishment of juvenile courts in the United States are Herbert H. Lou, *Juvenile Courts in the United States* (Chapel Hill, 1927); Anthony M. Platt, *The Child Savers: The Invention of Delinquency* (Chicago, 1969); Joseph M. Hawes, *Children in Urban Society: Juvenile Delinquency in Nineteenth-Century America* (New York, 1971); Robert M. Mennel, *Thorns and Thistles: Juvenile Delinquents in the United States, 1825–1940* (Hanover, N.H., 1973); Steven L. Schlossman, *Love and the American Delinquent: The Theory and Practice of "Progressive" Juvenile Justice, 1825–1920* (Chicago, 1977); Ellen Ryerson, *The Best Laid Plans: America's Juvenile Court Experiment* (New York, 1978); David J. Rothman, *Conscience and Convenience: The Asylum and Its Alternatives in Progressive America* (Boston, 1980); John R. Sutton, *Stubborn Children: Controlling Delinquency in the United States, 1640–1981* (Berkeley and Los Angeles, 1988); Eric C. Schneider, *In the Web of Class: Delinquents and Reformers in Boston, 1810s–1930s* (New York, 1992); Charles Larsen, *The Good Fight: The Life and Times of Ben B. Lindsey* (Chicago, 1972). Only Platt looks specifically at women reformers.

4. For a review of this literature, see Elizabeth J. Clapp, "Welfare and the Role of Women: The Juvenile Court Movement," *Journal of American Studies* 3 (December 1994): 359–83.

children. Many reformers during the 1890s had begun to recognize that existing methods rarely solved the problem of juvenile delinquency and often exacerbated it. The Juvenile Court Law embodied the fundamental idea that the state must exercise guardianship over a child found under such adverse social and individual circumstances as might develop into crime. It formally established separate courts for the hearing of children's cases, provided for the appointment of probation officers by the courts, and placed on a legal footing the belief that the justice system should treat children as children rather than as criminals.[5]

Women played a central role in the juvenile court movement throughout the United States, sometimes as individuals but more often as members of women's clubs, settlement houses, and national organizations. The extent of their involvement varied, but it was rare for a state to pass juvenile court legislation without at least the active support of local women. Nor were female juvenile court reformers homogeneous. Certainly, most came from middle-class backgrounds and espoused maternalist values; but they displayed quite different perceptions of the problem they sought to solve, and their approaches differed quite markedly from those of the male reformers. Thus, this book goes beyond the simple task of writing women back into the history of the juvenile court movement and seeks to examine the interaction between gender consciousness and the shaping of social welfare reform. These pages suggest, too, that although gender consciousness was a highly significant element in prompting women to pursue this reform, other factors were also important.

The kind of gender consciousness that prompted women to become involved in social welfare reform during the Progressive Era has recently been labeled "maternalism" by a number of historians of women.[6] The concept of maternalism accepted, even idealized, women's traditional role as wife and mother but at the same time insisted that women had a duty to extend their female skills and concerns beyond their own homes. The discourse of

5. "An Act to Regulate the Treatment and Control of Dependent, Neglected and Delinquent Children," July 1, 1899, as outlined in Report of the Chicago Bar Association Committee on Juvenile Courts, Chicago, October 28, 1899, pp. 5–6, typescript, Manuscript Division, Chicago Historical Society.

6. Definitions of maternalism may be found in Seth Koven and Sonya Michel, "Womanly Duties: Maternalist Politics and the Origins of Welfare States in France, Germany, Great Britain, and the United States, 1880–1920," *American Historical Review* 95 (October 1990): 1076–1108; Sonya Michel and Robyn Rosen, "The Paradox of Maternalism: Elizabeth Lowell Putnam and the American Welfare State," *Gender and History* 4 (Autumn 1992): 364–86; Seth Koven and Sonya Michel, "Introduction: 'Mother Worlds,' " in Seth Koven and Sonya

maternalism insisted on women's role as universal mothers, making it the duty of all mothers to look after all children—not just their own. Maternalism thus provided both a motivation and a means by which many American women entered politics in the Progressive Era. By emphasizing women's unique expertise in the area of child welfare, female reformers were able to demand legislative reform to protect children. Female juvenile court reformers varied considerably, however. Whereas most were prompted to become involved in social welfare reform because they believed it to be their duty as mothers to do so, not all were mothers. Nor did all women reformers interpret this maternal duty in quite the same way. Although most of these women came from middle-class backgrounds, they displayed quite different perceptions of the problem they aimed to solve.

By examining the different groups of women reformers involved in the juvenile court movement, it becomes clear that there were two distinct types and uses of the maternalist approach, and these two paths had a distinct effect on the priorities of those pursuing reform. One group, whom I call the "traditional maternalists," clearly operated within the ideals of motherhood and domesticity that the maternalist ideal dictated, and this gender consciousness prompted them to find new ways of dealing with children in trouble with the law. The other group, the "professional maternalists," took a much more pragmatic approach. Although they used the language of maternalism, their training in social science and their close examination of life in the poor neighborhoods of America's cities was of more importance in shaping their perceptions of the problem than was their gender consciousness.[7]

Although differences existed between them, the approach of the women reformers as a whole revealed marked discrepancies from those of the male reformers involved. The women were much more willing to use the state to

---

Michel, eds., *Mothers of a New World: Maternalist Politics and the Origins of Welfare States* (New York, 1993), 1–42; Theda Skocpol, *Protecting Soldiers and Mothers: The Political Origins of Social Policy in the United States* (Cambridge, Mass., 1992); Molly Ladd-Taylor, *Mother-Work: Women, Child Welfare, and the State, 1890–1930* (Urbana, 1994), 1–14; Linda Gordon, *Pitied But Not Entitled: Single Mothers and the History of Welfare, 1890–1935* (Cambridge, Mass., 1994); Gwendolyn Mink, *The Wages of Motherhood: Inequality in the Welfare State, 1917–1942* (Ithaca, 1995).

7. On the uses of the language of motherhood, see Molly Ladd-Taylor, "Toward Defining Maternalism in U.S. History," *Journal of Women's History* 6 (Fall 1993): 110–13, and Ladd-Taylor, *Mother-Work*, 3–7. While my definitions of the two kinds of maternalism are very similar to Ladd-Taylor's, I have chosen to use rather different terminology to describe these two groups of female reformers.

create new institutions to deal with the problem of wayward children than were their male counterparts. Male reformers were most often involved in the juvenile court movement as the supporters of the women reformers' initiatives. It was rare for men to initiate reform themselves. There were some exceptions, the most prominent being Judge Ben Lindsey of Denver. Far from typical of juvenile court reformers, Lindsey operated within the boundaries of an older masculine tradition of reform. His construction of masculinity dictated a different perspective on the treatment of juvenile delinquents—one not in tune with new ideas about child rearing or the nature of childhood and that differed markedly from that of the women reformers. The establishment of the juvenile courts was thus the product of a variety of different strategies. This book will therefore examine cases where maternalism was a strong factor in prompting women to push for reform in the law's treatment of wayward children and cases where other factors were more important.

Maternalism evolved from an earlier tradition of female reform in the United States that had gradually developed over the course of the nineteenth century and that grew out of pervasive middle-class attitudes toward women's proper role in society. This role had been defined over the years following the American Revolution until, by 1840, Alexis de Tocqueville could report, "In America, more than anywhere else in the world, care has been taken constantly to trace clearly distinct spheres of action for the two sexes. . . . You will never find American women in charge of the external relations of the family, managing a business, or interfering in politics. . . . If the American woman is never allowed to leave the quiet sphere of domestic duties, she is also never forced to do so."[8]

The idea of separate spheres for the two sexes permeated contemporary language, although Tocqueville's assertion that women were confined to the domestic sphere has been shown not to reflect the reality of many women's lives. Nonetheless, scholars have used this concept of the separation of spheres as a key to explaining women's role in history. These scholars, like Tocqueville, argued that men and women occupied separate realms—men the public sphere of work and politics; women the private, domestic sphere. Although the separate spheres idea became firmly entrenched as a major interpretative device of women's history, recent historians have demanded a more rigorous analysis of what this actually meant and have asked whether

---

8. Alexis de Tocqueville, *Democracy in America,* 2 vols. (New York, 1966; first published, 1840), 2:778.

or not it was accurate. Some have even begun to question whether it remains a useful analytical device.[9]

Historians of gender have consequently sought to explain the role of women in nineteenth-century American society not simply in terms of a clearly delineated domestic sphere but in the interface between gender and society and the dynamic nature of that relationship. Further, they have broadened the definition of women's place by addressing such factors as race, class, and ethnicity, explaining that gender roles, especially those of women, were social constructs that served specific functions in American society. Thus, men and women gradually recast their ideas about the proper behavior and role of women in society as economic, social, and indeed, ideological factors reshaped the United States in the late eighteenth and early nineteenth centuries.[10]

In the years following the Revolution, male and female writers and social thinkers strongly debated what the role of women in the republic should be. Since the male leaders of this new republic clearly were not prepared to accord women any new legal or political status, it was often women themselves—writers and educators—who sought to define women's relationship to the state. Thus, women's domestic role was endowed with political meaning in terms of "Republican Motherhood." Woman's prime purpose in the new republic was to educate her sons to be virtuous and moral citizens, thus ensuring the future welfare of the state. Women were therefore to be the nurturers and protectors of future citizens—a role quite distinct from that of men.[11]

The ideology of Republican Motherhood was bolstered, in the early nineteenth century, by Protestant clergymen who gradually began to perceive that women could be their allies in the battle against the increasing secularization of society. Thus, religious anxiety and self-interest prompted these

9. Ellen Du Bois et al., "Politics and Culture in Women's History," *Feminist Studies* 8 (Spring 1980): 26–64; Nancy A. Hewitt, "Beyond the Search for Sisterhood: American Women's History in the 1980s," *Social History* 10 (October 1985): 299–321; Linda K. Kerber, "Separate Spheres, Female Worlds, Woman's Place: The Rhetoric of Women's History," *Journal of American History* 75 (June 1988): 9–11; Joan W. Scott, "Gender: A Useful Category of Analysis," *American Historical Review* 91 (December 1986): 1053–75; Amy Dru Stanley, "Home Life and the Morality of the Market," in Melvyn Stokes and Stephen Conway, eds., *The Market Revolution in America: Social, Political, and Religious Expressions, c. 1800–1880* (Charlottesville, 1996), 74–96.

10. Kerber discusses this in "Separate Spheres," 9–39.

11. Linda Kerber, *Women of the Republic: Intellect and Ideology in Revolutionary America* (Chapel Hill, 1980); Ruth Bloch, "The Gendered Meaning of Virtue in Revolutionary America," *Signs* 13 (Autumn 1987): 37–58; Linda Kerber, "A Constitutional Right to Be Treated

clergymen repeatedly to declare that women's pious influence was crucial for the continued well-being of society.[12] By the early nineteenth century, most churchgoers were female. Women also played a significant part in encouraging other family members to participate in the religious revivals that constituted the Second Great Awakening. Protestant clergymen—who in Puritan times had regarded women as temptresses and inciters to evil—now argued that, far from tempting men away from the paths of good, women were instrumental in bringing men back to God. These clergymen and women writers used sermons, popular literature, and advice literature to begin constructing a discourse in which woman's role was redefined as being the moral guardian of the family. Women, in these terms, were believed to be responsible for the ethical and spiritual character of the home, as well as its comfort and tranquillity. In this sphere, women were the acknowledged superiors of men. Many ministers began to argue that only women could be an uplifting influence over home and children, providing a source of moral values and a counterforce to the growing commercialism and self-interest of the outside world.[13]

By the early nineteenth century, social and economic factors as well as ideological ones were playing an important part in reshaping women's position in society. The growth of industry and a market economy in the early nineteenth century had a profound impact on gender roles. Women's sphere, which had previously been defined ideologically by Protestant clergymen and women writers in terms of Republican Motherhood, began to undergo a reconstruction in the face of these social and economic changes. Proponents of the new capitalist order now began to construct women's sphere in purely private terms. Whereas men occupied the public arena of work and politics, the woman's place was now seen to be in the private world of home and family, and her economic role in the family was no

---

Like American Ladies: Women and the Obligations of Citizenship," in Linda K. Kerber, Alice Kessler-Harris, and Kathryn Kish Sklar, eds., *U.S. History as Women's History: New Feminist Essays* (Chapel Hill, 1995), 24–25.

12. Mary P. Ryan, *The Cradle of the Middle Classes: The Family in Oneida County, New York, 1790–1865* (New York, 1981), 60–104; Nancy Cott, *The Bonds of Womanhood: "Woman's Sphere" in New England, 1780–1835* (New Haven, 1977), 126–59; Ruth H. Bloch, "American Feminine Ideals in Transition: The Rise of the Moral Mother, 1785–1815," *Feminist Studies* 4 (June 1978): 101–26.

13. Barbara Welter, "The Cult of True Womanhood, 1820–1860," *American Quarterly* 18 (Summer 1966): 150–74; Glenna Matthews, *"Just a Housewife": The Rise and Fall of Domesticity in America* (New York, 1987), 35–65.

longer recognized.[14] Thus, preindustrial patterns in which all members were acknowledged as contributors to the family economy and in which gender roles enjoyed a certain amount of fluidity were now replaced by a more rigid pattern of gender differentiation.

As a result, apologists for the emerging capitalist order constructed a discourse defining women as nonparticipators in the economy, though alongside this new discourse the older one of the moral mother continued. The cultural disassociation of women from economic productivity that had begun in the late seventeenth century became much more widespread and apparent as a result of the economic upheavals generated by the market revolution in the late eighteenth and early nineteenth centuries.[15] Although women generally still did participate in the market economy, both from within the home and outside it, middle-class women increasingly adopted the discourse of economic nonparticipation. Thus, the emerging middle classes, both male and female, frowned on participation in the market economy by women of other classes and denied it in their own case.[16] As Jeanne Boydston has noted, what had originated in the New England colonies of the late seventeenth century as the gendered division of labor had become by the early nineteenth century the gendered definition of labor in the culture of the new republic. Only men were involved in the cash economy, and women began to discount their own contribution to the economic needs of their families.[17] This had been necessary because, as Amy Dru Stanley has argued, the spread of wage labor, which had traditionally been regarded as a dependent status and therefore as feminine, had threatened to make men more like women. Thus, defenders of the new market relations in the North constructed an ideology of separate spheres in which home and work were

14. Cott, *Bonds of Womanhood;* Bloch, "American Feminine Ideals in Transition," 101–26; Ryan, *Cradle of the Middle Class;* Stanley, "Home Life and the Morality of the Market," 74–96. On the economic and social upheavals of the time, see Charles Sellers, *The Market Revolution: Jacksonian America, 1815–1846* (New York, 1991).

15. Jeanne Boydston, *Home and Work: Housework, Wages and the Ideology of Labor in the Early Republic* (New York, 1990); Joan Jensen, *Loosening the Bonds: Mid-Atlantic Farm Women, 1750–1850* (New Haven, 1986); Sellers, *Market Revolution,* 243–45.

16. Boydston, *Home and Work;* Christine Stansell, *City of Women: Sex and Class in New York, 1789–1860* (Urbana, 1987; first published, 1982); Nancy Grey Osterud, *Bonds of Community: The Lives of Farm Women in Nineteenth-Century New York* (Ithaca, 1991). Lori Ginzberg has also shown how some middle-class women received wages for their charity work: Ginzberg, *Women and the Work of Benevolence: Morality, Politics and Class in the Nineteenth-Century United States* (New Haven, 1990), 53–59.

17. Boydston, *Home and Work,* 51–55.

counterpoised. The masculine sphere of work was constructed in terms of independent wage labor and its relationship to the market economy. In opposition to this was the female domestic sphere in which women were dependent and nonproductive and home life was distinct from the market economy.[18]

This construction of an ideology of separate spheres was an important element in the emergence of a middle-class identity in the first half of the nineteenth century. By defining woman's role as domestic and private, quite separate from the worlds of the marketplace and public life, the middle-class self-consciously established itself as a class apart.[19] Middle-class women refined the concept of female domesticity so that they were elevated to the status of "Angels of the Home." As housewives and mothers, middle-class women had come to be seen as morally superior to both men and women of other classes. They were the guardians of the nation's virtue.[20]

While a number of historians have seen this domestic ideology as isolating and confining for middle-class women (because it restricted them to the limited roles of housewife and mother within their own homes), more recent scholarship has suggested this was not the case.[21] The emphasis on domesticity and motherhood actually allowed women to become involved in activities beyond their own firesides. Moreover, the ideology of Republican Motherhood was used to justify a demand for women's education, as educational reformers both male and female argued that women needed to be properly educated themselves in order to educate their sons. In other areas, too, women were able to expand the limits of their prescribed sphere beyond their own homes, gradually creating a space for themselves in voluntary activities and reform—areas not claimed by the male sphere of commerce and politics.[22]

A female reform tradition consequently developed during the nineteenth

18. Stanley, "Home and the Morality of the Market," 74–96.

19. Ryan, *Cradle of the Middle Class;* Sellers, *Market Revolution,* 237–69; Ginzberg, *Women and the Work of Benevolence,* 1–10; Stansell, *City of Women,* xii–xiii; Stuart M. Blumin, "The Hypothesis of Middle-Class Formation in Nineteenth-Century America: A Critique and Proposals," *American Historical Review* 90 (April 1995): 299–338.

20. Ginzberg, *Women and the Work of Benevolence,* 19–18; Welter, "The Cult of True Womanhood," 150–74; Bloch, "American Feminine Ideals in Transition," 101–26.

21. Welter, "The Cult of True Womanhood," 150–74; Barbara Berg, *The Remembered Gate: Origins of American Feminism: The Woman and the City, 1800–1860* (New York, 1978); Skocpol, *Protecting Soldiers and Mothers,* 322–23.

22. Kathryn Kish Sklar, *Catherine Beecher: A Study in American Domesticity* (New Haven, 1973); Barbara M. Solomon, *In the Company of Educated Women: A History of Women and*

century that arose out of certain perceptions of "woman's place." From the early nineteenth century onward, this tradition drew on assumptions about female moral authority and superiority, together with the ability of middle-class white women to speak for other women. Although in theory such women were limited to the confines of their own homes, in practice many middle-class women were involved in social activism to varying degrees. Grassroots female associations organized the raising of funds for charitable purposes, visited the poor, and generally attempted to improve society through moral suasion. There existed, too, a more radical and controversial brand of women's activism that sought women's rights and a greater role for women in society but challenged established prescriptions for women's behavior. Yet this attracted only a small minority of women activists. For the most part, female social activism remained within the confines of women's sphere and utilized a discourse that emphasized women's difference from men.

By the end of the nineteenth century many middle-class women had established a tradition of constructing ideological justifications to explain their involvement in activities beyond the immediate confines of their own homes, thereby accounting for their involvement in community activism and cultural activities. In the last years of the nineteenth century a new discourse began to emerge that idealized woman's role as mother and that had considerable influence in dictating the kind of activism middle-class women undertook.[23] The ideal of "educated" or "scientific" motherhood drew on the older ideologies of Republican Motherhood and domesticity but also reflected the marked transformation in attitudes toward childhood and child rearing that had been occurring throughout the nineteenth century.

In colonial New England, the idea that children were born innately sinful was the dominant influence on attitudes toward them. Consequently, it had been the duty of parents to suppress their children's natural depravity and break their wills.[24] There was also little recognition of childhood as a period of life distinct from adulthood. Children were generally considered to be little adults. They were expected to be hardworking members of the family and community from an early age and to remain deferential and obedient to

---

Higher Education in America (New Haven, 1985); Cott, Bonds of Womanhood, 151–59; Ryan, Cradle of the Middle Class, 210–25.

23. Sheila M. Rothman, Woman's Proper Place: A History of Changing Ideals and Practices, 1870 to the Present (New York, 1978), 97–98; Ladd-Taylor, Mother-Work, 3–7.

24. Steven Mintz and Susan Kellogg, Domestic Revolutions: A Social History of American Family Life (New York, 1988), 1–2.

their parents well into adulthood. Although special laws made parents responsible for ensuring that their children received the guidance and education that would enable them to become upright and God-fearing members of the community, little else in the society recognized childhood as a distinct or special period of life. Children were expected from a young age to be responsible for their actions.[25]

By the early nineteenth century, society had become much more secular, and many of the attitudes of colonial times were rejected. A new conception of childhood began to emerge, influenced by writers of the European Enlightenment, such as Jean Jacques Rousseau and Johann Pestalozzi. This new idea emphasized the naturalness and individuality of children. Children were considered to be more innocent, and childhood itself was perceived as a period of life worth not only recognizing and cherishing but extending. These new conceptions about the nature of childhood came at a time when social and economic changes were influencing the constitution of family relationships. As the market economy moved the locus of production from the home and adult men gradually went out to work, children as well as their mothers began to be perceived as dependents and nonparticipators in the economy. Middle-class families began to limit the size of their families as children ceased to contribute to the family economy and instead became burdens on it.[26] Enlightenment ideas about childhood, however, ensured that children, possibly for the first time, were seen as special—the main reason for the existence of the family.

As new emphasis was placed on the special nature of childhood, the responsibility for the proper rearing of children was placed on parents—particularly mothers. Whereas previously advice books on child rearing had been aimed at fathers, now large numbers of such books were published by clergymen, doctors, and women writers and aimed at mothers.[27] The ideology of Republican Motherhood further testified to the new importance placed on mothers as the primary rearers of children. As mothers assumed this responsibility, advice writers shifted their focus. Emphasis was now placed on the nurture and development of a child's conscience and individ-

25. John Demos, *A Little Commonwealth: Family Life in Plymouth Colony* (New York, 1970), 131–44.

26. Sellers, *Market Revolution*, 239–42; Boydston, *Home and Work*, 99–104; Viviana Zelizer, *Pricing the Priceless Child: The Changing Social Value of Children* (New York, 1985).

27. John Demos, *Past, Present, and Personal: The Family and the Life Course in American History* (New York, 1986), 41–67; Bloch, "American Feminine Ideals in Transition," 101–26; Kerber, *Women of the Republic*; Ryan, *Cradle of the Middle Class*, 157–62.

uality, rather than on breaking his will. Mothers were to cherish their children and carefully regulate their childhoods in preparation for adulthood. The primary purpose of child rearing became the internalization of moral prohibitions, behavioral standards, and a capacity for self-governance that would prepare the child for the outside world. Moreover, since childhood was seen by these advice writers as an important period in the formation of an adult's character, care had to be taken that children were subjected to the proper influences. Children were considered to be especially impressionable; if not protected from evil influences, they were likely to develop wayward tendencies.[28]

As the nineteenth century progressed, a consensus emerged among northern middle-class families that only a gradual process of maturation within the protected confines of the home could ensure a smooth transition to adulthood; childhood was to be prolonged until the process was complete.[29] Middle-class children ceased to have any economic value to their families, for children rarely contributed to the family economy. Their emotional value, however, was perceived as priceless. In the last decades of the nineteenth century, children's lives were increasingly "sacralized"—invested with a great sentimental, even quasi-religious, meaning.[30]

This new emphasis on childhood was promoted by such new institutions as the kindergarten, which was inspired by the ideas of Friedrich Froebel and stressed the socialization of the child through play. The kindergarten idea was first introduced in the United States in the late 1840s, but it was not until after the 1876 Centennial Exposition, where the advocates of the kindergarten had presented an exhibition of their methods, that Froebel's ideas became popular. Froebel's major contribution was to divide the process of early education between birth and the age of six into distinct stages of physical and mental development: infancy, early childhood, and childhood. For each of these stages he developed distinct educational tasks. Froebel declared the child to be essentially good by nature, a bundle of possibilities at the beginning of life. As a result of these ideas, Froebel and his followers developed a new theory of childhood education—symbolic educa-

28. Ryan, *Cradle of the Middle Class,* 157–62; Sylvia D. Hoffert, *Private Matters: American Attitudes Toward Childbearing and Infant Nurture in the Urban North, 1800–1860* (Urbana, 1989).

29. Carl N. Degler, *At Odds: Women and the Family in America from the Revolution to the Present* (New York, 1980), 66–68; Mintz and Kellogg, *Domestic Revolutions,* 21, 47–49, 58–60.

30. Zelizer, *Pricing the Priceless Child,* 3–11.

tion. This advanced the idea that the child's thoughts preexisted as feelings and emotions, but these feelings could not be cultivated directly; only through the strenuous training of intellectual faculties were these feelings given general form, thus allowing them to become ideas. Having formed his own ideals through symbolic training and directed play, the child learned to adapt these ideals to others before leaving the kindergarten.[31]

Although the middle classes did not always welcome the kindergarten idea as suitable for their own children — because it stressed the importance of the trained kindergarten teacher rather than the mother in instructing the child — most accepted it as a means of training immigrant children and other children of the slums. With the establishment of free kindergartens in working-class neighborhoods in the 1870s, the advocates of kindergartens began to suggest that the proper training of these children might eventually lead to the elimination of urban poverty. These advocates believed they could not only socialize the slum child in the habits of cleanliness and discipline but, through evening classes, educate working-class mothers in the principles of Froebelian child nurture. Thus, through the child and his now-educated mother, the family could be taught "proper" — that is, middle-class — ideals of family life. It was further believed that by recovering the child before the stamp of the slum was irrevocably placed on him, he could be taught habits of virtue; thus the creation of future generations of paupers and criminals would be prevented.[32]

At a time when the influx of vast numbers of immigrants from Southern and Eastern Europe was causing great anxiety about the future dominance of Anglo-Saxon Protestant culture in the United States, the immigrant child was an obvious target for Americanization. The kindergarten idea was widely accepted among middle-class reformers as a way of inculcating their own values and ideas into poor and immigrant children. It was also seen as a way of lifting these children out of lives of degradation. Thus many of the settlement houses established during the 1890s founded free kindergartens as one of the earliest efforts to help their neighbors in the slums. Women's clubs also frequently supported kindergartens financially.[33]

By the late nineteenth century, children had become recognized as a distinct group whose interests were no longer identical with those of their par-

31. Michael Steven Shapiro, *Child's Garden: The Kindergarten Movement from Froebel to Dewey* (University Park, 1983), 50–60.

32. Ibid., 85–96.

33. See, for instance, Julia C. Lathrop, "Hull House as a Sociological Laboratory," *Proceedings of the National Conference of Charities and Correction* (1894), 313–19; Minutes of

ents or the greater community. The kindergarten movement and the child study movement of the 1890s, led by the psychologist G. Stanley Hall, served to nurture a greater awareness of the unique nature of childhood and the basic emotions and interests characteristic of the child. As a by-product, woman's role as an educated mother was greatly enhanced, for Hall insisted that the mother should respond differently to each stage of the child's growth. New ideas about the nature of childhood tended to be confined to the middle classes, however. It was not until the twentieth century that these theories began to filter through to the working classes.[34] The new emphasis on the economic dependence of children was regarded as undesirable and impractical among working-class parents who relied on their children's labor to contribute to the family's economic survival. This increased awareness of the importance of childhood was also reflected in the belief that children were indispensable in the battle for the nation's destiny. Children were seen as embryonic citizens who represented the future of the country; if neglected they were likely to be a threat to the future of the nation.

It was against this background that the new ideal of educated motherhood emerged and the discourse of maternalism was constructed. The child who held the future destiny of the nation in his hands had to be carefully nurtured by a mother who was fully conversant with the new theories of child study and the newly accepted principles of child rearing. The child was no longer a simple creature but a complex one whose every development had to be carefully watched and guided. Thus, motherhood was increasingly idealized, while at the same time concern grew about those children who did not have the advantages of a mother trained in scientific motherhood. These newer ideals of childhood awakened middle-class women to the fact that many children, especially those of the immigrant and working classes, often lived in appalling conditions that clearly did not conform to these ideals. Since these children also represented the future of the country, it became clear to many of these women that if such conditions were allowed to continue, social instability might well be the result. This concern about the possible consequences to society of allowing children to grow up in ignorance of proper social standards prompted many middle-class women to seek means to ensure that the lives of all children should conform to their own ideals of childhood.

---

the Board Meeting, May 21, 1884, box 1, vol. 7, Chicago Woman's Club Papers, Manuscript Division, Chicago Historical Society.

34. Zelizer, *Pricing the Priceless Child.*

Although it was not until the late nineteenth century that female reformers began to bring this perspective to the problem of juvenile delinquency and to see it as a problem of such pressing magnitude that it required a new solution, delinquency had been a source of concern to many observers since early that century. The fears aroused by the increasingly urban character of the United States—including fears that poverty would lead to crime and that poverty itself was a kind of deviancy—had proved strong motivators among those who from the early nineteenth century began to single out dependent and delinquent children as a group requiring special attention. It was not until the urbanization of the early nineteenth century that juvenile delinquency was recognized as a phenomenon requiring separate treatment from adult crime. Whereas in rural communities misbehavior among children would be contained by social pressures, in cities, with all their opportunities for petty misdemeanors and more serious offenses, juvenile delinquency, however minor, came to be viewed in a more serious light.[35]

The first institution that sought to deal with the problem of wayward children was the New York House of Refuge, founded in 1825. Similar institutions followed in Boston in 1826 and Philadelphia in 1828. Their establishment marked a recognition that children should be treated differently from adults, for these three institutions were based on the belief that by separating youthful offenders and vagrants who showed tendencies toward criminality from the temptations to idleness and crime in the city, they would become virtuous and reformed. Hence, the children in these institutions were kept under strict discipline while they were supposedly taught how to be good citizens.[36] The houses of refuge had difficulty sustaining their original principles, but it took some time before they were replaced by other institutions. They gradually deteriorated until they became little more than prisons for juveniles, placing more emphasis on discipline than efforts to reform the characters of their inmates.

The second generation of institutions designed to deal with the problem of wayward children were the state reformatories. The Massachusetts State Reform School for Boys, established in 1847, differed little from the houses of refuge except that it was the first fully state-supported institution for juveniles in trouble with the law. By the mid-nineteenth century, however, in-

35. David J. Rothman, *The Discovery of the Asylum: Social Order and Disorder in the New Republic* (Boston, 1990; first published, 1971); Sutton, *Stubborn Children*, 43–44; Hawes, *Children in Urban Society*, 160–62.

36. Grace Abbott, *The State and the Child*, 2 vols. (Chicago, 1938), 2:325–26; Rothman, *Discovery of the Asylum*, 234–36. See also Robert S. Pickett, *House of Refuge: Origins of Ju*

fluenced by European examples, reformers began to advocate reform schools that would truly live up to their name by functioning as institutions of learning rather than prisons.[37] The development of industrial schools and reformatories, though in theory marking a shift away from punishment toward prevention and reformation, rarely fulfilled the hopes placed in them.

By the 1850s, as the wider society increasingly stressed the importance of the home and the family in bringing up children to be good citizens, those reformers concerned with the problem of juvenile delinquency began to look to the family as a model.[38] This manifested itself in two ways. On the one hand, some reformers, influenced by European examples, advocated the establishment of institutions built on the cottage or family system. The aim was to build institutions in the countryside on the cottage system with each cottage housing a small number of children and presided over by houseparents, thus providing a family atmosphere.[39] On the other hand, another group of reformers began to question the efficacy of all institutions, believing they had a detrimental influence on the children housed in them. Instead they advocated non-institutional means of dealing with wayward children. Reformers such as Charles Loring Brace argued that the family was the natural place for the children, and the most wholesome environment for the child was the farm. Brace developed a placing-out system in which children were to be placed in the families of farmers, not as apprentices as earlier systems had done but as members of the family, to receive the nurture and love of a family. Through the Children's Aid Society, founded in 1853, Brace organized a system of sending children to the West, carefully screening the families in which children were placed and following the progress of children placed in those families.[40]

---

venile Reform in New York State, 1815–1857 (Syracuse, N.Y., 1969). The first legal definition of juvenile delinquents appears in the charter of the New York House of Refuge.

37. The three European examples that seem to have had the greatest influence on developments in the United States were the industrial schools established by Mary Carpenter in England, the French Agricultural Colony at Mettray, and the "Rauhe Haus" near Hamburg in Germany. A full discussion of these may be found in Hawes, Children in Urban Society.

38. Welter, "The Cult of True Womanhood," 151–74; Matthews, "Just a Housewife," 35–65; Steven Mintz, A Prison of Expectations: The Family in Victorian Culture (New York, 1983), 29–39.

39. See, for instance, R. R. Reeder, "To Country and Cottage: The Effect on Institution Children of a Change from Congregate Housing in the City to Cottage Housing in the Country," Charities 13 (October 1, 1904): 16–18, and (November 5, 1904): 123–24; Schneider, In the Web of Class.

40. Mintz and Kellogg, Domestic Revolutions, 39–64; Ann Vandepol, "Dependent Children, Child Custody, and the Mothers' Pensions: The Transformation of State-Family Rela-

There were criticisms of both systems. Whereas in practice many of the institutions failed to live up to their ideals, and the size of the "family" in each cottage gradually increased, the placing-out system was also open to abuse.[41] Throughout the last decades of the nineteenth century the debate between the advocates of reformatories and those of the placing-out system dominated the question of how best to deal with the problem of dependent and delinquent children. While the debate continued to be waged, the number of reform and industrial schools continued to grow, and child-placing agencies proliferated.

By the last decade of the nineteenth century, however, some reformers had begun to seek alternatives to the reform schools and child-placing agencies. Each had its advocates, but a growing number of reformers had come to believe that neither method was having any fundamental effect on crime rates among city children. Although by the end of the nineteenth century it was recognized that children required separate treatment from adult offenders, the emphasis was still placed on the reformation of juvenile offenders rather than the prevention of juvenile delinquency. The idea of the juvenile courts was by no means an obvious development from such methods of dealing with dependent and delinquent children, for the juvenile courts shifted the focus from the reform of juvenile offenders to an emphasis on treating children as children, rather than as criminals, within the justice system.

Thus, while the creation of the juvenile courts needs to be placed in the continuity of earlier attempts to deal with the problem of dependent and delinquent children, it also represented a departure from these earlier solutions. However, the juvenile court movement does fit clearly within the con-

---

tions in the Early Twentieth Century," *Social Problems* 29 (February 1982): 221–35. For an alternative view of Brace, see Paul Boyer, *Urban Masses and Moral Order in America, 1820–1920* (Cambridge, Mass., 1978), 95–104; Hawes, *Children in Urban Society,* 93, 98–108; editorial, *New York Times,* November 28, 1888, p. 4; "Country Homes for Children: Work of the Children's Aid Society Since Its Founding," *New York Times,* January 10, 1897, p. 12.

41. Homer Folks, "Home Care for Delinquent Children" [1891], in Savel Zimand, ed., *Public Health and Welfare, the Citizen's Responsibility: Selected Papers of Homer Folks* (New York, 1958), 1–8; Supt. L. D. Drake, "Juvenile Delinquency and Its General Treatment," *Proceedings of the National Conference of Charities and Correction* (1900), 208–11; Galen A. Merrill, "Some Recent Developments in Child-Saving," *Proceedings of the National Conference of Charities and Correction* (1902), 226–30; Edwin P. Wentworth, "The Origin and Development of the Juvenile Reformatory," *Proceedings of the National Conference of Charities and Correction* (1901), 245; Homer Folks, "Family Life for Dependent Children" [1893], in Zimand, ed., *Public Health and Welfare,* 9–22.

text of the female tradition of reform. It was one of the earliest of a number of maternal and child welfare reforms pursued by maternalist reformers during the Progressive Era, though its emphasis differed from that of the other social welfare reforms of the Progressive Era in that it focused specifically on the child. The movement was heavily influenced both by new ideas about the nature of childhood emerging in the late nineteenth century and by the great emphasis on the role of women as educated child-rearers. Its central concern was the function of women as mothers, and this emphasis provided both the justification for middle-class women to become involved as reformers and the rationale behind the reform. Thus, it was culturally determined female values—that is, maternalism—that shaped the juvenile court movement. But as this book seeks to show, there were different versions of maternalism affecting the priorities of the women reformers involved. I do not mean to suggest that male reformers were absent from the juvenile court movement, but their perspective on the problem of juvenile offenders differed from that of the women involved.

Thus, this book provides an analysis of the juvenile court movement during the Progressive Era, primarily exploring the role of women in the movement and the importance of gender consciousness in this reform. It is broadly divided into three parts: Chapters 1 and 2 examine the origins of the pioneer court in Chicago; Chapters 3, 4, and 5 consider the influence of the Chicago court on the spread of the juvenile court idea; Chapter 6 explores the operation of the juvenile courts in the first decade of their existence and the way in which their approach to wayward children was contested and resolved. This is illustrated through a case study of the Chicago Juvenile Court. Three broad traditions of reform are identified in the book: first, the "traditional maternalist" approach; second, the female social science tradition, which I have identified as "professional maternalism," and which took a more pragmatic attitude toward gender consciousness; and third, the quite separate male philanthropic tradition. Thus, through a close investigation of the origins of the juvenile courts, this study examines the difference in visions of child welfare between male and female reformers, and, what is more important, goes beyond this point to explore the nuances within maternalism itself. Further, it examines the way in which gender consciousness was an essential element in shaping legislation to deal with the problem of dependent and delinquent children in Progressive Era America.

1

The Role of the Chicago Woman's Club

The court that opened its doors to the public on July 1, 1899, appeared much like other courts in Chicago. There was, however, one big difference—all the defendants were children. Judge Tuthill, who presided over the court, stressed to all of the children who came before him that he did not intend to administer punishment alone but was their friend. Moreover, sitting beside the judge were several women from the Chicago Woman's Club who advised him on the background of the various children. In some cases Judge Tuthill, instead of sentencing a child to the industrial school at Glenwood or the John Worthy School, released him on condition that one of these women watch over him and bring him back to the court if he did anything wrong.[1] This opening session of the Chicago Juvenile Court represented a departure from earlier methods of dealing with dependent and delinquent children, not just in Chicago but throughout the United States. It not only marked the hard-won recognition by the state of Illinois of its duty toward children but symbolized a new attitude toward young people in a justice system that now saw them as children in need of help rather than as criminals to be punished.

The Chicago Juvenile Court was not a sudden invention by a single re-

---

1. The great majority of delinquent children brought before the juvenile courts were boys. They were most often charged with offenses such as incorrigibility, burglary, robbery, truancy, and disorderly behavior. Although girls were charged with similar offenses, the juvenile courts generally treated them differently, for reasons that will be explained later. Hence, the masculine pronoun has been used throughout the book to refer to all children. This also follows the usage employed by the reformers themselves.

former; rather, it was an evolution encouraged by the cooperation of a number of groups of concerned individuals in the city. This chapter will explore the part played by the Chicago Woman's Club, the motives of its leaders, and its role both in lobbying for reform and in initiating some of the informal methods that culminated in the Juvenile Court Law.

The concerns of the various groups of reformers who cooperated to produce the Juvenile Court Law of 1899 differed in emphasis. The leaders of the Chicago Woman's Club were prompted by their own identification as mothers and the perceptions of family life and childhood this produced. These women were "traditional maternalists," or what Molly Ladd-Taylor has called "sentimental maternalists."[2] They were clearly committed to the ideals of motherhood and domesticity that late nineteenth-century society dictated for middle-class women, while at the same time they believed these ideals required them to extend their maternal instincts beyond their own homes and apply their domestic values to society at large. Their increasing concern with child welfare was a reflection of the emphasis placed on the importance of childhood within the wider society. Childhood was to be cherished and carefully regulated as a preparation for adulthood. Intellectual currents and the child study movement of the late nineteenth century placed the responsibility for the proper rearing of children on educated mothers.[3] It is therefore unsurprising that the women of the Chicago Woman's Club should have been imbued with ideas about the importance of motherhood and should consider it their responsibility to ensure that not only their own children but all children should be reared properly. They regarded it as their womanly duty to extend their mothering skills beyond their own homes to the wider society. Thus, child welfare work seemed particularly appropriate to women who pursued reform through a gender consciousness that emphasized their role as mothers responsible for society's dependents. Their maternalism propelled them into the public sphere of reform to work on behalf of those in need, especially women and children.

Prompted by these maternalist instincts, members of the Chicago Woman's Club carried out charitable work in the slums of Chicago and in the city's jail and police stations. Their work caused them to believe that families in

2. Although my description of traditional maternalism is very similar to what Ladd-Taylor calls "sentimental maternalism," I believe my terminology is more appropriate to this context.

3. Club women were acquainted with the ideas of the child study movement and the kindergarten movement. See for instance, Minutes of the Club Meeting, April 22, 1896, box 20, volume 90, Chicago Women's Club Papers, Manuscript Division, Chicago Historical Society (hereafter cited as CWC Papers).

the poorer sections of the city were on the point of breakdown as a result of the pressures of urban life. This view was reinforced by the apparent growth in the rate of juvenile delinquency in Chicago, and it became increasingly clear to these women that new methods of dealing with dependent and delinquent children were required. While at first they worked within existing structures, they gradually became aware that the law itself needed to be rewritten so as to treat the young as children in need of help and protection, rather than as criminals to be punished.

The Chicago Woman's Club was founded in February 1876 by Mrs. Caroline Brown, a native of Boston, and several of her friends. The objects of the club were, as its historians stated, "a desire to enlarge our vision, to enable us to share in the wider interests of the community, to do our share of the world's work; we wished to prevent wrong and harm to those unable to help themselves, to bind up wounds, to create that which was lovely, to take the place of the unsightly."[4] It was neither a political nor a suffrage organization but one that sought to better the world and its members through charity, philanthropy, and culture. With this aim in mind, the founders established four committees: Home, Education, Philanthropy, and Reform. Two more were added later. Each member of the club had to belong to one of these committees.[5]

The Chicago Woman's Club was not a unique organization in either Chicago or the United States as a whole. It was part of a wider trend among middle-class women, begun before the Civil War, to organize themselves into voluntary associations of various kinds. At first most of these associations had been church related, but gradually they grew more secular in orientation. Through their voluntary associations women became more involved in community activities, and some groups began to push for reform of various kinds. By the time of the Civil War, women were accustomed to voluntary activity and were able to use the talents they had fostered in these benevolent associations to enter a larger sphere of usefulness and help with the war effort. It was not, however, until after the war that there was a real explosion in the number of women's organizations of all varieties.[6]

The tremendous growth in women's organizations in the cities of late

4. Henriette Greenbaume Frank and Amalie Hofer Jerome, *Annals of the Chicago Woman's Club for the First Forty Years of Its Organization, 1876–1916* (Chicago, 1916), 9.

5. Minutes of the Board Meeting, and March 2, 1876, box 1, vol. 1, CWC Papers.

6. Anne Firor Scott, "On Seeing and Not Seeing: A Case of Historical Invisibility," *Journal of American History* 71 (June 1984): 7–21; Margaret Gibbons Wilson, *The American Woman in Transition: The Urban Influence, 1870–1920* (Westport, Conn., 1979), 91–92; Anne Firor Scott, "Women's Voluntary Associations: From Charity to Reform," in Kathleen D. McCarthy,

nineteenth-century America was the result of changes in the wider society and within middle-class households that gave women more time and desire to become involved in activities outside their homes. Many of the middle-class women who lived in cities such as Chicago were better educated than their mothers had been. Moreover, an increasing number of these women were college-educated and had experienced the closeness of female friendship and the organized female activities of college life.[7] In forming themselves into clubs, these women sought female companionship and intellectual stimulation. These organizations consisted broadly of two types: religious associations and, a new phenomenon, the secular women's club or association. A number of these secular clubs were concerned with "self culture," and during the 1870s and 1880s many remained uninterested in careerist or reform causes. Gradually, however, these clubs began to turn their focus away from self-improvement toward community activism.[8]

The first of the women's clubs to promote self-improvement and a degree of activism began in 1868 in New York and Boston. Sorosis and the New England Woman's Club were formed with the idea that women should organize to assist one another and to be of use to the world. Karen Blair has also suggested that they provided a forum where the demand for women's rights could be expressed and through which members justified both self-improvement and action to erode sexism by invoking the domesticity and morality ladies were supposed to embody.[9] Although such conscious feminism might have been true of the East Coast clubs, the Chicago Woman's Club was much less forthright and indeed fairly timorous in its early years: "Some of us who were neither teacher, physician nor lawyer," explained the club's historians, "but simply home-women, quite content to remain within the sphere of woman, then defined as limited to the fire-side, were timid at the thought of venturing out of the lines of family ties and the circle of

ed., *Lady Bountiful Revisited: Women, Philanthropy and Power* (New Brunswick, 1990), 35–54.

7. Barbara Welter, "The Cult of True Womanhood, 1820–1860," *American Quarterly* 18 (Summer 1966): 150–74; Suzanne Lebsock, "Women and American Politics, 1880–1920," in Louise A. Tilly and Patricia Gurin, eds., *Women, Politics and Change* (New York, 1990), 35–62; Glenna Matthews, *"Just a Housewife": The Rise and Fall of Domesticity in America* (New York, 1987), 21–22; Sheila M. Rothman, *Woman's Proper Place: A History of Changing Ideals and Practices, 1870 to the Present* (New York, 1978), 5–7, 41–42.

8. Scott, "Women's Voluntary Associations," 35–54; Theda Skocpol, *Protecting Soldiers and Mothers: The Political Origins of Social Policy in the United States* (Cambridge, Mass., 1992), 323–33.

9. Karen J. Blair, *The Clubwoman as Feminist: True Womanhood Redefined, 1868–1914* (New York, 1980), 8–15; Wilson, *The American Woman in Transition*, 93–97.

friends, which we had inherited and acquired in home and school,—it seemed a daring step to adventure into club-land."[10] Such timidity did not, however, prevent a large number of middle-class women from joining the club.

The membership of the club was taken from the middle class—at first mainly married women with children past the nursery age. It did not, in the beginning, have the fashionable character it later acquired. As the club grew in stature, however, it began to attract not only those women who required occupation for their leisure hours but also that increasing class of professional women who were making innovations in the accepted social patterns of their sex. Whereas in the 1870s the club was composed mainly of middle-class housewives, during the 1880s many of Chicago's social leaders—such as Mrs. Charles Henrotin, Mrs. Potter Palmer, and Mrs. William Chalmers—entered the club. The membership also included prominent professional women: lawyers such as Mrs. Myra Bradwell and Mrs. Catherine Waugh McCulloch; physicians like Sarah Hackett Stevenson and Julia Holmes Smith; journalists such as Mrs. Helen E. Starret, Mary Kraut, and Mrs. Caroline S. Twyman; as well as an increasing number of social workers and settlement house workers, including Miss Jane Addams, Miss Julia Lathrop, and Miss Mary McDowell. Membership was fairly exclusive, and limitations were put on the number admitted each year. Moreover, prospective members had to be sponsored by an existing member, and their acceptance into the club was often dependent on the importance of their sponsor.[11]

Typically the leaders of the Chicago Woman's Club in the late 1880s and 1890s were white, middle-class, and Protestant. The majority were married and had several children who, by the time their mothers became heavily involved in the club, were beyond the earliest years of childhood. Nevertheless, many of the professional women were unmarried, and not all were Protestant—for instance, Mrs. Henriette Greenbaume Frank, president of the club in the early twentieth century and the club's historian, was the daughter of a prominent Jewish banker in Chicago. Most, however, were middle-class, and the leaders, if not the rank and file, were either the wives of prominent Chicago men or prominent in their own right. The exceptions

10. Frank and Jerome, *Annals of the Chicago Woman's Club*, 9–10.

11. Jane Addams experienced this question of the exclusivity of the Chicago Woman's Club when a prominent member suggested she join. Addams is quoted in Allen F. Davis, *American Heroine: The Life and Legend of Jane Addams* (New York, 1973), 55. Details about club members may be found in Dorothy Edwards Powers, "The Chicago Woman's Club" (master's thesis, University of Chicago, 1939), 55–63.

tended to be settlement house workers, introduced to the club by their more socially prominent colleagues.

Among the social elite who gave the Chicago Woman's Club its fashionable character and its more glamorous leadership was Mrs. Palmer. She was born Bertha Honoré, in Louisville, Kentucky, in May 1849, the daughter of Eliza Jane and Henry Hamilton Honoré. When she was six, the family moved to Chicago, where her father invested in real estate and became one of the city boosters. She was educated at fashionable schools in Chicago and on the East Coast. In 1870 she married Potter Palmer, who had moved to Chicago from New England in 1852; made a fortune in dry goods, real estate, and cotton trading during the Civil War; and took a leading role in rebuilding Chicago after the great fire of 1871. They had two sons, in 1874 and 1875. The couple held a position of social prominence in the city and were regarded as members of the pre-fire aristocracy. Mrs. Palmer was involved in a number of cultural undertakings and was also active in practical endeavors for public welfare. She came to national prominence as chairman of the Board of Lady Managers of the World's Columbian Exposition, held in Chicago in 1893.[12]

Ellen Martin Henrotin was also born outside Chicago, in Portland, Maine, and spent much of her childhood in England, where her father had inherited property. She attended schools in London, Paris, and Dresden. Her family returned to the United States and in 1868 settled in Chicago, where in September 1869 she married Charles Henrotin, the son of a Belgian physician. They had three sons. Charles Henrotin was already well-established in a financial career when he married Ellen Martin, and this career brought him eventually to the presidencies of his own bank and the Chicago Stock Exchange, as well as to a leading position in Chicago society. Mrs. Henrotin, like Mrs. Palmer, was involved in the social and cultural activities of Chicago and also some of the various reform projects of the Chicago Woman's Club, which she joined in the early 1880s. She, too, was prominently associated with the World's Columbian Exposition, as vice president of the women's branch. As a result of her success with the Exposition, she was elected in 1894 as president of the General Federation of Women's Clubs, an office she held for four years.[13]

---

12. Biographical details taken from Edward T. James, Janet Wilson James, and Paul S. Boyer, *Notable American Women, 1607–1950: A Biographical Dictionary*, 4 vols. (Cambridge, Mass., 1971), 3:8–10.

13. Ibid., 2:181–83; Lana Ruegamer, "The Paradise of Exceptional Women: Chicago Women Reformers, 1863–1893" (Ph.D. diss., Indiana University, 1982), 158–61.

Of a different breed were the professional women, such as Dr. Sarah Hackett Stevenson, who grew to prominence in her capacity as a physician. She was born in a rural county of Illinois in 1841, the daughter of a farmer, and educated at Mount Carroll Seminary and the State Normal University, in Illinois, from which she graduated in 1863. She taught school for a number of years and then moved to Chicago and London following medical courses, gaining her M.D. in Chicago in 1874. In 1881 she became the first woman appointed to the staff of Cook County Hospital and in 1893, the first woman appointed to the Illinois Board of Health. Her example did much to advance the cause of medical education for women. She was welcome in the upper circles of Chicago society and served as president of the Chicago Woman's Club in 1893.[14]

Many club members were socially prominent, living in the fashionable areas of Michigan Avenue and Lake Shore Drive, as well as the equally well-to-do suburbs of Hyde Park. Although a large number were the wives and daughters of rich men, several had gained social and civic prominence through their own activities. The Chicago Woman's Club was, therefore, an organization for elite women that tended to reflect prevailing ideas about women's role. During the 1890s few of the club's members were radical feminists who sought greater involvement in the world of politics as a means of gaining equality with men in the public sphere. It was not until the early twentieth century that any significant number of members endorsed the fight for suffrage, and then only as a maternalist measure. The Chicago Woman's Club was in fact a traditional maternalist organization that worked within the accepted bounds of women's role in society.

Many club members were also fairly conservative in their social ideas and reflected the concerns of their class. As members of the social elite they wanted to preserve the existing structures of society but were anxious that if they did not help alleviate the poverty they encountered in the city, first through their charitable work and later through various social reforms, social unrest would ensue. Although the club itself was not a charitable organization, it was instrumental in the founding of the new Chicago Charity Organization Society in 1893, and when the Bureau of Charities was founded in 1896, many club members became friendly visitors and directors of the bureau.[15] Participation in both the Charity Organization Society

14. James, James, and Boyer, *Notable American Women*, 3:374–76.
15. Kenneth L. Kusmer, "The Functions of Organized Charity in the Progressive Era: Chicago as a Case Study," *Journal of American History* 60 (December 1973): 657–78; *Annual Reports of the Chicago Bureau of Charities*, 1894–95, 1896–97.

and the Chicago Woman's Club gave women the emotional support that allowed them to play a greater part in the community outside their homes and
that eventually involved them in reform activity within a maternalist framework. In the beginning, however, the Chicago Woman's Club had no such
ambitions. Women's clubs were still a relatively new phenomenon in the
cities of America in the years after the Civil War, and women entered them
with a degree of timidity.[16]

The Chicago Woman's Club was established in February 1876 and was
clearly influenced by the organization of Sorosis and the New England
Woman's Club. Indeed, at the meeting to found the club, the bylaws and
constitution of the New England Woman's Club were read aloud to provide
a model on which to base the new association.[17] Although it was in part a
cultural club concerned with self-improvement—as evidenced by the formation of the Art and Literature Committee, which organized classes—it was
from the beginning concerned with questions of reform and philanthropy.
According to the club historians, "It has broadened the views of women
and has tended to make them more impersonal and has widened their sympathies. They have learned to assume responsibility outside of home interests, and to consider the study of conditions in city and state as an extension
of their concern—constituting as they do the larger home. The idea of practical work for the community was fundamental in the minds of the founders. It required several years of concerted action to prepare the members
for active co-operation in practical work."[18]

Cultural and reform activities were often interrelated, as the club's historians noted: "The Club became the mature woman's college. These classes
served a two-fold purpose—they brought the members together in a more
intimate way and stimulated them to continue to give attention to serious
topics of study, and gave a feeling of solidarity. Out of these attempts at
widening our intellectual horizon and our appreciation of art in all its
phases, came the desire to share with others. . . . All were interested in the
work of Philanthropy and Reform."[19] The club provided a sense of sisterhood and support for those women who wished to reform society. It also inspired self-confidence in those who previously had been content to center

---

16. Frank and Jerome, *Annals of the Chicago Woman's Club*, 9–10; Skocpol, *Protecting Soldiers and Mothers*, 323–33.

17. Minutes of the Board Meeting, February 17, 1876, box 1, vol. 1, CWC Papers. For more on Sorosis and the New England Woman's Club, see Blair, *The Clubwoman as Feminist*.

18. Frank and Jerome, *Annals of the Chicago Woman's Club*, 15.

19. Ibid., 10–11.

their lives around their homes, giving these women the confidence to become involved in active efforts for reform. Women were thus able to extend their traditional charitable role of the "lady bountiful" to more systematic and "scientific" charitable enterprises—and thus to efforts to reform society.

From the beginning the club was concerned with matters affecting women and children, most particularly those among the poorer and criminal classes. Thus, at an early meeting on January 4, 1877, after selected readings from Charles Loring Brace's work *The Dangerous Classes of New York,* a discussion concluded that the only hope of preventing crime, and most especially prostitution, lay in the training and education of children. As a result, one of the first actions of the club was an attempt to persuade the mayor to appoint women to vacancies on the school board.[20] Members' interests soon diversified to include discussions on prison reform and on how to prevent crime and poverty through the industrial education of children and through kindergartens. Although reformers did not find any of these issues particularly new, they were so to club members. In the earliest years, while members presented papers on the role of women as reformers, practical efforts remained largely an individual affair.[21] Then in 1881, the Philanthropy Committee expressed a desire to do something practical and formed a society for the diffusion of psychological and hygienic knowledge among women.[22] The committee also began visiting the jail and asked the endorsement of the club in its efforts to secure an assistant matron to look after women prisoners. The club gave its endorsement with the proviso "That in undertaking such practical work it is not the purpose of the Club to become a Charity Organization but rather a discoverer of the best methods of advancing humanitarian principles and of helping individuals and organizations become self-sustaining."[23]

Both the Philanthropy Committee and the Reform Committee of the club continued their visits to the jail and police stations and their practical work in investigating conditions in these institutions, as well as securing matrons to look after women and children imprisoned there. In 1892 the Reform Committee took a further practical step to alleviate conditions in the jail. At

20. Minutes of the Board Meeting, January 4, 1877, April 4, 1877, and May 2, 1877, box 1, vol. 1, CWC Papers.
21. Minutes of the Board Meeting, February 15, 1877, box 1, vol. 1, CWC Papers; January 16, 1878, box 1, vol. 2, CWC Papers.
22. Annual Report, 1880–81, box 1, vol. 4, CWC Papers.
23. Directors' Meeting, February 13, 1884, box 1, vol. 6, CWC Papers.

the request of Mrs. Dennison Groves, the Chicago Woman's Club assumed the responsibility of the jail school she had begun.

Mrs. Groves was not a member of the club, although she became an honorary member in 1892, but she had been involved in a number of philanthropic enterprises—such as helping to found the Chicago Waif's Mission and the Chicago YWCA—and was clearly a wealthy woman. She had become interested in the plight of children in the Cook County Jail on a visit there in 1886. She had found quite small boys confined in the same quarters with murderers, anarchists, and hardened criminals and went to the superintendent of the jail to ask if these boys might be placed in a separate room. As her daughter recalled, "He replied that he had no space. After a day or two of thought; she asked and received permission to give instruction in reading and writing, in the Bible and singing, each morning for about three hours."[24] With the aid of her personal friends, Mrs. Groves employed a regular teacher. In 1892 the Chicago Woman's Club assumed payment of the salary given to the teacher, Miss Florence Haythorne. The sheriff allowed her to teach the boys in the corridor of the jail every morning.[25]

Mrs. Groves was also a publicist on behalf of the boys in the city and county jails. During the 1880s she wrote a number of articles for the *Chicago Tribune* and the *Inter Ocean* in which she pointed out the evils of the jail system as it affected children and suggested that a detention manual training school be established in Cook County so that boys who had committed crimes would not be driven to deeper crime and degradation.[26] Little was done by Cook County, though the Chicago Woman's Club also lobbied for such a school. Clearly these women were motivated by more than a humanitarian concern with the misery and degradation experienced by children in the Chicago jails. They were worried that without the benevolent influence of the school teacher, they would be contaminated by the atmosphere of vice and crime. Moreover, in pushing for a manual training school in the jail, they sought to ensure that boys confined there would learn a trade and thus not be forced into lives of crime. For, it was believed that the lack of a trade was a major cause of idleness and criminality.

The club did not merely concentrate on such informal methods of alleviating the problems in which it was interested. In March 1885, Mrs. J. B. Adair gave a paper before the club on "The Office of Women in the Reform

24. Letter to Mrs. Clement from Julia M. Lucas, December 8, 1922, Grace Groves Clement Papers, Manuscript Division, Chicago Historical Society.

25. Frank and Jerome, *Annals of the Chicago Woman's Club*, 127.

26. "Tribute to the Work of Mrs. Dennison F. Groves" [1923?], typescript, Grace Groves Clement Papers.

and Care of Criminals." This was followed by a discussion revealing that Illinois had no reform school for girls and that "In case [*sic*] of light offenses comparatively good girls were classed with such vicious company that their futures became inevitably blighted." The discussion ended with the adoption of a resolution endorsing a bill before the legislature.[27] As the club became more confident in its own abilities, it moved from merely endorsing measures already before the legislature to initiating legislation of its own, such as the juvenile court bill. It did not, however, abandon less formal methods of dealing with the problems with which it was concerned.

Although the club continued to have a wide range of interests and activities, charitable work and particularly efforts to prevent children from becoming hardened criminals were a dominant concern throughout the 1880s and 1890s. This interest was marked by the formation in 1886, in conjunction with a number of other women's clubs, of the Protective Agency for Women and Children, "an undertaking in the opinion of some the greatest we have yet attempted."[28] The club also continued to endorse legislation relating to the welfare of women and children and tried to fight contaminating influences by educating boys in the county jail. They took great interest in working to establish institutions to prevent dependent children from becoming criminals.

. The club was also coming to be recognized in the wider community as an agency that worked for the welfare of children. Thus, it helped raise funds to build a home for dependent children when asked by the men on the school's board of directors. It appealed for funds in the newspapers and through its own subscriptions raised money to build one of the cottages at the school. Its work was acknowledged by the board of directors of the Glenwood School when an inscription with the words "Erected by the Woman's Club" was placed on the school building. This acknowledgment did not come without considerable prompting by the club, however, and it is significant that the club should have demanded this recognition. As one member noted, she "wanted the boys to learn that women had their interests at heart, and that [it was] only through the efforts of the Chicago Woman's Club . . . [that Glenwood] School had come into existence."[29]

27. Frank and Jerome, *Annals of the Chicago Woman's Club,* 46; March 18, 1885, and Minutes of the Board Meeting, May 20, 1885, box 1, vol. 7, CWC Papers.

28. Frank and Jerome, *Annals of the Chicago Woman's Club,* 11; Annual Report, March 2, 1887, box 1, vol. 8, CWC Papers.

29. Frank and Jerome, *Annals of the Chicago Woman's Club,* 83–88; Regular Meeting, April 24, 1889, and Special Meeting, January 29, 1890, box 1, vol. 11, CWC Papers.

Clearly club members considered such work to be appropriate to their status, for they were beginning to move beyond purely fund-raising and supportive activities to request places on the governing bodies of institutions that dealt with children.[30]

Club members did not often articulate their reasons for this increasing interest in the welfare of children, and it is therefore difficult to chart the evolution of their thinking. Judging by their activities and by the priority given child welfare in the club's *Annals,* it is clear this issue was of increasing importance to club members. As the club historians wrote, "Not only those fortunately placed in life were its care, but the step-children of fortune, those who needed mothering and guidance."[31] By the last years of the nineteenth century, many members were devoting considerable attention to projects aimed at preventing children from becoming hardened criminals. Their concern about the nature of childhood in the slums seems to have been prompted more by their gender consciousness than by more general anxieties about social breakdown. It seemed to many of the women involved in the various charitable enterprises of the Chicago Woman's Club that the rapid industrialization and urbanization of American society, especially obvious in Chicago, was having a detrimental effect on the family. Moreover, the vast influx of immigrants from Eastern and Southern Europe from the 1880s onward led to fears that traditional American ideals based on Protestantism would be eroded—especially because these families, which were mainly Catholic, seemed to produce large numbers of children who did not behave as middle-class American children were expected to.

Prompted by both maternalist ideas and the middle-class emphasis on child nurture within the confines of a protected family environment, members of the Chicago Woman's Club sought a solution to the problem of dependent and delinquent children. They were shocked by what they saw of family life in those poorer sections of the city they had observed when visiting Chicago's police stations and city jail and during their charitable work in poor and immigrant neighborhoods.[32] Quite apart from the apparently

30. See, for instance, Meeting of the Board of Directors, February 27, 1890, box 1, vol. 11, CWC Papers.

31. Frank and Jerome, *Annals of the Chicago Woman's Club,* 11, 14; Annual Report, May 20, 1896, box 2, vol. 17, CWC Papers. This identification has been described as "maternalism" by a number of historians. See, for instance, Seth Kovan and Sonya Michel, "Womanly Duties: Maternalist Politics and the Origins of Welfare States in France, Germany, Great Britain, and the United States, 1880–1920," *American Historical Review* 95 (October): 1079; Skocpol, *Protecting Soldiers and Mothers,* 317–20.

32. Annual Report, May 20, 1896, box 2, vol. 17, CWC Papers.

high rate of juvenile delinquency in these parts of the city, other factors seemed to suggest that families there were breaking down, for the situation clearly did not conform to middle-class ideals of family life.

Members of the club were horrified to discover that in many families, both parents went out to work, leaving their children to roam the streets all day. Clearly these mothers were not fulfilling their child-rearing functions. Children were sent out to work in factories at a young age, and many were also seen on the streets selling newspapers and hawking various wares. Moreover, in a large number of the cases Chicago's charitable organizations handled, the father had deserted his family and the mother either had to work to feed her family or ask for alms.

As a result, several club members were not slow to point out that many working-class and immigrant families did not conform to the ideal of the American family and that if something were not done, the whole of society would ultimately suffer. For this reason the club concentrated many of its efforts on ways to educate working-class mothers about their responsibilities in rearing children and in ensuring that their young offspring conformed to middle-class ideas about how children should behave. This explains club members' involvement in supporting free kindergartens in the poorer areas of Chicago and their growing interest in dealing with the problem of dependent and delinquent children.[33] Moreover, their concern about the apparent breakdown in working-class and immigrant families and their consequent interest in seeking a solution to the problem of dependent, neglected, and delinquent children seemed further justified by the apparent rise in crime rates in the poorer sections of Chicago.

The period from 1876 to 1898 saw a rapid increase in the population of Chicago: in 1876 it stood at 500,000; by 1890 it had reached 1,000,000; and by 1898 it was 1,875,000.[34] As the city's population grew, so also did crime rates, and it was not only the figures for adult arrests that increased. In 1876, 153 children under ten and 5,945 between the ages of ten and twenty were arrested. By 1898, these figures had risen to 508 children under the age of ten, and 15,161 between the ages of ten and twenty. The number of child arrests actually increased little in proportion to the population, although it is likely that the number of arrests did not reflect the num-

---

33. Lucy L. Flower, "The Duty of the State to Dependent Children," *Proceedings of the Illinois Conference of Charities and Correction* (1896), 9–16; Frank and Jerome, *Annals of the Chicago Woman's Club*, for instance, 162–63.

34. Population figures for 1876 and 1898 are taken from the *Reports of the Superintendent of Police of the City of Chicago to the City Council* for those years; that for 1890 is from U.S. Bureau of the Census, *Eleventh Census, 1890*, "Population," pt. 2, p. 117.

ber of crimes committed.[35] What the arrest figures did reflect, however, was an increasing anxiety about crime among city children. The problem of crime among children appeared to be very visible, especially in crowded areas. It seemed that more children were being held in police stations and the city prison, and the numbers cited in police reports and in newspapers were larger. This may, of course, have been simply because the police found it easier to arrest children—especially when, in some cases, policemen were rewarded for the number of arrests made. But it may also reflect a move among the police to arrest children for petty depredations that would not have been recognized as offenses in a rural community. Indeed, the cases of many of these children were dismissed at their court hearing. Thus, whether or not there was a proportionate increase in the amount of juvenile crime in Chicago, it gave the appearance of having escalated, and members of the Chicago Woman's Club were not prepared to accept these higher figures complacently. "Just think of it. Think what it means to us as well as to them, and then say, if you can, 'I cannot help it. I am not my brother's keeper,'" argued one of its members.[36]

Among those most consistently concerned with the question of dependent and delinquent children was Mrs. Lucy Flower, who became a member of the club in the early 1890s. Lucy Coues was the adopted daughter of Samuel Elliott Coues and his second wife, Charlotte. Both were natives of

35. Here are the figures for arrests of children and young people under the age of twenty for the years 1876 to 1898 from *Reports of the General Superintendent of Police of the City of Chicago to the City Council*:

Year ending December 31	1876	1877	1878	1879	1880	1881
Under 10 years	153	104	141	182		243
Aged 10–20 years:	5,945	6,714	5,259	5,079		6,510

Year ending December 31	1882	1883	1884	1885	1886	1887
Under 10 years	305	242	211	117	191	155
Aged 10–20 years	6,894	6,433	6,508	6,373	6,650	7,384

Year ending December 31	1888	1889	1890	1891	1892	1893
Under 10 years	228	248	231		430	475
Aged 10–20 years	8,695	9,092	10,862		15,570	17,389

Year ending December 31	1894	1895	1896	1897	1898	
Under 10 years	282	296	326	301	508	
Aged 10–20 years	16,760	15,218	16,695	16,274	15,161	

36. Flower, "The Duty of the State to Dependent Children," 11.

New Hampshire, where Samuel was a prosperous merchant and had many friends who were reformers. Lucy was educated in local schools until 1853, when the family moved to Washington, D.C. There she attended the Parker Collegiate Institution until family illness prevented her from continuing. In 1859 she moved to Madison, Wisconsin, where she taught school and in September 1862 married James Flower, a rising lawyer. They had three children before the family moved to Chicago in 1873. James Flower continued to prosper as a lawyer, gaining renown as the senior partner in a prominent Chicago law firm. He also became prominent in Republican circles. Mrs. Flower was heavily involved in charitable enterprises, first in church-related work but later as a board member of the Chicago Half-Orphan Asylum and the Home for the Friendless, and a founder of the Illinois Training School for Nurses.[37] It is unsurprising, therefore, that she became involved in the reform work of the Chicago Woman's Club.

Mrs. Flower, both as a member of the club and as an individual, was a keen lobbyist who advocated solutions to the problem of dependent and delinquent children. She made clear her belief that criminal youths were the result of poor homes and bad child rearing and that unless the state stepped in to find these boys good homes at an early age, they would become a danger to society. Thus in a newspaper article in January 1887, she claimed, "Every *boy* who grows up depraved and vicious is a danger to the State. As a voter, he has as much voice in public matters as you; as a criminal, he costs the State more for trials, convictions and board in prison than would suffice to take twenty boys and, by finding suitable homes and securing to them protection and training in infancy, make of them honest, self-supporting citizens."[38] She reiterated this argument in 1896 at the Illinois Conference of Charities: "Every child allowed to grow up in ignorance and criminality or in pauperism tends to lower the standards of the community in which he lives, as the evil of his life does not end with him but may be transmitted to his posterity, and the extent of his influence be incalculable."[39]

Mrs. Flower believed that it was the right of every child to be properly reared, as were the majority of middle-class children. No child naturally knows good or evil, she argued; these must be learned. In a normal family

---

37. Biographical details on Lucy Flower are from James, James, and Boyer, *Notable American Women*, 1:635–37; Ruegamer, "The Paradise of Exceptional Women," 156–58.

38. "The Dependent Children of Illinois," clipping, January 1887, scrapbook 2, Lucy Flower and Coues Family Scrapbooks, Manuscript Division, Chicago Historical Society (hereafter Flower Scrapbooks).

39. Flower, "The Duty of the State to Dependent Children," 11.

(one conforming to middle-class values) a child is taught what he can and cannot have, but the moral sense of a child cannot develop properly when he lives in an atmosphere of drunkenness and profanity. It therefore seemed natural to Mrs. Flower and her colleagues in the Chicago Woman's Club that the state should ensure that all children have a proper training for adulthood. "Has not the child, simply as a child, some inherent rights, some claims on society for at least a chance to be decent and upright?" she questioned. "I am sure he has and that we as [C]hristian men and women fail of our plain duty when we do not endeavor by every means in our power to secure to every child that which should be his inalienable right, viz: food, clothing and shelter, until such time as he can earn them for himself, and such physical, mental and moral training as is necessary to enable him to be a self-supporting, upright citizen."[40]

Attitudes like these expressed by Mrs. Flower prompted a general feeling among club members that juvenile delinquency was a symptom of a larger crisis among lower-class families. Whereas in part they were influenced by fears that neglected and dependent children were incipient offenders and therefore a danger to society, they also believed it was their duty as mothers to seek a practical solution to the problem of criminal youth.[41] Thus, during the 1880s the Philanthropy and Reform Committees of the club became involved in jail visits and in efforts to secure matrons within the jail and the police stations.[42] The role of the matrons seems to have been originally to provide a warden of the same sex as protection for women in the police stations, but this idea was extended to provide protection for children as well. It was also believed that these female matrons would look after the interests of the children there, ensuring they were not exposed to the worst influences of these places.

During the early 1890s the Philanthropy and Reform Committees further extended their activities in the jail by undertaking the support of the jail school. These practical efforts sought to counteract the contaminating influences of the jail as well as introduce the beneficial influences of the matrons and the school teacher.[43] The club's endorsement of legislation to establish a reformatory institution for women and girls, and their fund-raising efforts for the home for dependent children, should also be seen in this

40. Ibid., 11.
41. Minutes of the Board Meeting, November 3, 1880, box 1, vol. 4, CWC Papers; Annual Report, May 19, 1894, box 20, vol. 89, CWC Papers.
42. Frank and Jerome, *Annals of the Chicago Woman's Club,* 42, 76–77.
43. Ibid., 76, 127.

light. None of these endeavors was, however, a panacea, and the Philanthropy and Reform Committees continued to seek a solution to the problem of dependent and delinquent children.

The Reform Committee continued its interest in the boys housed in the jail, and it was as a result of this interest that Mrs. Perry Smith, the wife of a railroad capitalist and lawyer, spoke to the club in November 1892 of the difficulties encountered by the Jail Committee in helping boys who had been jailed, often for petty offenses.[44] She observed that various organizations had been appealed to—such as the Helping Hand and the Glenwood School—but they could not help. She asked that some of the rich women of the club establish a manual training school for this class of child. It is also significant that Mrs. Perry Smith recommended a juvenile court be established "so as to save these boys from the contamination of association with older criminals." Mrs. Coffin, the chairman of the Jail Committee, further stated, "We need Reform Prisons—we need the Juvenile Court, open every morning—for this, the Club should work."[45] It is unclear what either of these women meant by a juvenile court at this juncture, but it is perhaps symptomatic of the way their thoughts were beginning to turn. Gradually throughout the 1890s, while they continued to develop other means of confronting this problem, the idea of a juvenile court evolved within the Chicago Woman's Club.

Whereas previously the efforts of the club had been concentrated on reforming children in the jail and on preventing crime by educating these children, either in the jail or in manual training or industrial schools, by the mid-1890s they began to search for means of changing the actual machinery of justice. One newspaper noted in 1893 that the women who had succeeded in introducing night matrons in the jail and in police stations were now agitating for the passage of a law similar to that in Massachusetts, which compelled the trial of juvenile delinquents within twenty-four hours of arrest.[46] Possibly as a result of this agitation and because a club committee conferred with lawyers regarding the great delay that attends the trial of boys in jail, one judge was prevailed upon to hold separate court sessions just for the trial of boys.[47] Thus in November 1894, Miss Haythorne, the

44. For more on Perry Smith, see Bessie Louise Pierce, *A History of Chicago, 1871–1893* (Chicago, 1957), 61.

45. Frank and Jerome, *Annals of the Chicago Woman's Club*, 125–26; Club Minutes, November 23, 1892, box 20, vol. 88, CWC Papers.

46. "To Save Children from the Jails," p. 44, clippings, 1893, folder 506, scrapbook 1, Hull House Association Papers, Special Collections, University of Illinois, Chicago.

47. Club Minutes, February 27, 1895, box 20, vol. 89, CWC Papers.

jail school teacher, "reported that she had been encouraged by the assurance that cases of boys would be tried at once by Judge Tuthill, who would hold court for the purpose on Saturday mornings."[48]

Concern that children be tried speedily and at separate sessions of the court had sprung from a realization that they were associating with hardened criminals from the moment of their arrest until their release—which occurred after either the judge dismissed them or they had served their sentence. Thus, by insisting that children be tried speedily and in separate courts, it was hoped that the contamination of children by older criminals would be avoided, at least until sentence was passed. The hearing of children's cases before those of adults or in an entirely separate session was accomplished on an informal basis but not sanctioned by legislation, as it had been in New York since 1892. It depended merely on the agreement of the state's attorney and on the willingness of Judge Tuthill himself.

In 1895 the Chicago Woman's Club, led by Mrs. Flower, Mrs. Henrotin, and Miss Lathrop, tried to formalize this embryo juvenile court through legislation. As Mrs. Flower recalled,

> Several of those interested in children, among them Miss Lathrop and myself, were very much exercised over the inequalities and injustices of the administration of the law to juvenile offenders, and we attributed this largely to the fact that the cases were handled by so many different justices, each with different ideas of the responsibility of juvenile offenders and more or less affected by political influences. So the idea gradually developed that it would be a good thing if all children's cases could be taken from the police courts and tried by a higher judge.[49]

They sought to obtain a law that would establish a separate court for the trial of children's cases. A draft law was presented to some lawyer associates, but the attorneys could see no way by which such a court could be formed in accordance with the rights guaranteed under the Illinois constitution and so judged that such a law would be unconstitutional. It was therefore abandoned, but informal methods continued.[50] One significance of this legal effort, however, is to illustrate some of the reasons

48. Frank and Jerome, *Annals of the Chicago Woman's Club*, 159.

49. Letter from Mrs. Lucy L. Flower, May 1917, vol. 2, Louise deKoven Bowen Papers, Manuscript Division, Chicago Historical Society (hereafter Bowen Papers).

50. Letter from Mrs. Flower, May 1917, and memorandum by Julia C. Lathrop, May 3,

women reformers believed a separate court was needed for juvenile cases, for it was meant not only to keep children separate from adult offenders at all times but also to achieve a certain amount of uniformity in the treatment of such cases. Moreover, by having only one court deal with all children's cases, it was hoped that if a child who had been dismissed on one charge came before the court again, his case would not be dismissed without proper consideration. Up to this point, children had been appearing before different police courts. Since no records were kept, reformers believed each child had been able to offend without fear of punishment, because before each new court he had a clean slate. The abandoned bill also provided for the introduction of a probation system for children, which would have allowed a more direct influence on the lives of poor youths.

Although this attempt to secure legislation formally to create a juvenile court and probation system was, for the moment, abandoned, members of the club continued to seek ways to change the treatment of dependent and delinquent children. Mrs. Flower visited Massachusetts to study the probation system there, for probation had been a formal part of the Massachusetts state justice system for young offenders since 1869, and courts in Massachusetts had been obliged to appoint probation officers since 1891.[51] Massachusetts had also introduced separate hearings for delinquent children in 1875. The state therefore offered alternative models for ways to deal with delinquent children. The club also secured permission from the state's attorney to have one judge hold a morning session once a week for boys only. To this session, Miss Haythorne, the jail school teacher, having investigated every phase of each case, brought her records of the boys to be tried.[52] Done presumably to help the judge decide on the disposition of each case, her efforts also foreshadowed the work of probation officers after the Juvenile Court Law was passed.

The club also campaigned for a new compulsory education, or truancy, law, since they considered the existing one ineffective. This was because the law did not outline the minimum number of weeks a child should attend school. Nor did it have any machinery to enforce the law, and no prosecutions had been made under it. The club also sought a parental school to

1917, vol. 2, Bowen Papers; Julia C. Lathrop, "The Development of the Probation System in a Large City," *Charities* 13 (January 7, 1905): 344–45.

51. Mrs. Flower's visit to Massachusetts is mentioned in Lathrop, "The Development of the Probation System in a Large City," 344–45. Details of the Massachusetts reform may be found in Grace Abbott, *The Child and the State*, 2 vols. (Chicago, 1938), 2:330.

52. Frank and Jerome, *Annals of the Chicago Woman's Club*, 177, 179.

which persistent truants could be sentenced and where they would receive an education under constraint.[53]

The Chicago Woman's Club continued to be prominent in leading the agitation for an improvement in the condition of women and children in Chicago. The agitation began in January 1896 with a proposal that the club have monthly meetings for the study of laws regarding women and children. Proponents argued that Illinois was behind other states in this regard. At a special meeting on January 15, 1896, Mrs. Henrotin proposed a congress of city clubs that would evaluate the condition of childhood in Chicago. She particularly noted that the existing truancy law was ineffectual, that Illinois was backward in the treatment of criminal children, and that prevention rather than reformation was required. She urged the club to take the initiative in this matter and invite the city clubs to come together.[54] At further meetings it was agreed that Mrs. Flower would contact the other women's organizations in the city and ask them to unite with the club in a symposium on the subject of the condition of child life in Illinois and the steps necessary to improve these conditions.[55]

The resulting meeting of more than fifty representatives of the many women's organizations in Chicago and its suburbs was held on January 31, 1896, in the Chicago Woman's Club rooms. The meeting was a clear example of how women's informal networks could be utilized to lobby for a matter of concern to women, and it reflected the degree of interest in the matter among women's associations.[56] The main aim of the meeting was to arouse public awareness of the conditions of children in Illinois. Mrs. Henrotin emphasized the possibilities of preventive as much as reformative work with children, advising that men be secured to do effective lobbying in the legislative halls. Mrs. Flower proposed a mass meeting at which a series of papers would be presented showing what ought to and could be done relative to the "child problem."[57]

To consolidate the message of the meeting, an appeal was sent out signed by Lucy Flower, Ellen Henrotin, and Dr. Sarah Hackett Stevenson, among

53. "Compulsory Education," *Hull House Bulletin* (February 1897): 6; Jane Addams, "Woman's Work for Chicago," *Municipal Affairs* 2 (September 1898): 505.

54. Special Meeting, January 15, 1896, box 2, vol. 17, CWC Papers.

55. Special Meeting, January 24, 1896, box 2, vol. 17, CWC Papers; Club Meeting, January 22, 1896, box 20, vol. 90, CWC Papers.

56. Compare this with Skocpol's explanation for the spread of mothers' pensions in Skocpol, *Protecting Soldiers and Mothers,* chap. 8.

57. "With Up-to-Date Women: Club Representatives Confer on the Child Problem," clipping, February 1, 1896, scrapbook 3, Flower Scrapbooks.

others, addressed to "The Women and Women's Clubs of Illinois." This document is particularly significant in showing the concerns of these women about child life in the poorer sections of Illinois. It stated that among the duties of women were the care and protection of social dependents, and the neglect of children was social suicide. Moreover, it conveyed the position of the club that all women were interested in children, and their condition was of the utmost importance to the state. "In all large cities one condition exists which is comparatively unknown in small communities," the appeal claimed, "namely, numbers of children who, through the death, neglect, poverty, weakness or criminality of parents or guardians, do not attend school, have practically no home training or control, and through such neglect drift into criminality. There are hundreds of such children in Chicago and elsewhere throughout the State, growing up to constitute an ignorant and criminal class, dangerous to the welfare of the whole country."

The appeal went on to describe the conditions of children and the connection between these conditions and the growth of crime and pauperism in the state. It concluded with an appeal to mothers:

> Those who have children know that no child should be considered a criminal until his reasoning faculties are developed and until some opportunity has been given him of knowing good and evil. In the cities of the state thousands of children are, through the death, neglect, indifference or criminality of parents, left entirely to the education of the streets, with no training in right doing, but every inducement for wrong, and our laws recognize no difference between the untrained child of seven who throws a stone or steals an apple and the adult criminal who is drunk, disorderly or who commits petty theft.

It was the duty of the state to provide these children with a better start in life, since their parents had failed to do so.[58] It was time also that the state recognized the delinquent child as a different kind of offender from the adult criminal. The women of the state should investigate local conditions and use their influence with members of the legislature to secure laws to protect children.

A further meeting of the various women's clubs was held on May 9,

---

58. "To the Women and Women's Clubs of Illinois," leaflet, February 15, 1896, 7–10, scrapbook 3, Flower Scrapbooks.

1896. Papers were presented by Mrs. Flower, Miss Haythorne, Miss Mc-Dowell, as well as a representative of the Teachers' Club, and a number of men, including Superintendent Mark Crawford of the bridewell (the city jail),[59] and sociologist Professor Albion S. Small of the University of Chicago. The papers sought to describe the conditions of child life in Illinois and thereby arouse public opinion to do something about it. The meeting ended with a call on members of the legislature to enact laws protecting dependent and delinquent children—particularly to prohibit the retention of children in the poorhouses of the state, to forbid the confinement of children in the jails or bridewell in association with adult criminals, and to establish a parental school for truant children.[60] It is perhaps significant that there was not a call for the establishment of separate courts for children or for a probation system at this time, possibly because there were still questions as to how such a court could be made constitutional.

Throughout the later 1890s the Chicago Woman's Club continued to lobby, more or less successfully, for various measures to reform the conditions of children in Illinois, and especially in Chicago. As well as arousing public sentiment in favor of change, they persuaded the county board to take over the expense of the jail school, they suggested that needy children should be placed in approved family homes rather than institutions, and they campaigned for vacation schools and playgrounds to keep children off the streets.[61] They also supported Mrs. Flower's successful efforts to obtain a compulsory education law.[62] Much of their time was spent agitating for the building of separate dormitories and a manual training school for boys at the bridewell. In this they were supported by the bridewell's superintendent, Mark Crawford. The manual training school, named the John Worthy School after the husband of a Chicago Woman's Club member, was opened within the bridewell in 1897. It provided schooling and industrial training for the boys during the day, but they were still returned to the cells of the

---

59. In discussing Chicago's institutions of confinement, I use the term "bridewell" to refer to the Chicago city prison and "jail" to designate the Cook County institution used as a place of confinement following trial. In other contexts, "jail" is used generically.

60. "To Save the Child: Women's Clubs of Chicago Tackle an Important Problem," clipping, May 10, 1896, scrapbook 3, Flower Scrapbooks.

61. These efforts can be followed in Minutes of the Board Meeting, box 2, vol. 17, CWC Papers; Minutes of the Board Meeting, box 3, vol. 19, CWC Papers; Club Minutes, box 20, vol. 92, CWC Papers.

62. Club Minutes, Box 20, vols. 89 and 91, CWC Papers; *Hull House Bulletin* (February 1897, April 1897, and March 1898); Frank and Jerome, *Annals of the Chicago Woman's Club,* 158–76.

main prison at night, where they continued to associate with adults. The school did not, therefore, achieve its purpose, and until the dormitories, which finally secured the separation of juveniles from adult offenders, were opened in June 1899, it was regarded as little better than the county jail.[63]

These measures were, however, fairly limited in actually dealing with the problem of juvenile crime and its prevention. They did not produce a fundamentally different way of dealing with child offenders, nor did they succeed in keeping children apart from adult criminals. Although failing to bring Illinois in line with other states' provisions for delinquent children, these changes did, however, help produce the atmosphere in which a change in methods of dealing with young offenders could be attempted.

It was not until 1898 that agitation for reform came to a head. The Chicago Woman's Club began the year with a request for further meetings to discuss the question of dependent children.[64] In April 1898 the Reform and Philanthropy Committees formed a joint committee—with Julia Lathrop as chairman—which aimed to concentrate its efforts on probation for children in police stations. Miss Lathrop recommended that members assist in establishing a probation law in the justice courts, so that children who were not criminals would not be sent to the bridewell. The most satisfactory way to do this was to have the justice appoint some member of the club as the offender's guardian for a certain length of time, giving him freedom only if he lived up to all agreements made.[65] This suggests that club members may have already been doing such work; significantly, it appears that probation for juvenile offenders was increasingly the central concern of the club. In becoming directly involved in the lives of poor children brought before the courts, club women could help to guide these children toward what they considered to be the proper behavior of a child.

The club was not alone in seeking a change in the methods of dealing with child offenders, and indeed, without the help of other interested groups, among them certain influential male reformers, it is unlikely they could have secured any legislation. They did, however, produce an atmosphere conducive to a change in the law regarding dependent and delinquent

63. Club Minutes, Box 20, vol. 90, CWC Papers; "With Up-to-Date Women: Club Women Likely to Secure Separate Dormitory for Bridewell Boys" and "Plea for Waifs: Bridewell Supt. Crawford on Training School," undated clippings, scrapbook 3, Flower Scrapbooks; memorandum by Julia Lathrop, May 3, 1917, vol. 2, Bowen Papers. On the opening of the dormitories, *Chicago Tribune*, June 28, 1899, and July 1, 1899.

64. Minutes of the Board Meeting, February 9, 1898, box 3, vol. 19, CWC Papers.

65. Club Minutes, October 26, 1898, box 21, vol. 93, CWC Papers; Frank and Jerome, *Annals of the Chicago Woman's Club*, 187–88.

children, leading the agitation that produced the juvenile court bill. They also played an important role in lobbying for the Illinois legislature's passage in 1899 of what became the Juvenile Court Law. Moreover, together with the women of the Hull House community they had established informal methods of dealing with juvenile offenders before legislation was secured. Thus, although the club continued to lobby for reform by sending delegates to the Illinois Conference of Charities in November 1898—which concentrated on the question "Who Are the Children of the State?"—it was just as concerned with developing informal methods of treating juvenile delinquents.[66]

At the end of December 1898 the Joint Committee on Probation Work for children in police stations reported that in cooperation with the Children's Home and Aid Society, the salary of a probation officer had been raised so that he could work in the East Chicago Avenue police station. Mr. Carl Kelsey of Boston, who was familiar with the work, was secured for the position. Members of the club would cooperate with him by looking out for the children after Mr. Kelsey had secured a suspended sentence and investigated the case. The club member would then visit the child's home and his teachers and see that he was kept in school and off the streets and otherwise watched and guided.[67] Thus, by paying the salary of a probation officer and securing a man who had experience working in an established probation system, the Chicago Woman's Club made steps toward a more formal use of probation in Chicago, although work by volunteers continued in other police stations.

As individuals, rather than as delegates of the club, Mrs. Flower and Miss Lathrop, and possibly a few others, were involved in drawing up the juvenile court bill. The committee that wrote the measure did so under the auspices of the Chicago Bar Association, and it was Judge Harvey B. Hurd who actually drafted the bill, although the final version that was presented to the legislature in February 1899 was a composite of the views of committee members and represented the cooperation of several organizations.[68] The document was known as the Chicago Bar Association bill, for even though women reformers had been instrumental in promoting the need for such

66. Club Minutes, October 26, 1898, and January 25, 1899, box 21, vol. 93, CWC Papers.
67. Club Minutes, December 28, 1898, January 25, 1899, and April 29, 1899, box 21, vol. 93, CWC Papers; Minutes of the Board Meeting, February 8, 1899, box 3, vol. 20, CWC Papers; Frank and Jerome, *Annals of the Chicago Woman's Club*, 188.
68. Memorandum by Julia Lathrop, May 3, 1917, and letter from Lucy Flower, May 1917, vol. 2, Bowen Papers; Timothy D. Hurley, *Juvenile Courts and What They Have Accomplished*

legislation, they realized that the bill was less likely to pass the legislature as a woman's measure than as a bar association bill. Although women could campaign for reform, especially in matters relating to children, legislation too closely identified as a woman's measure was likely to be treated with suspicion by a male legislature.[69] Nevertheless, a group from the club was sent to Springfield to lobby for the bill's passage, though they were not allowed to appear before the legislature.[70]

The act that passed and came into effect on July 1, 1899, was entitled "An Act to Regulate the Treatment and Control of Dependent, Neglected and Delinquent Children," and it clearly acknowledged the viewpoint of its originators—the women reformers—in its conclusion: "This act shall be liberally construed to the end that its purpose may be carried out, to-wit: That the care, custody and discipline of a child shall approximate as nearly as may be that which should be given by its parents, and in all cases where it can properly be done, the child to be placed in an approved family home and become a member of the family by legal adoption or otherwise."[71]

By the time the Juvenile Court Law became operational in July 1899, the Chicago Woman's Club had been campaigning for changes in the law as regards children for some years. The leaders of the club realized that if their efforts to improve the conditions of childhood in Illinois were to be successful, the sanction of law was required. Their efforts visiting the jail, supporting the jail school and the John Worthy School, and their charitable work in the poorer sections of Chicago suggested to them that many working-class and immigrant parents were not rearing their children to be good citizens and, moreover, that these children were being forced to grow up too fast and were not being properly nurtured, and so were becoming a danger to society. This seemed apparent in the increasing rates of juvenile delinquency in the poorer sections of Chicago. It was therefore the duty of society, through its laws, to ensure that neglected and delinquent children were

(Chicago, 1904), 20; Report of the Chicago Bar Association Committee on Juvenile Courts, typescript, October 28, 1899, Manuscript Division, Chicago Historical Society.

69. Letter from Lucy Flower, May 1917, vol. 2, Bowen Papers; Harriet S. Farwell, *Lucy Louisa Flower: 1837–1920: Her Contribution to Education and Child Welfare in Chicago* (privately printed, 1924), 30; Timothy D. Hurley, *The Origins of the Illinois Juvenile Court Law* (Chicago, 1907), 18.

70. Minutes of the Board Meeting, February 8, 1899, box 3, vol. 20, CWC Papers; Club Minutes, February 15, 1899, February 22, 1899, and March 1, 1899, box 21, vol. 93, CWC Papers.

71. "An Act to Regulate the Treatment and Control of Dependent, Neglected and Delinquent Children," as quoted in Hurley, *Origins of the Illinois Juvenile Court Law,* 26–39.

brought up in a proper fashion, even if this meant removing them from their natural home. Mrs. Flower emphasized this in stating that the rights of children and those of the state were of greater importance than those of their parents: "To my mind it presents no difficulty, for I believe the good of the child and the right of the state to control its citizenship are superior to any claim of the parent who is unfit or who willfully fails to perform his duty to his child."[72]

Accordingly, in seeking to reform the law in Illinois with regard to dependent and delinquent children, the Chicago Woman's Club was concerned that the children of the slums were not conforming to their ideas about how children should behave and that if they continued to lead lives of criminality and pauperism, they would undermine society itself. Clearly, the child's natural family was the best means of ensuring that these children were properly nurtured and grew up to be good citizens, but the fact that children were being brought before police courts suggested that some of these families needed help. With those families beyond the means of a visiting helper, it was essential that the child be removed from the influence of its own family and placed either with another approved family or in an institution. Thus, in seeking the reforms that eventually led to the establishment of a juvenile court and a probation system in Chicago—reforms aimed to ensure that the child was treated as a child by the law, with its best interests protected—leaders of the Chicago Woman's Club were motivated by a desire to see that the children of the slums lived and behaved as did their own children.

In many senses the reformers of the Chicago Woman's Club reflected the bias of their social class in their view of the cause of and solution to the problem of young offenders. Of more importance, however, was their gender identification. It was as mothers that they sought to help the children of the slums. The main concern of these women was to make working-class and immigrant families conform to their middle-class ideas about child rearing, for they believed the child who committed an offense was clearly suffering from a lack of proper nurture. Rather than seeking to appropriate the functions of the working-class family, as some historians have suggested, women of the club felt these families required help because, being poor, they were disintegrating under the impact of industrialization and urbanization and the struggle for survival in the slums of the city.[73] It was their

72. Flower, "The Duty of the State to Dependent Children," 14.

73. Christopher Lasch, *Haven in a Heartless World: The Family Besieged* (New York, 1977), 13–16.

own role as mothers, not only of their own children but of all children, that prompted these reformers to believe that the children of the slums were suffering from the breakdown of their families. Thus it was their duty, as mothers, to protect these children.

2

The Hull House Community

Among the women who sat with Judge Tuthill on the bench of the first session of the Chicago Juvenile Court on July 1, 1899, were several from Hull House, a social settlement in Chicago's Nineteenth Ward. They, like their colleagues from the Chicago Woman's Club, had been heavily involved in the creation of the court, especially the development of the probation system Judge Tuthill was soon to pronounce the keystone that supported the arch of the juvenile court.[1] In recognition of her expertise as a volunteer probation officer, Judge Tuthill appointed Mrs. Alzina Stevens of Hull House as the first probation officer of the new court, and it was to her custody that the first case considered suitable for probationary care was committed. The formal introduction of probation into the new system for juvenile justice in Chicago was not a new feature in the United States, but it marked a recognition in Illinois of the inadequacy of existing methods of dealing with juvenile offenders. Moreover, it reflected the concern of women reformers that existing custodial methods of dealing with children who broke the law were unsuitable for many of them and the belief that probation would allow these children to experience the proper influences of childhood.

In focusing their attention on developing a probationary system centered on Hull House, the settlement women made a substantial contribution toward the evolution of the Juvenile Court Law of 1899. This chapter will explore how the Hull House community was involved in securing this law, the reasons they felt a change in the law regarding dependent and delinquent children was necessary, and their motivations in campaigning for reform. In

---

1. Richard S. Tuthill, "The Juvenile Court Law in Cook County," *Proceedings of the Illinois Conference of Charities* (1900), 10–16.

many respects they were prompted by the same concerns as their fellow reformers in the Chicago Woman's Club, but substantial differences existed
between the two groups. Although the Hull House women may be described as "maternalists," their perspectives and priorities were different
from those of the "traditional maternalists" of the Chicago Woman's Club.
Many of the Hull House reformers had college educations and backgrounds
in the social sciences that, together with their experience of living in
Chicago's Nineteenth Ward, influenced their pursuit of reform. Their identification as women and the social expectation that they would be mothers
were often secondary to these factors in guiding their social activism. Thus,
although the Hull House women, the "professional maternalists," wrapped
themselves in traditional maternalist ideology, it may sometimes have been
little more than a rhetorical device or strategic posture.

Despite this difference in perspective, the women of Hull House were
closely connected with the Chicago Woman's Club in many of its ventures
to improve the lot of dependent and delinquent children. On a personal basis the connection between the two agencies was very close. Several members of the Hull House community were also members of the Chicago
Woman's Club—notably Jane Addams, Florence Kelley, and Julia Lathrop.
Similarly, prominent members of the Chicago Woman's Club, particularly
Lucy Flower and Louise deKoven Bowen, were benefactresses of Hull
House and were involved in its various activities.[2] At times the two groups
worked together so closely that it is difficult to differentiate between the initiatives of the two organizations. This interaction between Hull House and
the Chicago Woman's Club was an important factor in the various efforts
made to alleviate the problem of juvenile crime and in the eventual agitation
for a juvenile court law.

Jane Addams and her friend Ellen Gates Starr moved into what became
known as Hull House on 18 September 1889. They were soon the nucleus
of a thriving social settlement in Chicago's Nineteenth Ward.[3] Hull House
was not the first settlement house in the United States, but it became arguably its most famous, due in large part to the character of the women
who lived there during the 1890s.

Most important among the residents of Hull House was its chief resident,
Jane Addams. She was the youngest daughter of John Addams, who was a

2. Kathryn Kish Sklar, "Who Funded Hull House?" in Kathleen D. McCarthy, ed., *Lady
Bountiful Revisited: Women, Philanthropy and Power* (New Brunswick, 1990), 94–115.
3. Jane Addams, *Twenty Years at Hull House* (reprint, New York, 1961; first published,
1910), 79.

prominent member of the community of Cedarville, Illinois. He was also active politically and had served eight terms as a senator in Illinois and was an early member of the Republican Party in Illinois and a supporter of Abraham Lincoln. Jane Addams was educated in local schools and then attended Rockford Female Seminary. The years immediately after she graduated from college were a period of uncertainty and illness in which she sought to find something important to do with her life. The result was ultimately the establishment of Hull House with her college friend Miss Starr.[4]

Julia Lathrop came from a similar background. She was born in Rockford, Illinois, on June 29, 1858, the daughter of William and Sarah Adeline Lathrop and the eldest of five children. The family traced its roots back to John Lothrop, a dissenting minister who emigrated to the colony of Massachusetts in 1634. William Lathrop had a law practice in Rockford and helped organize the Republican Party in Illinois. He served in the Illinois state legislature at Springfield and later in Congress. Julia Lathrop was educated in local schools and attended Rockford Seminary for a year before transferring to Vassar College, from which she received her degree in 1880. During the next decade she worked as a secretary in her father's law office, where she read some law and became secretary of two local companies. In 1890 she decided to join Jane Addams at Hull House.[5]

Florence Kelley, another Hull House resident, was born in Philadelphia on September 12, 1859, the third child of William Kelley and his second wife, Caroline. William Kelley was of Irish Protestant stock, a self-educated lawyer and judge, and a Jacksonian Democrat whose opposition to slavery led him into the Republican Party in 1854 and to a long career in Congress. Florence Kelley received much of her early schooling at home due to illness. She entered Cornell University in 1876 and received her degree in 1882. She attempted to enter the University of Pennsylvania Graduate School as a preliminary to studying law but when refused entry on the ground of her sex went instead to Zurich, where she read law. While a student in Zurich, Kelley became a socialist and met and married Lazare Wischnewetzky, a Russian medical student and socialist, in June 1884. The couple returned to

4. Jane Addams's family background and her life before the establishment of Hull House are dealt with in Addams, *Twenty Years at Hull House*, 19–74; Allen F. Davis, *American Heroine: The Life and Legend of Jane Addams* (New York, 1973), 3–52.

5. Biographical details taken from Edward T. James, Janet Wilson James, and Paul S. Boyer, *Notable American Women, 1607–1950: A Biographical Dictionary,* 4 vols. (Cambridge, Mass., 1971), 2:370–72; Jane Addams, *My Friend, Julia Lathrop* (New York, 1935), 2–45.

America in 1886 and had three children, but they became increasingly es-
tranged, and the marriage ended in separation in 1891. As a result, Florence
Kelley with her three children moved to Illinois, where she soon obtained a
divorce and late in 1891 became a resident of Hull House.[6]

Many Hull House residents shared a similar upbringing: they were from
middle-class families and had been college educated. The life of Alzina Parsons Stevens, who became a resident of Hull House in 1893, however, had
been very different. She was born on May 27, 1849, in Parsonsfield, Maine,
a town founded by her paternal grandfather, but the family fell on hard times
when Alzina was a child, and she was forced to work in a textile factory at
the age of thirteen. There she lost a finger in an industrial accident. She had
little formal education, but at age eighteen learned the printing trade and
went to work as a newspaper proofreader and typesetter. She became involved in the labor movement and in 1877 organized and became the first
president of a woman's labor group, as well as one of the leading spirits of
the Knights of Labor in Toledo, Ohio. In 1892 she moved to Chicago and
soon became a resident of Hull House. Like Florence Kelley, she had married at an early age, but this had ended in divorce.[7]

Mary Kenney, like Alzina Stevens, had found employment in the printing
and binding trades in order to support herself and her invalid mother. After
moving to Chicago in the late 1880s and working in several binderies in the
city, she became convinced that women must organize for better hours and
working conditions. It was through her efforts to organize women book-
binders into a union of their own that she became associated with the Hull
House community. While only a semi-resident herself, Mary Kenney worked
closely with other residents to improve working conditions for women and
to establish a cooperative boarding club for working girls. She remained involved in the labor movement and in 1892 was appointed the first woman
general organizer for the American Federation of Labor. Though the A F of
L had little interest in organizing women, Miss Kenney became a leading labor activist and continued her close association with Hull House.[8]

Jane Addams, Julia Lathrop, and Florence Kelley were fairly typical of
settlement house residents in the United States during the 1890s. But while

6. Biographical details are taken from James, James, and Boyer, *Notable American
Women*, 2:316–19; Kathryn Kish Sklar, ed., *The Autobiography of Florence Kelley: Notes of
Sixty Years* (Chicago, 1986); Kathryn Kish Sklar, *Florence Kelley and the Nation's Work: The
Rise of Women's Political Culture, 1830–1900* (New Haven, 1995).

7. Biographical details are taken from Davis, *American Heroine*, 79–80; Addams, *My
Friend, Julia Lathrop*, 146–47.

8. Biographical details are taken from James, James, and Boyer, *Notable American*

the majority of settlement house workers came from middle-class, often small-town environments and had been college educated, a significant minority were from less-privileged backgrounds. These, like Alzina Stevens and Mary Kenney, were often prominent in the labor movement and, although working-class, were members of occupational and organizational elites.[9] Hull House was perhaps unusual among the settlement houses in that its residents came from a wider social background than others. It drew its members from among middle-class, college-educated young people; trade unionists; and very occasionally, its neighbors, working-class immigrants. It was, however, the college-educated residents who gave the settlement its character, and it was middle-class values that predominated.[10]

Another feature of Hull House was that, like a number of other American settlement houses, it was dominated by women. Indeed, a striking fact about American settlements was that although numerous men went into settlement work in the 1890s, many houses were run and staffed primarily by women.[11] For the first three years of its existence, all residents of Hull House were women, though several men were involved as nonresidents. It was not until around 1894 that men came into residence in a cottage on Polk Street, dining at Hull House itself and giving as much of their time as was consistent with their professional or business life.[12] It is also significant that many of the women settlement workers were unmarried or, like Florence Kelley and Alzina Stevens, divorced. Some married couples lived in the settlements, but they tended to be exceptions.[13]

Young people of both sexes entered the settlements for a number of rea-

Women, 2:655–56; Davis, American Heroine, 78–80; Sklar, Florence Kelley and the Nation's Work, 186, 197–98.

9. Kathryn Kish Sklar, "Hull House in the 1890s: A Community of Women Reformers," Signs 10 (Summer 1985): 668–69; Allen F. Davis, Spearheads for Reform: The Social Settlements and the Progressive Movement, 1890–1914 (New York, 1967), 38.

10. Recent works on settlement houses that look at the lesser-known houses and the middle-class bias of most settlements include Ruth Hutchinson Crocker, Social Work and Social Order: The Settlement Movement in Two Industrial Cities, 1889–1930 (Urbana, 1992); Mina Carson, Settlement Folk: Social Thought and the American Settlement Movement, 1885–1930 (Chicago, 1990); and Rivka Shpak Lissak, Pluralism and Progressives: Hull House and the New Immigrants, 1890–1919 (Chicago, 1989).

11. Carl N. Degler, At Odds: Women and the Family in America from the Revolution to the Present (New York, 1980), 320; Sklar, Florence Kelley and the Nation's Work, 171–205. For an alternative view, see Crocker, Social Work and Social Order, 216–17.

12. "Hull House: A Social Settlement," in Hull House Maps and Papers, by the Residents of Hull House (New York, 1895), 229.

13. Davis, Spearheads for Reform, 34; Margaret Gibbons Wilson, The American Woman in Transition: The Urban Influence, 1870–1920 (Westport, Conn., 1979), 100.

sons, both selfish and benevolent. The settlement concept itself came from England. Its main idea was that well-educated, middle-class young people should set up residence in slum neighborhoods and, by living among the poor as neighbors, be in a better position to help them. Many of the pioneer settlement workers in America were idealists who believed they had a mission to solve the problems of the crowded city.[14] Their motives were not purely altruistic, however. Recognizing this, Jane Addams argued that young people did not enter settlement work purely out of a benevolent desire to help the poor. Rather, the settlement experiment served a dual purpose, for through it the need of college-educated young people to find an outlet for their otherwise frustrated talents and energy was combined with what Addams considered to be a sincere desire to help those trapped in poverty. The settlement experiment gave these young people a sense of adventure and mission, a feeling of getting back to basic elements their own lives lacked.[15] Thus, the settlement impulse was a multifaceted one, but, as Addams argued, its aims were straightforward:

> It aims, in a measure, to develop whatever of social life its neighborhood may afford, to focus and give form to that life, to bring to bear upon it the results of cultivation and training; . . . It is quite impossible for me to say in what proportion or degree the subjective necessity which led to the opening of Hull House combined the three trends: first, the desire to interpret democracy in social terms; secondly, the impulse beating at the very source of our lives, urging us to aid in the race progress; and thirdly, the Christian movement toward humanitarianism. . . . Many more motives may blend with the three trends; possibly the desire for a new form of social success due to the nicety of imagination, which refuses worldly pleasures unmixed with the joys of self-sacrifice; possibly a love of approbation.[16]

For college-educated women in particular, the settlements fulfilled a very obvious need. Higher education had a profound impact on the first and second generation of female graduates, and this impact manifested itself in a number of ways. Many of these women found it difficult to find a place in society after they had graduated. Their families expected them to settle down and have families of their own, whereas their education suggested

---

14. Davis, *Spearheads for Reform*, xi, 38.
15. Addams, *Twenty Years at Hull House*, 94–98; Davis, *American Heroine*, 57.
16. Addams, *Twenty Years at Hull House*, 97–98.

that there were wider horizons to be explored. Settlement work provided an ideal outlet for these women. The knowledge they had acquired at college, joined with the principles of educated motherhood and the growing emphasis on child study, encouraged college graduates to confront the problems that industrialization, urbanization and immigration had posed. They aimed to go beyond philanthropy and charity to influence and educate through direct and personal encounters. However, their emphasis was rather different from that of older charity workers. They no longer preached virtue, frugal housekeeping, and temperance to their neighbors but instead instructed them in hygiene and child development. They also went beyond purely practical work to investigate the conditions in which these neighbors lived and worked. This change of emphasis came about in part because women's colleges were steeped in the traditions of educated motherhood but also because by the end of the nineteenth century, many women's colleges had begun to introduce a social science curriculum that influenced college graduates to use more "scientific" methods in their charity work.[17]

In essence, for college-educated women the settlement movement supplied an outlet for their talents and training. Life in a settlement often also provided an alternative to family life for its residents, at least until they married and established families of their own. Settlement work quickly became an attractive occupation for single middle-class women, and it was soon widely accepted as a proper occupation for these women. To society it appeared as an extension into the slum of the traditional role of women as mother and housekeeper, and settlement workers did little to upset this assumption.[18]

The community life fostered by the settlements proved an important source of support for the women who lived in them and was also instrumental in their development as reformers. As Kathryn Kish Sklar has shown, Hull House gave women reformers an emotional and economic substitute for family life and linked them with other women of their own class and educational background, thereby greatly increasing their political and social ties. Hull House also had many effective ties with other women's

17. Sheila M. Rothman, *Woman's Proper Place: A History of Changing Ideals and Practices, 1870 to the Present* (New York, 1978), 5–7.

18. John P. Rousmaniere, "Cultural Hybrid in the Slums: The College Woman and the Settlement House, 1889–1894," *American Quarterly* 22 (Spring 1970): 45–66; Mary M. Kingsbury, "Women in New York Settlements," *Municipal Affairs* 2 (September 1898): 458–62; Jane Addams, "Woman's Work for Chicago," *Municipal Affairs* 2 (September 1898): 502–8; William Hard, "Chicago's Five Maiden Aunts: The Women Who Boss Chicago Very Much to Its Advantage," *American Magazine* 62 (1906): 481–89.

organizations. Further, it enabled women reformers to cooperate with male reformers and their organizations, allowing them to draw on male support without submitting to their control. Because Hull House was largely funded by the residents themselves and wealthy women sympathetic to the residents' goals, their freedom of action was unrestricted. Finally, it provided a creative setting for the women reformers to pursue and develop a reform strategy.[19]

As a result, in a period when women still did not have the vote, the settlement gave women reformers the mutual support and ability to reach beyond female institutions to enter the political realm dominated by men. Although it is unlikely that all women settlement house workers were as concerned to gain political power as Sklar suggests, it remains true that the network of women reformers centered around settlements such as Hull House gave female reformers the support and contacts that enabled them to seek legislative redress for some of the problems of their neighborhoods.

Thus, the settlement movement allowed women reformers to move more fully into civic life, but they still did so as women. Even though they emphasized their professionalism and the scientific nature of their work, the Hull House women reformers drew on the traditions of women's sphere in their practice of social activism. The settlement emphasized women's qualities of compassion, nurture, and sympathy and to an extent also drew on maternalist ideology with its emphasis on the role of women as mothers.[20] However, the interpretation of this ideology was quite different from that espoused by the Chicago Woman's Club. For unlike the traditional maternalists of the Chicago Woman's Club, the majority of the Hull House women were not mothers themselves, and they rejected a sentimental view of motherhood in favor of a more scientific approach. Often their use of maternalist rhetoric was little more than a strategic posture. Thus, while they acknowledged the centrality of feminine qualities in their work, they placed much greater emphasis on their professional expertise as social scientists.[21]

The social science methods and philosophy advocated by Hull House

19. Sklar, "Hull House in the 1890s," 658–77; Sklar, "Who Funded Hull House?" 94–115.

20. See, for instance, the use of maternalist rhetoric by Julia Lathrop and Florence Kelley in "To the Women and Women's Clubs of Illinois," February 15, 1896, Illinois Federation of Women's Clubs, 1896, reel 41, Jane Addams Papers, microfilm.

21. Molly Ladd-Taylor, "Toward Defining Maternalism in U.S. History," *Journal of Women's History* 5 (Fall 1993): 110–13; Barbara Sicherman, "Working It Out: Gender, Profession, and Reform in the Career of Alice Hamilton," in Noralee Frankel and Nancy S. Dye, eds., *Gender, Class, Race, and Reform in the Progressive Era* (Lexington, Ky., 1991), 127–47.

women remained gendered nonetheless, drawing on a growing tradition of women social scientists. By the 1890s college-educated women had been involved in this field for several decades, but it was in the settlement movement that women social scientists were able to find an institutional base. Whereas male social scientists within the universities found themselves increasingly circumscribed in their ability to advocate the kind of social reforms their research suggested to them because of limits on academic freedom, women in the settlement movement had considerable freedom of action. As Sklar has shown, female settlement workers confidently used the research methods they learned at college and at the same time drew on the older social science heritage their male academic counterparts had been forced to abandon. Thus they combined practical work to help the poor of America's largest cities with advocacy for social change that often took the form of campaigns to enact structural legislative reform.[22] For many of these women, the ultimate aim was to change society itself. As Florence Kelley argued, settlement workers must "Seek to understand the laws of social and industrial development, in the midst of which we live, to spread this enlightenment among the men and women destined to contribute to the change to a higher social order, to hasten the day when all the good things of society shall be the goods of the children of men, and our petty philanthropy of today superfluous—this is the true work for the elevation of the race, the true philanthropy."[23]

Although the female social scientists at Hull House placed great emphasis on collecting data about their neighborhood, their main purpose was not an objective, scientific study of conditions. Rather, they used this scientific data to provide a careful analysis of a social problem and to demand reform. Their demands drew on female traditions of social activism and often took the form of a moral imperative. Thus, women settlement house workers used social science methods to shed new light on social problems and draw conclusions from their findings; but these conclusions were gendered in that

22. Kathryn Kish Sklar, "*Hull House Maps and Papers*: Social Science as Women's Work in the 1890s," in Martin Bulmer, Kevin Bales, and Kathryn Kish Sklar, eds., *The Social Survey in Historical Perspective, 1880–1940* (Cambridge, Eng., 1991), 115; Kathryn Kish Sklar, "The Historical Foundations of Women's Power in the Creation of the American Welfare State, 1830–1940," in Seth Koven and Sonya Michel, eds., *Mothers of a New World: Maternalist Politics and the Origins of Welfare States* (New York, 1993), 65; Sklar, "Who Funded Hull House?" 94–115. The influence of social science on Hull House women may be clearly seen in *Hull House Maps and Papers*. See also Mary Jo Deegan, *Jane Addams and the Men of the Chicago School, 1892–1918* (New Brunswick, 1988).
23. Sklar, ed., *Autobiography of Florence Kelley*, 104.

they often focused on the needs of women and children and demanded reform as an immediate moral necessity.[24]

It is therefore unsurprising that some of the earliest efforts of the Hull House residents were directed toward helping the women and children of the neighborhood. One of the first moves was to open a free kindergarten for the children of the area. A day nursery grew out of an increasing awareness that in some families women had to work outside the home and so needed somewhere to leave their children while at work. It is suggestive of attitudes of the Hull House reformers in the early 1890s that the day nursery was justified in terms of the proper role of the mother in the family—it was necessary for these women to work outside their homes because of the willful or enforced idleness, or the temporary or permanent absence, of their husbands.[25] The assumption was that otherwise these mothers would not willingly work outside their homes. Other measures also sought to help women and children: the opening of a public playground located on a piece of empty land close to Hull House and supervised by a Hull House resident; the establishment of various clubs for children and young people; and attempts to provide some alternative to the commercialized entertainments of the area, which were regarded as detrimental to the morals of young people.[26] Hull House never concentrated its efforts entirely on the neighborhood women and children, for it was also involved in other activities to improve the neighborhood generally and to provide cultural clubs for all its residents. Nevertheless, it was the facilities they provided for women and children that were most numerous, and it was in an attempt to protect women and their families that they first campaigned for reform legislation.

Living as they did in a neighborhood where many of the immigrants lived a fairly marginal existence and where unemployment could spell disaster for many families, Hull House residents soon became aware of the need for more than just stopgap measures to help these families. They also soon gained the impression that under the impact of industrialization, urbaniza-

24. Sklar, "Hull House Maps and Papers," 116–29; Deegan, Jane Addams and the Men of the Chicago School, 33–34; Hull House Maps and Papers, 3–14. See also, Ellen Fitzpatrick, Endless Crusade: Women Social Scientists and Progressive Reform (New York, 1990).

25. Julia Lathrop, "Hull House as a Sociological Laboratory," Proceedings of the National Conference of Charities and Correction (1894), 313–19. On day nurseries, see Sonya Michel, "The Limits of Maternalism: Policies Toward American Wage-Earning Mothers During the Progressive Era," in Koven and Michel, eds., Mothers of a New World, 277–320.

26. Julia Lathrop, "Hull House as a Sociological Laboratory," 315–16; circulars, folder 507, scrapbook 2, 1894, Hull House Association Papers, Special Collections, University of Illinois at Chicago; Addams, Twenty Years at Hull House, 83–86, 127–30.

tion, and immigration, the family as they saw it was under threat. In this they shared many of the same perceptions as the women of the Chicago Woman's Club, but their experience of living in the Chicago slums and their involvement in compiling social surveys of the area gave them a more realistic understanding of the problems these families faced. Nonetheless, their perceptions were colored by their own assumptions about "proper"—namely, middle-class—family life. It is therefore unsurprising that they should have become so concerned with the problem of neglected, orphaned, and delinquent children in the neighborhood.

It soon became clear to Jane Addams and her colleagues that the lives of slum children did not conform to their preconceived image of childhood. They believed children should remain dependent until they had been fully prepared for adult life by means of a loving and nurturing family and a formal education. Their experience among the children of the neighborhood, and especially the apparent increase in the incidence of crime among these children, led them to think that immigrant and working-class families were on the point of breakdown. Jane Addams, in particular, recognized the pressures the slum exerted on family life and the problems that developed between immigrant parents and their Americanized children, but her sympathies were most often with the children and what she saw as the denial of their right to childhood. Thus, she felt that the strictness of some immigrant parents could lead directly to the delinquency of their children, especially in those cases where parents sent their offspring out to work and did not allow them any money of their own, expecting them instead to hand over all their wages.[27] In other cases the temptation of goods on display was too much for children living in poverty: "many younger children . . . are constantly arrested for petty thieving because they are too eager to take home food or fuel which will relieve the distress and need they so constantly hear discussed," wrote Jane Addams. "The coal on the wagons, the vegetables displayed in front of the grocery shops, the very wooden blocks in the loosened street paving are a challenge to their powers to help out at home."[28] In still other cases, immigrant customs brought these children to grief: "The honest immigrant parents, totally ignorant of American laws and municipal regulations, often send a child to pick up coal on the railroad tracks or to stand at three o'clock in the morning before the side door of a restaurant which gives away broken food, or to collect grain for the chickens at the base of elevators and standing cars. The latter custom ac-

27. Addams, *Twenty Years at Hull House*, 179–80.
28. Ibid., 180–81.

counts for the large number of boys arrested for breaking the seals on grain freight cars."[29]

Jane Addams was perhaps more articulate than other Hull House residents in expressing what she understood as the problems of immigrant and working-class children in the slums. But, some of her fellow residents, also recognizing that many of the problems of dependent and delinquent children were the result of a maladjustment to city life, sought means to deal with these problems. As a result, a body of expertise grew up informally around Hull House, which provided a basis from which the juvenile court could be built.

Most prominently involved in efforts to find a solution to the problem of dependent and delinquent children was Julia Lathrop. Her experience as a resident of Hull House and a member of the Illinois Board of Charities—her appointment to which was due to her involvement with Hull House—had shaped her perceptions of the problem and the answers she sought. The solutions the Hull House women advocated to the problem of juvenile delinquency and dependency initially had a different emphasis from those of the Chicago Woman's Club until the two groups merged to campaign for legislative change. Whereas the women of the club at first were mainly involved in helping children already involved with the courts and penal institutions by providing a school in the jail and lobbying for a law that would embody new ideas about childhood, some residents of Hull House were striving to prevent children from ever appearing before the courts and acting as probation officers to those already in trouble with the police. Although Hull House residents were also lobbying for a change in the law as regards dependent and delinquent children, their most significant contribution was arguably that of developing an informal probation system around Hull House. This provided a body of probation officers who would form the nucleus of the probation system introduced in the Juvenile Court Law of 1899.

Julia Lathrop moved into Hull House in 1890, and it is probable that her motives in joining the settlement were similar to those of many other young people in the settlement movement. During the panic and depression of 1893 she became a volunteer county agent, helping to investigate relief applicants in the Nineteenth Ward. In 1893 she was appointed, by Governor Altgeld, as the first woman member of the Illinois Board of Charities, a post she held—apart from an interval of four years—until 1909. For her, the

---

29. Ibid., 181.

post was not a political sinecure, and she set about visiting every one of the state and county charitable institutions. She soon came to the conclusion that the reason some state institutions did not operate effectively and failed to benefit those who needed their help was because of the political spoils system. This meant those appointed to many positions in charitable institutions were chosen because of their political allegiance rather than their suitability for the job. She began to campaign for an end to the spoils system but with little success, and in 1901 she resigned from the State Board of Charities in protest at further encroachments by politicians on the state's charitable institutions.[30] She only agreed to accept the post again when the new governor promised something would be done about the spoils system. This campaign against political corruption was not unique to Miss Lathrop or even to Chicago but was a recurrent theme among many women and male reformers in the late nineteenth century; it foreshadowed the insistence by those who drew up the juvenile court legislation of 1899 that the new probation officers should not be paid by the state so that these positions would not become part of the spoils system.

Her experience as a member of the Illinois Board of Charities not only brought Miss Lathrop to distrust the political spoils system but also gave her firsthand experience of the conditions in the poorhouses and lunatic asylums of the state. Her reactions to the presence of children in county poorhouses and jails were recorded in the reports that the Board of Charities presented to the governor of Illinois every two years. Thus, in their report for 1894 the board noted that there was no law in Illinois that prevented the housing of children in the poorhouses, and this was detrimental not only to the children themselves but to society. Miss Lathrop's influence on the report is clearly seen in its explanation that the conditions of the poorhouse were not only meager and uncomfortable but those of an institution, not a home; thus, the children had no chance to learn the lessons a good home could teach. Moreover, there could be no worse school for citizenship than an almshouse, for there the child was surrounded by idleness, stupidity, and near criminality, as well as irresponsible authority on the part of the superintendents.

As a solution the board suggested a law that no child between the ages of two and sixteen be permitted in an almshouse. Instead, dependent children

---

30. Addams, *My Friend, Julia Lathrop*, 94–109; Julia Lathrop, "The Cook County Charities," in *Hull House Maps and Papers*, 143–61; letter to Hon. Richard Yates, Governor, July 19, 1901, folder 306, Residents and Associates—Julia Lathrop, Correspondence, Hull House Association Papers, Special Collections, University of Illinois at Chicago.

should be placed in proper families that had been carefully inspected before the child was placed in them.[31] Here, Miss Lathrop and her colleagues on the Board of Charities were reflecting certain assumptions about what did and did not constitute the correct environment in which a child should be brought up. Clearly an almshouse was not, in their opinion, a suitable environment, and children should be removed even if it meant separating them from their parents. Reformers felt it to be their duty to judge what was in the child's best interests, and this often meant condemning some parents as unfit, even if only because of their circumstances. Some women reformers shortly came to the conclusion that poverty alone was not a sufficient reason to condemn a mother as unfit to bring up her children, yet the distribution of payments to mothers to alleviate their poverty remained heavily dependent on whether they lived up to the moral standards of middle-class reformers.[32] This recommendation to remove children from the almshouses was repeated in the reports for 1896 and 1898, and in 1897 a bill was presented to the legislature in an attempt to secure this reform, but with little success.[33]

The bill of 1897 was sponsored by the Board of Charities and as such was not clearly identified as a women's measure, but it received the endorsement of both the Hull House community and the Chicago Woman's Club. In commenting on both Miss Lathrop's reappointment to the Board of Charities and on the bill before the legislature, the *Hull House Bulletin* outlined their ideas about the state's duty to dependent children: "Curiously enough there is no law in Illinois forbidding the presence of children in the poor house, and hundreds of children pass through the poorhouses of Illinois every year. Dependency would seem the natural right of every child, but when the natural family relation breaks down, either by reason of the death or neglect of parents, society must contrive in some way to make good the lack."[34] This attitude was clearly stated by Julia Lathrop herself in a speech before the Illinois Conference of Charities in 1896, in which she

31. Board of State Commissioners of Public Charities of the State of Illinois, *Thirteenth Biennial Report,* 1894, pp. 47–48.

32. Linda Gordon, "Single Mothers and Child Neglect, 1880–1920," *American Quarterly* 37 (Summer 1985): 173–92; Joanne L. Goodwin, "An American Experiment in Paid Motherhood: The Implementation of Mothers' Pensions in Early Twentieth-Century Chicago," *Gender and History* 4 (Autumn 1992): 323–42.

33. Board of State Commissioners of Public Charities of the State of Illinois, *Fourteenth Biennial Report,* 1896, pp. 62–65; *Fifteenth Biennial Report,* 1898, pp. 61–72.

34. *Hull House Bulletin* (April 1, 1897): 6, Special Collections, University of Illinois at Chicago.

argued that the state should extend to the poor child without property the same protection it gave the rich orphan. The state should say to the child, "You are the ward of the State; your interests shall be constantly in mind; . . . the State will not forget you nor forget to know all the time that you have a proper home, a genuine education and as fair a chance in life as possible."[35]

Her experiences as a member of the Illinois Board of Charities clearly showed Miss Lathrop that dependent children in Illinois were not treated as her ideas of childhood suggested they should be. Moreover, if something were not done, these children might become criminals, since they were not receiving the proper home influences to shape them into good citizens. She continued to campaign for legislation to prohibit the presence of children in poorhouses in the state. There had been a clause in the juvenile court bill of 1899 that aimed to do just that, but it was thrown out in the committee stage of the bill. Miss Lathrop continued this campaign, even as her interests shifted to the problem of delinquent children in Chicago. The attempt to remove children from poorhouses was part of a long-running campaign, for many other states already had such legislation. Julia Lathrop's attitude toward this question differed little from that of her male colleagues, though her rhetoric was much more maternalist in its orientation.[36]

Whereas her involvement as a member of the Illinois Board of Charities showed Miss Lathrop the need for legislation to help the dependent children of the state, her experience as a member of the Hull House community made her realize the need for legislation to help delinquent and near-delinquent children. She was not alone among the women of Hull House in this. As a member of the Board of Charities she was able to establish contacts with male reformers, politicians, and men of influence, which she could use in her attempts to secure legislative reform.

Florence Kelley and Alzina Stevens were also influenced by their experiences as state office holders in their growing awareness of the nature of child life in Chicago. In 1893 Governor John Altgeld appointed Florence Kelley as Chief Factory Inspector and Mrs. Stevens as Assistant Factory Inspector for Illinois. In their visits to factories and sweatshops around Illinois

35. Julia Lathrop, "Discussion," *Proceedings of the Illinois Conference of Charities* (1896), 62.

36. For instance, the *Reports of the Illinois Board of Charities* refer constantly to the need to remove children from the contaminating influence of the poorhouses: see, for example, the reports for 1887, pp. 52–83, when Julia Lathrop was not a member, and for 1894, pp. 47–48, when she was.

they were confronted with what they saw as the victims of industrialization:
the toiling children of these factories. Although the immediate result of their
tours of inspection were reports about the horrors of child labor and attempts to limit it, their familiarity with the conditions of child life in the factories and sweatshops gave them an insight into other aspects of child life in
the city. Thus, while their reports were full of specific demands for an end to
child labor and the enforcement of compulsory education laws, they also
reveal a concern about the quality of life for children in the slums of
Chicago.[37] Consequently, Florence Kelley and Mrs. Stevens began to seek
ways to alleviate what they saw as the distress of these children. They, like
the women of the Chicago Woman's Club, were fearful that such aspects of
industrialization and urbanization as child labor and juvenile delinquency
were symptoms of a breakdown in the family, and this largely explains their
motivation for trying to strengthen family life in the slums by such measures
as probation and compulsory education.

The Hull House women were involved in many of the efforts for reform
in the treatment of dependent and delinquent children that were initiated by
the Chicago Woman's Club. In several of these efforts, the Hull House
women, especially Miss Lathrop, were very much to the forefront. The relationship between the Chicago Woman's Club and the Hull House community was a symbiotic one. The women of Hull House had a greater knowledge of the temptations and conditions that led to juvenile crime, and they
had a certain expertise to draw on, both as a result of this experience and in
their work as factory inspectors and on the State Board of Charities. The
Chicago Woman's Club provided much of the support, both financial and
moral, necessary in their combined reform efforts. Several of the leaders of
the Chicago Woman's Club also supplied a number of the initiatives for reform legislation on which the juvenile court bill was eventually built. Thus,
in 1895 Miss Lathrop was involved with Mrs. Flower and Mrs. Henrotin in
an initiative to enact legislation that would introduce a probation system
and a juvenile court to deal with all children's cases in Chicago.[38] Similarly,

---

37. For instance, Florence Kelley and Alzina Stevens, "Wage Earning Children," in *Hull
House Maps and Papers*, 49–76; Alzina Parsons Stevens, "The Child, the Factory and the
State," *Arena* 10 (June 1894): 117–35. On Kelley's work as a factory inspector, see Sklar, *Flo-
rence Kelley and the Nation's Work*, 237–64.

38. Julia Lathrop dismissed her own involvement in this initiative as merely being a member
of the audience, but Mrs. Flower recalled Miss Lathrop's participation as much greater. Memorandum by Julia C. Lathrop and letter from Mrs. Lucy L. Flower, May 1917, vol. 2, Papers of
Louise deKoven Bowen, Manuscript Division, Chicago Historical Society (hereafter Bowen Papers).

Miss Lathrop and Florence Kelley were involved with Mrs. Flower in organizing mass meetings, in 1896, of the women's clubs of Illinois to discuss
the conditions of childhood in the state and in producing the appeal to the
women of Illinois that resulted from the meeting.[39] Throughout the 1898–
99 campaign to secure the Juvenile Court Law, the two agencies worked together. The Hull House community, however, also developed its own
method of dealing with the problem of criminal youth in its neighborhood:
an embryonic probation system.

Probation was not a new idea in the United States when it was introduced
for Illinois children by the Juvenile Court Law of 1899. It had been developed in Boston during the 1840s by John Augustus as a means of dealing
with offenders convicted of trivial offenses. First used informally for adult
offenders, it was gradually extended to include children; in 1878 probation
was recognized by statute. By 1899, however, very few states had adopted
probation as a way of dealing with offenders.[40]

It was clear that the women of Hull House were aware of developments
in Massachusetts, and this may be what prompted them to start an informal
probation system in Chicago. Informal and formal contacts at conferences
of settlement workers and the annual National Conference of Charities and
Correction ensured the spread of news about the latest innovations among
the national charitable and reform community. Moreover, Julia Lathrop
corresponded with Emily Balch of Wellesley College, Massachusetts, and
received reports from her on the workings of the Massachusetts system of
justice as regards children and the use of probation.[41] Mrs. Flower also visited Massachusetts to investigate the probation system and brought back a
report of how it worked.[42] The abandoned Illinois juvenile court bill of

39. January 24, 1896, box 2, vol. 17, Chicago Woman's Club Papers, Manuscript Division,
Chicago Historical Society (hereafter CWC Papers); June 22, 1896, box 20, vol. 90, CWC Pa-
pers; "With Up-to-Date Women: Women's Club Representatives Confer on the Child Prob-
lem," clipping, February 1, 1896, scrapbook 3, Lucy Flower and Coues Family Scrapbooks,
Manuscript Division, Chicago Historical Society (hereafter Flower Scrapbooks); "To the
Women and Women's Clubs of Illinois," leaflet, February 15, 1896, signed by Florence Kelley,
Julia Lathrop, Jane Addams, Lucy Flower, Ellen Henrotin, and Dr. Sarah Hackett Stevenson,
scrapbook 3, Flower Scrapbooks, pp. 7–10.

40. N. S. Timasheff, *One Hundred Years of Probation, 1841–1941. Part One: Probation in
the United States, England and the British Commonwealth of Nations* (New York, 1941); Carl
Kelsey, "How Does the Massachusetts Probation System Affect Children," *Proceedings of the
Illinois Conference of Charities* (1898), 65–66.

41. Correspondence with Emily Balch, Julia Lathrop Papers, Rockford College Archives,
Rockford, Illinois.

42. Julia C. Lathrop, "The Development of the Probation System in a Large City," *Charities*
13 (January 7, 1905): 344–49.

1895 included provision for the creation of a probation system in Chicago, but in its absence a probation system gradually began to develop in Chicago without the formal sanction of legislation.

In October 1896 the *Hull House Bulletin* reported that "Dr. Moore who has been in co-operation with the police stations for some months, will be at home from 8 to 9 o'clock every evening and will be glad to consult with parents who may desire her services." A similar announcement appeared regularly in the bulletin beginning in December 1897, advising that a resident of Hull House visited neighboring police stations and courts to aid in securing better conditions for wayward and incorrigible children. It went on to state that this resident would be available every evening at Hull House to meet with parents having trouble of this kind with their children.[43] In this informal way, a form of children's probation centered on Hull House grew up in the Nineteenth Ward. It seems to have begun simply as an extension of the work of the settlement, a means to help immigrant parents who were struggling with delinquent children and needed assistance dealing with the police stations and the courts. It is possible that Hull House residents at first acted as little more than a means of liaison between immigrant parents and the police, but this slowly developed into a system that not only helped children already in trouble with the police but tried to stop children from ever becoming involved with the courts. This work foreshadowed the role of probation officers after the passing of the Juvenile Court Law of 1899.

Until the passing of the Juvenile Court Law, judges were legally restricted in the way they could deal with children who came before the courts. A judge, on finding a child more than ten years old guilty of a crime, could sentence him to jail or some other reformatory institution, or the judge could impose a fine, which generally meant the child ended up in jail for failing to pay it.[44] By the mid-1890s, however, some judges were beginning to take a more lenient attitude toward juvenile cases, although as yet this had no legal basis. Judge Tuthill held separate court sessions for children at the request of the Chicago Woman's Club, but other judges also dealt differently with these cases, as and when they felt the necessity. Thus, a number of children were dismissed either to the care of their parents or, occa-

43. *Hull House Bulletin* (October 1896 and from December 1897 on). Dr. Dorothea Moore was a resident of Hull House.

44. Helen Ranklin Jeter, *The Chicago Juvenile Court* (Washington, D.C., Government. Printing Service, 1922), 2–3, outlines the legal position in Illinois as regards children before 1899.

sionally, to the supervision of a truant officer or one of the social workers at Hull House.

A number of social workers, apparently based at Hull House, kept records of cases in which they were involved in the local police stations from June 1897. These documents suggest that the dismissal of cases in which children were charged with criminal offenses was fairly frequent. They also reflect the use by the courts of various institutions, ostensibly established for dependent children, for delinquent children. Significantly, these records show Hull House residents investigating the background of the children's cases with which they were concerned and advising the judge on what action should be taken as a result of their investigations.[45] For instance, in June 1897 a boy of thirteen was brought before Judge Eberhardt on a charge of stealing iron, brass, and other items from a railroad company. It was suggested that the boy be sent to Feehanville, a Catholic institution for dependent children, but the case was continued; when it came up again before the court, a different judge dismissed the boy on the parents' promise to control him. Another thirteen-year-old boy who was before the court for stealing a basket of grapes and who had been locked up at the police station before had his case dismissed on his mother's promise to send the boy to his uncle on a farm at Kankakee. Other children were dismissed on condition that they attend school. Such a stipulation shows the importance attached to education as a means of preventing crime.

In other cases, the "probation officer" would request that a case be continued while she investigated the home conditions of the child and wrote a report to the judge to recommend the best action to be taken for the child. In May 1898 a twelve-year-old was brought before Judge Eberhardt for stealing. The case was continued at the probation officer's request, and after investigating the boy's family and finding that the boy was in the habit of selling papers and sleeping downtown, sometimes being away for as long as two weeks at a time, she recommended that the boy be sent to Feehanville, since he was clearly lacking the necessary home influences. The father agreed, and the boy went to Feehanville.[46]

Other cases suggest that the courts were powerless to enforce what action

---

45. These cases appear in a series of case studies in Case Studies (Restricted), supplement 1, folder 7, August 1899, Juvenile Protective Association Papers, Special Collections, University of Illinois at Chicago (hereafter JPA Papers); "An Interview with Hon. Oliver H. Horton on the Juvenile Court," *Juvenile Record* 2 (January/February 1901): 12–13.

46. All of these cases and those that follow are taken from Case Studies (Restricted), June 1897–August 1899, supplement 1, folder 7, JPA Papers.

they considered to be in the best interests of the child, especially in those cases where the offender was under ten, the parents were unwilling to co-operate, or the child's behavior was not strictly criminal. A child aged six was arrested for running wild and stealing from neighbors and was placed by the Catholic Visitation and Aid Society in Feehanville. After a couple of years, however, Feehanville refused to have him any longer, and the boy was sent home, where he behaved badly. His mother wished to send him to the Glenwood Industrial School, but it was suggested that if she was prepared to pay Mr. Bradley five dollars a month, she could have the boy kept at Al-lendale Farm. His mother refused to let him go, and the court was power-less to enforce its decision because the child was underage.

Not all cases were thwarted in this way, however, and on a number of oc-casions the parents themselves brought their children into court with com-plaints that they were incorrigible. This fact suggests that the court was not just a means by which middle-class social workers sought to impose social control on predominantly immigrant children. Clearly, parents who brought their children voluntarily into court for noncriminal offenses saw it as a means of enforcing parental control rather than as an instrument of class control. Immigrant parents could therefore use the courts for their own purposes. This must have been fraught with risks, however, for a child above the age of criminal responsibility—which at that time was ten years of age—brought before the courts by his parents for incorrigible behavior might well have been dealt with much more severely than the parents in-tended.[47]

The courts also dealt in various ways with the cases of children who were victims of neglect. A number of child offenders in the more obviously crim-inal cases were, however, sentenced to the House of Correction or sent for trial by the grand jury. Significantly, these case histories reflect the confu-sion within the correctional system at this time and the difficulties judges had enforcing sentences to institutions other than the bridewell or jail and dealing with children under ten, who were not legally responsible for their actions. They also suggest that some judges were more concerned than oth-

47. Anthony M. Platt suggests that the juvenile courts were instruments of social control: Platt, *The Child Savers: The Invention of Delinquency* (Chicago, 1969), 135–36. But see the following works, which suggest that welfare clients were able to use reformatory institutions and charitable agencies for their own purposes: Barbara Brenzel, *Daughters of the State: A So-cial Portrait of the First Reform School for Girls in North America, 1855–1905* (Cambridge, Mass., 1983); and Linda Gordon, *Heroes of Their Own Lives: The Politics and History of Family Violence* (London, 1989; first published, 1988).

ers about the circumstances of the children before them and took these circumstances into account in sentencing. Other judges, clearly convinced that education was of great importance in preventing children from becoming criminals, emphasized this in dismissing certain cases only after a period of time in which a record was kept of the child's school attendance. Child-saving organizations also safeguarded their own interests in the courts. This was especially true of the Catholic Visitation and Aid Society, which insisted on the need to place children in institutions of their own religious persuasion.

These case studies have a still greater significance in that they show a body of women acting for all intents and purposes as probation officers: appearing in court when children's cases were to be heard, investigating the home backgrounds of these children, and advising the judge how best to look after the interests of the child. Some children were even dismissed into the care of these women. Their efforts gave them an understanding of the problems of the justice system as it affected children and prompted them to lobby for legal sanction of their work. Thus, even before the passing of the Juvenile Court Law, a rudimentary probation system based around Hull House was in operation. The embryo probation officers, all of whom were volunteers and had no official status in the courts, provided a body of expertise on which those who established the Chicago Juvenile Court in 1899 could draw. It is therefore significant that Mrs. Stevens, who had been one of these embryo probation officers, was appointed as the first probation officer by Judge Tuthill in 1899.[48]

A formal probation system was established by the Juvenile Court Law of 1899, and several of the probation officers appointed under the new law were women who had acted in a volunteer capacity before the passing of the law.[49] For many, especially the women of Hull House, probation became the key element of the juvenile courts. It provided a noncustodial means of dealing with children in trouble and also, by allowing probation officers to exercise supervision over the lives of children, aimed to keep them out of further trouble. This clearly reflected the maternalist desire to ensure that children were properly raised. Another important aspect of probation was

48. Letter from Mrs. Lucy Flower, May 1917, vol. 2, Bowen Papers.

49. Henriette Greenbaume Frank and Amalie Hofer Jerome, *Annals of the Chicago Woman's Club for the First Forty Years of Its Organization, 1876–1916* (Chicago, 1916), 181; letter from Lucy Flower, May 1917, and memorandum from Julia Lathrop, May 3, 1917, vol. 2, Bowen Papers.

the investigation of the family and environmental backgrounds of the children who were to come before the juvenile court. Here the influence of the social science training of the Hull House women was evident. One key function of their research into living conditions, as far as these women were concerned, was to collect data for the purpose of constructive work that would ultimately improve the situation. By investigating the family and environmental backgrounds of children who were to appear before the juvenile courts, these women reformers aimed to provide the court with some insight into the life of the child and, by so doing, give court officials an idea of how to help him. All of these elements appear to have been present in the informal probation system centered around Hull House. What was missing, however, was any legal sanction for this work.

It was not until after the Juvenile Court Law came into operation in July 1899 that those involved in its development explained what they hoped to achieve from probation. At the Illinois Conference of Charities in November 1899, Mrs. Stevens noted that the first effort of the probation officer should be to keep the child in its own home, for both the child's and the parents' sake. However, the best interests of the child should be paramount, and this might mean that the child should be surrendered to an institution or home-finding society.[50] The development of the informal probation system clearly reflects the concerns of the Hull House women that children of the slums were not being given the opportunity to behave as children. In introducing what they considered to be the benevolent influence of a probation officer into the lives of children who were in danger of becoming criminal, the Hull House women hoped to prevent these young people from becoming so. The probation officer was to act not merely as an educational influence but as a means to ensure that the child's family recognized its responsibilities in properly bringing up the child.[51] For this reason, probation officers investigated a child's family before probation was suggested, seeking to discover whether the necessary qualities of family life, especially parental love and nurture, were present. This involved a considerable amount of interference into the lives of these families, for they were to be judged by the standards of the predominantly middle-class probation officers. To the women reformers, probation was an important way of ensuring that chil-

50. Mrs. A. P. Stevens, "The Juvenile Court Bill," *Proceedings of the Illinois Conference of Charities* (1899), 38–40.

51. This is suggested by Steven L. Schlossman, *Love and the American Delinquent: The Theory and Practice of "Progressive" Juvenile Justice, 1825–1920* (Chicago, 1977), 60–69.

dren were properly nurtured and treated as children, according to the reformers' understanding of what this meant. It also enabled them to help the child's family to adjust to the strains of urban and industrial life.

While such informal methods of dealing with delinquent children gradually developed around Hull House, there was also a growing conviction among certain residents that legislation was needed to deal with the problem. Like the Chicago Woman's Club, the Hull House residents were clearly prompted by their perception of women's role as mothers and the need to save the children of the slums. More important, though, their experience with these children showed the women reformers that current laws were not working, and existing institutions for the care of dependent and delinquent children were inadequate. Miss Lathrop was concerned that efforts by judges to minimize the sentences of delinquent children so they could be sent to institutions intended for dependent children, such as orphans, were backfiring. The presence of criminal children in these institutions only served to corrupt the noncriminal children for whom the institutions were intended. Moreover, it was a crime, according to Julia Lathrop, that children were sent to the city prison or ordered to pay a fine, which, if they were unable to pay, would result in their being sent to prison. Miss Lathrop expressed a further concern: "But often they were let off because justices could neither tolerate sending children to the Bridewell nor bear to be themselves guilty of the harsh folly of compelling poverty-stricken parents to pay fines. No exchange of court records existed and the same children could be in and out of various police stations an indefinite number of times, more hardened and more skilful with each experience."[52]

The understanding gained by the Hull House residents in acting as probation officers further persuaded them that the existing system as regards children was inadequate and inconsistent. It was also detrimental to the welfare of the children who became involved in it, and it would consequently have a dangerous effect on society.[53] For this reason, a change in the law for dependent and delinquent children was needed. Increasingly from 1897 onward, Hull House residents cooperated with the Chicago Woman's Club in their efforts for reform. Beginning in early 1898, Mrs. Henrotin and Mrs. Flower of the Chicago Woman's Club joined forces with Miss Lathrop

52. Julia Lathrop, as quoted in Addams, *My Friend, Julia Lathrop,* 132–33.
53. See, for instance, Addams, *My Friend, Julia Lathrop,* 132–35; Kelsey, "How Does the Massachusetts Probation System Affect Children?"; Julia Lathrop, draft of speech, approx. 1901, miscellaneous file, Julia Lathrop Papers.

to campaign for reform. Thus, in April 1898 Miss Lathrop became chairman of the Woman's Club Joint Committee on Probation Work for Children in Police Stations and coordinated their efforts to establish a form of probation for children. This culminated in the appointment of Mr. Carl Kelsey as probation officer, paid by the Chicago Woman's Club and the Illinois Children's Home and Aid Society to work in the East Chicago Avenue police station.[54]

Julia Lathrop did not confine her campaigning only to the Chicago Woman's Club. As a member of the Illinois Board of Charities, she was in a position to influence the agenda of the annual Illinois Conference of Charities. The conference of 1898 concentrated its entire program on the question "Who Are the Children of the State?" Various papers were read by members of the Board of Charities and superintendents of state institutions, as well as leading attorneys and experts in child saving, on aspects of the state's duties toward children. The conference concluded with a call by Frederick Wines, secretary of the Board of Charities and a noted penal reformer, for reform of the Illinois justice system as regards children:

> We make criminals out of children who are not criminals by treating them as if they were criminals. That ought to be stopped. What we should have, in our system of criminal jurisprudence, is an entirely separate system of courts for children, in large cities, who commit offences which would be criminal in adults. We ought to have a "children's court" in Chicago, and we ought to have a "children's Judge," who should attend to no other business. We want some place of detention for those children other than a prison.[55]

A resolution was drawn up by Miss Lathrop as chairman of the Conference Business Committee to push for legislative changes:

> The business committee desires to offer the following resolution:
>
> WHEREAS, It has been reported to this conference that committees of various organizations in the State have been and are engaged in the consideration of legislation for delinquent and dependent children, and

54. October 26, 1898, box 21, vol. 93, CWC Papers; December 28, 1898, box 21, vol. 93, CWC Papers.
55. Dr. Frederick Wines, "Discussion," *Proceedings of the Illinois Conference of Charities* (1898), 64.

WHEREAS, It is most fitting that all friends of such proposed legislation work harmoniously;

Therefore, in order to bring about co-operation, be it

Resolved, That the committee on legislation this day to be appointed take steps to bring about an early meeting of the other committees of the State dealing with the subject, and endeavor to agree upon the scope and form of the bills proposed to be submitted to the Legislature.[56]

The Legislation Committee of the conference was not very prominent in agitating for a new law to deal with dependent and delinquent children, but the conference was significant in bringing the issues before a wider audience, focusing attention on the need for new legislation, and increasing momentum toward reform.[57] By the time the conference met in November 1898, various other agencies had seized the initiative and had begun to seek legislative action. The conference was held back by more conservative members, such as superintendents of state institutions who opposed non-institutional methods of dealing with dependent and delinquent children.[58]

Even before the conference met, the Chicago Woman's Club had made overtures to the Chicago Bar Association. At its annual meeting on October 22, 1898, Ephraim Banning, an associate of Miss Lathrop's on the State Board of Charities, offered the bar association a series of resolutions that pointed out deficiencies in the care of delinquent children in Chicago: the presence of children in the jail and bridewell in close association with older, vicious criminals; the lack of any provision in Illinois for dependent children other than public almshouses; and the limitations of the judges, who were so overburdened with other work that it was difficult for them to give due attention to children's cases. Many of these statements clearly reflected the concerns of the Hull House and Chicago Woman's Club women. The resolutions were accepted by the bar association, which appointed a committee to draw up the necessary legislation.[59]

56. Speech by Julia Lathrop, *Proceedings of the Illinois Conference of Charities* (1898), 56.

57. The proceedings of the conference were widely reported in the Illinois Press: for instance, "Denounces Truant School: Superintendent Smith of the John Worthy School Censures Institution, Its Object and the School Board," *Chicago Tribune,* November 18, 1898, and "Chicago Club's New Protege," *Chicago Tribune,* November 20, 1898.

58. *Chicago Tribune,* November 18, 1898, p. 7.

59. "For Delinquent Children: Resolution Adopted by the Chicago Bar Association," undated clipping, p. 26, scrapbook 3, Flower Scrapbooks; William M. Lawton, "Father of the

The Hull House community and the Chicago Woman's Club provided the motivating force behind the campaign that produced the Illinois Juvenile Court Law. Their concerns are clearly apparent in the law, but other agencies, such as the Catholic Visitation and Aid Society and the Protestant Illinois Children's Home and Aid Society, led respectively by Timothy D. Hurley and Hastings H. Hart, were also involved in lobbying efforts, though apparently at a fairly late stage. These agencies seem to have been motivated by rather different concerns than those of the Hull House community and the Chicago Woman's Club, however. Judging by Hurley's 1891 bill, the two child-saving organizations were more interested in gaining the protection of the state for their own part in the juvenile justice system than in being early advocates of juvenile courts or probation.[60] The Chicago Bureau of Associated Charities was also involved in agitating for the law and thus presented a united front of reformers that gave demands for legislation more chance of success than if the measure had been strictly a women's bill. Although women might legitimately campaign for reforms closely connected with their interests, a measure too closely associated with women's concerns and lacking the endorsement of male reformers was unlikely to succeed in the entirely male legislature.[61]

Cooperation between female and male reformers was important in securing the passage of the juvenile court bill. The male reformers seemed happy to support the initiatives of the women and accepted their leadership, and the women reformers needed the legal expertise and political clout of the men to achieve their reform. Hull House seems to have played an important part in facilitating this cooperation. It acted as a meeting place for reform-minded people in Chicago and gave the women reformers involved in the agitation for what became the Juvenile Court Law numerous contacts and much expertise to draw on.[62] It also seems to have acted as a center of operations from which pressure was put on legislators at Springfield to pass the bill.[63]

Illinois Juvenile Court Law," *Juvenile Court Record* 8 (December 1907): 11; Report of the Chicago Bar Association Committee on Juvenile Courts, typescript, October 28, 1899, Manuscript Division, Chicago Historical Society.

60. Timothy D. Hurley, *Juvenile Courts and What They Have Accomplished* (Chicago, 1904), 17–18, 69–71.

61. Letter from Mrs. Lucy Flower, May 1917, and memorandum by Julia Lathrop, May 3, 1917, vol. 2, Bowen Papers.

62. This is explored further by Sklar in "Hull House in the 1890s" and "The Historical Foundations of Women's Power," 69–75. See also Jane Addams, "Women's Work for Chicago," 502–3.

63. Memorandum by Julia Lathrop, May 3, 1917, vol. 2, Bowen Papers. On an earlier ex-

The juvenile court bill was introduced into the Illinois House of Representatives by John R. Newcomer on February 8, 1899, and into the Senate by the Honorable Selon H. Case on February 15, 1899. It was known as the Chicago Bar Association bill so it would not be identified as a woman's measure.[64] A committee, on which no women served, was appointed to urge passage of the bill. The Hull House women continued to lobby on its behalf, however, trying to influence legislators and arouse public opinion. The bill did not pass the Judiciary Committee stage without substantial revisions, and delaying tactics in the House meant the bill was almost lost. It was only through the intervention of Governor Tanner and Speaker Sherman, who were pressured by Miss Lathrop and others from Hull House and the Chicago Woman's Club, that it was passed on the last day of the session.[65] Some features of the bill important to Miss Lathrop in particular were lost as a result of opposition to the bill. Most notable of these was one provision removing all children from the county poorhouses and another empowering judges to order a child boarded at public expense.[66] The resulting bill, though deficient in some respects, was hailed by the *Hull House Bulletin* as a great step forward in state provision for the care of children: "The whole measure is in a true sense preventive, and while it is compulsive at few points it will certainly mark a great and wise change in the care of unfortunate children if public interest gives its administration due support.[67]

The Juvenile Court Law of 1899 thus marked the culmination of a decade of efforts by the women of Hull House to deal with the problem of dependent, neglected, and delinquent children. Not all of their initiatives were directed toward legislation to correct what they saw as deficiencies in existing methods of treating such children. They strove to find informal ways of easing the life of children caught up in the problems of the slums by providing playgrounds, kindergartens, and social clubs as alternatives to the streets and commercialized entertainment. Their efforts to develop an informal probation system centered around Hull House and their agitation for the Juvenile Court Law should therefore be seen as part of a wider concern with child life in the slums.

----

ample of the role of Hull House in steering legislation through the state legislature, see Sklar, *Florence Kelley and the Nation's Work,* 234–36.

64. Letter from Mrs. Lucy Flower, May 1917, vol. 2, Bowen Papers.

65. Hurley, *Juvenile Courts and What They Have Accomplished,* 20; memorandum by Julia Lathrop, May 3, 1917, and letter from Mrs. Lucy Flower, May 1917, vol. 2, Bowen Papers; Report of the Chicago Bar Association Committee on Juvenile Courts.

66. Memorandum by Julia Lathrop, May 3, 1917, vol. 2, Bowen Papers.

67. *Hull House Bulletin* (April and May 1899): 10.

In seeking legislation to deal with the problem of dependent and delinquent children, particularly laws that would embody their ideas about the
nature of childhood and family life, the Hull House women worked closely
with the Chicago Woman's Club. They also utilized the contacts they had
made with other reformers, both male and female, through the reform community attracted to Hull House. In lobbying for reform, the Hull House
women called on many of the same arguments used by members of the
Chicago Woman's Club. The Hull House women emphasized their identification as women and the cultural expectation they would be mothers, as
well as the ideas of educated womanhood this entailed.

Other factors, however, seem to have been more important in motivating
them to demand reform. Their experience living among the families of one
of the poorest sections of Chicago gave the Hull House women a greater
awareness of the problems these families faced. Their use of social science
methods to investigate living and working conditions prompted them not
only to write about these conditions as part of social surveys but also to demand that something be done to ameliorate them.[68] The Hull House women
were particularly appalled by the effects of industrialization and urbanization on the lives of the children of the slums, and many of their reform activities were associated with ensuring that these children were given a better
start in life. The women were undoubtedly influenced by their gender identification, but wider concerns about social justice, though themselves gendered, were equally important. Thus, the Hull House women had a clearer
idea of what lay behind juvenile delinquency than did the members of the
Chicago Woman's Club and for this reason were as much concerned with
preventing children from ever getting into trouble as preventing their further contamination and development into criminality, once they were before the courts.

The distinction between the club women and the settlement women was
not always very sharp. In general terms it might be suggested that the settlement women were more likely to be single, and the club women were usually married. It is, however, significant that while an informal probation
system was being developed by Hull House, the club concentrated its efforts
on providing a jail school and separate court sessions for children. Both
were, however, ultimately concerned with overcoming the inadequacies of
the existing system of treating problem children and forcing the state to rec-

---

68. See, for instance, the articles in *Hull House Maps and Papers* written by Florence Kelley,
Alzina Stevens, and Julia Lathrop, 27–45, 49–76, 143–61.

ognize its duty toward these children. Moreover, whether focusing their efforts on supporting the child's own family through probation or on finding the child another home, both groups were anxious to ensure that all children received the proper love and nurture that these women regarded as the right of children.

Their campaign to secure legislation to embody these ideas was prompted by a recognition that they needed legal sanction for informal practices and a desire that the state take the responsibility for protecting family life. Thus, in reviewing the reasons for the law, Miss Lathrop suggested that the Juvenile Court Law came out of "an almost simultaneous expression of a slowly matured, popular conviction that the growing child must not be treated by those rigid rules of criminal procedure which confessedly fail to prevent offenses on the part of adults or to cure adult offenders." Moreover, she argued, "Obviously, the new method of dealing with neglected children should take into account not an isolated child, but a child in a certain family and amid certain neighborhood surroundings, and a judge should base his action upon the value or the danger to the child of his surroundings."[69] The Juvenile Court Law of 1899 sought to embody these concerns.

69. Julia Lathrop, introduction to Sophonisba Breckinridge and Edith Abbott, *The Delinquent Child and the Home* (New York, 1912), 5.

3

The Spread of the Juvenile Court Idea, I

The Female Influence

Illinois did not remain the only state with a juvenile court law for very long. Many of the conditions that had influenced the women reformers in Chicago also existed in other cities in the United States, and various charitable and reform bodies had been expressing alarm about the question of how to deal with wayward children for some time. The legislation adopted in Illinois in 1899 clearly met a perceived need in the United States to find a solution to the problem of dependent and delinquent children, for within a few years of the passing of the Illinois Juvenile Court Law, several other states enacted similar laws. By 1909, twenty-two states had passed juvenile court laws, many of them modeled on the Illinois law. Significantly, the earliest states to adopt such legislation in the wake of the Chicago example did so as the result of initiatives by female reformers espousing "maternalist" rhetoric. Indeed, in the early years, women, either as individuals or as members of women's organizations, proved much more willing to embrace new methods of dealing with problem children through legislative measures than were most men.

This chapter explores the female influence on the early spread of the juvenile court idea. It examines the role of both local and national women's associations in publicizing the need for solutions to the problem of juvenile delinquency and agitating for legislative reform. Maternalist reformers only maintained a high profile in the juvenile court movement for a few years before male reformers, most notably Judge Ben Lindsey, seized the limelight. Nonetheless, women continued to play a significant role in the movement, both as initiators of reform and as publicists. The role of women in the juvenile court movement testifies to the strong networks of communication among women reformers and also to the fact that the juvenile court idea seemed to fit well with the maternalist concerns of many women's organizations in the first decade of the twentieth century.

The level of interest shown in the juvenile court idea outside Illinois in the immediate aftermath of the establishment of the Chicago Juvenile Court is illustrative of the sources of support for the juvenile court movement in general. Whereas national women's organizations quickly reported and praised the passing of the Illinois Juvenile Court Law, the National Conference of Charities and Correction took much longer to acknowledge it.[1] This is especially noteworthy because the children's section of the National Conference of Charities and Correction had been debating the question of how to find a new method of dealing with dependent and delinquent children throughout the 1890s. These debates had been dominated by conflict between advocates of reformatory institutions and those supporting child-placing agencies, who sought non-institutional methods of dealing with these children.[2] The conflict between backers and opponents of institutional care became increasingly intense within the conference until, in 1899, a truce was declared in the Committee on Dependent and Neglected Children.[3] What the debates clearly pointed to was the need for an alternative method of dealing with both dependent children and those in trouble with the law. Reform initiatives did not, however, begin at the National Conference of Charities and Correction. It was not until 1901 that the Illinois Juvenile Court Law was mentioned at the conference, and even then, it was only referred to in passing: "In 1899, Illinois enacted a law similar to the Massachusetts probation law, but more comprehensive. Its chief feature was the establishment of a court to deal with both dependent and delinquent children."[4] Another year elapsed before there was any discussion of juvenile courts at the conference, by which time a number of

1. See, for instance, Report of the Illinois State Federation to the Fifth Biennial, June 4–9, 1900, Convention Records (Proceedings—Reports) 1900/06/04–1902/05/08, General Federation of Women's Club Papers, Archives of the General Federation of Women's Clubs, Washington, D.C. (hereafter GFWC Papers); and reports in *Club Woman* 3 (November 1898): 68–69. The first mention of the Illinois Juvenile Court Law in the *Proceedings of the National Conference of Charities and Correction* (hereafter PNCCC) appears in "Reports from the States: Illinois," PNCCC (1901), 26.

2. See, for instance, PNCCC for the years 1891, 1898, and 1899.

3. J. M. Mulry, "The Care of Destitute and Neglected Children," PNCCC (1899), 166–70.

4. "Reports from the States: Illinois," 26.

states had secured juvenile court legislation through the initiative of women reformers.[5]

Although leaders of the General Federation of Women's Clubs were quick to bring the Illinois initiative to the attention of its members, it was at the state level that reformers began to seek new methods of dealing with dependent and delinquent children. The second state to secure legislation to formally establish a juvenile court system was Pennsylvania. There, agitation for reform was centered in Philadelphia and led by Mrs. Hannah Kent Schoff, leader of the Pennsylvania branch of the National Congress of Mothers. This group of women reformers, like those of the Chicago Woman's Club, were traditional maternalists. They were largely unconcerned with social science methods and with exploring the wider effects of industrialization and urbanization—interests that characterized the professional maternalists of the Hull House community. If anything, the brand of maternalism espoused by Mrs. Schoff and the National Congress of Mothers was even purer than that of the Chicago Woman's Club. It accepted, even idealized, women's traditional role as wife and mother but at the same time insisted that women had a duty to extend their female skills and concerns beyond their own homes. In idealizing motherhood, it sought to teach middle-class mothers the most up-to-date and "scientific" methods of child rearing while at the same time arousing middle-class mothers to the necessity of improving conditions for all children, not just their own. Thus, it was with an overt avowal of her identity as a mother that Mrs. Schoff led the campaign for a new method of dealing with children in trouble with the law—first in Philadelphia and then, on the national stage, as president of the National Congress of Mothers.

It is important to examine the National Congress of Mothers in the context of the origins of juvenile courts in the United States, not so much because this organization was a pioneer in seeking new methods of dealing with children in trouble with the law but because under the leadership of Mrs. Schoff, it played a significant part in spreading the juvenile court idea. It was as one of the foremost national exponents of traditional maternalism that the National Congress of Mothers adopted the juvenile court idea and advocated the passing of juvenile court laws across the United States. It did

---

5. "Minutes and Discussion," *PNCCC* (1902), 423–25. By 1903, Pennsylvania (1901), Wisconsin (1901), and Missouri (Winter 1902–3) had all passed juvenile court laws modeled on the Illinois law.

so because the juvenile court idea fit perfectly with its maternalist agenda. Thus, an examination of the role of the National Congress of Mothers in the agitation for juvenile court legislation will further illustrate the way in which traditional female concern with motherhood could be translated into a demand for legislative reform.

The National Congress of Mothers was founded by Mrs. Alice McLellan Birney, who, as she sought guidance in the rearing of her own children, was appalled at both the dearth of good literature on the subject and how the lives of many children were warped through parental ignorance. She studied the works of G. Stanley Hall and Friedrich Froebel and, in 1895, pondering the question of how mothers could be educated and the nation made to recognize the supreme importance of the child, conceived the idea of a great gathering of mothers in the nation's capital. In August 1895 she successfully presented the idea to a group of mothers at the Chautauqua, New York, summer school.[6] The idea immediately struck a chord among many middle-class women. That it did so suggests widespread concern among such women not only about how to rear their own children but, more significantly, about the dangers to society of vast numbers of children living in the slums of America's cities, apparently without "proper" nurture or guidance. In this respect the timing of the meeting was significant, for the United States was in the midst of an economic depression characterized by widespread unemployment, industrial unrest, and poverty.[7] Although they may not have been directly affected by the economic downturn, many of these women must have been alarmed at the possibility of social unrest. This sense of unease, accompanied by concerns about children growing up in poverty, ignorance, and without a proper regard for American ways, prompted many middle-class women to seek means of alleviating these problems. To the women who met at the Chautauqua summer school, the idea of a national gathering of mothers clearly seemed one way of doing so.

The women who met together in Washington, D.C., in December 1896 to organize the proposed meeting of mothers were not, however, ordinary mothers. The meeting was held at the home of Mrs. Phoebe Hearst, widow

6. Biographical details of Mrs. Birney are taken from Edward T. James, Janet Wilson James, and Paul S. Boyer, eds., *Notable American Women: 1607–1950: A Biographical Dictionary*, 4 vols. (Cambridge, Mass., 1971), 1:147–48.

7. On the sense of crisis in the 1890s, see, for instance, Robert H. Wiebe, *The Search for Order, 1877–1920* (New York, 1967), 76–110; Paul Boyer, *Urban Masses and Moral Order in America, 1820–1920* (Cambridge, Mass., 1978), 123–31.

of newspaper publisher and U.S. senator George Hearst and mother of publisher William Randolph Hearst.[8] The first meeting was chaired by Mrs. Adlai Stevenson, the wife of the vice president, and attended by women whose husbands and relatives were prominent in political circles.[9] These were, then, some of the foremost women in the country, by virtue of their husbands' status, and consequently it is not surprising that when the first meeting of the National Congress of Mothers was held in Washington, D.C., on February 17, 1897, it attracted considerable media attention.[10]

The National Congress of Mothers has been little studied by historians, despite the fact that during the first two decades of the twentieth century, it played a critical role in popularizing more scientific methods of child rearing and advocated child welfare reforms.[11] It certainly was not a radical movement but instead was representative of conservative women who asserted that their primary duty and fulfillment was to be found as mothers in the home. They believed women already had influence and therefore did not need to enter the public sphere of politics, nor did they need the vote. Even those early leaders of the congress who were married to prominent politicians seem to have had little interest in entering politics; any use they might have made of their political connections was exercised in private. Their main concern was to assert woman's traditional role as wife and mother. They also saw it as the duty of middle-class women to take the lead in awakening others to their responsibility to provide every child with the best possible environment.[12] There is a certain irony in the fact that though they espoused a conservative view of womanhood, many leaders of the National Congress of Mothers made a career for themselves outside the home by campaigning for the organization, in a similar fashion to advocates of women's suffrage.

8. On Mrs. Hearst, see James, James, and Boyer, *Notable American Women*, 2:171–73.

9. Meeting, December 11, 1896, National Congress of Mothers, minutes, National Congress of Parents and Teachers Records, Special Collections, University of Illinois at Chicago (hereafter NCM Papers). See also Molly Ladd-Taylor, *Mother-Work: Women, Child Welfare, and the State, 1890–1930* (Urbana, 1994), 48–49.

10. *New York Times*, February 18, 1897, p. 6, and February 21, 1897, p. 16.

11. Only recently have scholars begun to study the National Congress of Mothers. See, for instance, Theda Skocpol, *Protecting Soldiers and Mothers: The Political Origins of Social Policy in the United States* (Cambridge, Mass., 1992), 333–40; Ladd-Taylor, *Mother-Work*, 44–73. It receives only a very brief mention in Anne Firor-Scott, *Natural Allies: Women's Associations in American History* (Urbana, 1992), 150, 155.

12. Mrs. Theodore W. Birney, "Address of Welcome," *The Work and Words of the National Congress of Mothers: First Annual Session* (New York, 1897), 6–10; Ladd-Taylor, *Mother-Work*, 48–49.

The congress received considerable support from the press. The *New York Times,* for instance, praised the first meeting in Washington for touching on subjects of wide significance and dealing with matters it considered highly appropriate for women.[13] The reception of its leaders at the White House and the apparent endorsement of the president this reception conferred gave the new organization a further boost. The attendance of the wives of the president and vice president at sessions of the congress and the fact that its meetings were overcrowded testified to the fact that the National Congress of Mothers answered a need among elite women in American society.[14] Posing no threat to accepted perceptions of the role of women, the organization bolstered the idea of woman as nurturer of children and clearly worked within nineteenth-century ideals of womanhood. Indeed, the congress made it clear that its aims were quite different from those of the wider women's rights movement.

In her opening address to the first meeting of the National Congress of Mothers, Mrs. Birney examined the purposes of the fledgling organization. She noted that although women currently were involved in many different kinds of projects, they could not and should not separate themselves from the child question. Indeed, it was only because women were not properly educated and trained to the possibilities of home life that they sought occupation elsewhere. Mrs. Birney argued that it was time for women to turn their full attention to the study of the child: "It has therefore seemed to us good and fitting that the highest and holiest of missions—motherhood—the family interest upon which rests the entire superstructure of human life— and the element which may indeed be designated as the foundation of the entire social fabric, should now be the subject of our earnest and reverent consideration. I refer to what is called child study—that broad, deep theme, most worthy, in all its varying phases, of our study and attention, because the fundamental one."[15]

The main purpose of the congress was thus "to recognize the supreme importance of the child," which meant to equip mothers to respond appropri-

13. See, for instance, two editorials in the *New York Times,* February 18, 1897, p. 6, and February 21, 1897, p. 14.
14. "Commentary on the Congress," *The Work and Words of the National Congress of Mothers,* 255–58. These elite women remained associated with the National Congress of Mothers. See the list of honorary vice presidents in "National Congress of Mothers, 1897–1907," pamphlet, carton 9, Mrs. Phoebe Hearst Papers and Correspondence, Manuscript Collections, Bancroft Library, University of California, Berkeley. The list includes Mrs. Adlai Stevenson, President Roosevelt, and Mrs. Phoebe Hearst.
15. Birney, "Address of Welcome," 6–7.

ately to such a complex creature. To further emphasize this point, the psychologist G. Stanley Hall addressed the congress on the great importance of child study and the proper rearing of children, noting that this was especially the province of women.[16] The meeting heard further papers on the importance of the mother's role in many aspects of their children's lives, as speakers sought to promote the education of middle-class mothers in the latest child-rearing theories and practices. To this end, and in criticizing the existing curricula in women's colleges, speakers advocated courses for women students in domestic science and promoted university chairs in child study to extend the work of Professor Hall. They also recommended the establishment of local mothers' congresses for child study.[17]

The initial purpose of the National Congress of Mothers was therefore to boost the importance of the proper education of middle-class mothers in order to enable them to practice the latest child-rearing methods. Many delegates, however, suggested that such mothers had a further role — that privileged mothers were obligated to ensure that all children benefit from proper methods of child rearing. As one speaker advised, it was of universal importance to the future of the individual and the nation that women accept as their divine burden responsibility for the childhood of all children.[18] One way of doing this was to establish kindergartens for the children of the slums. Many considered direct intervention into impoverished households essential in order that children be raised as good citizens. As one delegate at the meeting in 1897 observed, "Your children belong to me, to the neighbors, to everybody else, to everyone with whom they come in touch. You can not keep them to yourself. . . . They are only lent to you to care for, to help, until they can stand on their own feet and live their own lives independently of you."[19] Consequently, it was the duty of better-educated mothers to help the children of the poor and their mothers.

The attitude of some delegates toward slum mothers is indicative of the middle-class bias of the National Congress of Mothers. To these women,

16. G. Stanley Hall, "Some Practical Results of Child Study," *The Work and Words of the National Congress of Mothers*, 165–71.

17. *The Work and Words of the National Congress of Mothers;* "The Child Question," *New York Times*, February 21, 1897, p. 14.

18. Mrs. Mary Lowe Dickinson, "Response to Address of Welcome," *The Work and Words of the National Congress of Mothers*, 18.

19. As quoted in Steven L. Schlossman, *Love and the American Delinquent: The Theory and Practice of "Progressive" Juvenile Justice, 1825–1920* (Chicago, 1977), 76; David J. Rothman, *Conscience and Convenience: The Asylum and Its Alternatives in Progressive America* (Boston, 1980), 208–9.

the family life of the poor represented the antithesis of everything the National Congress of Mothers stood for. Drawing on the tradition found among women's benevolent associations of "friendly visiting" among the poor, delegates suggested that the best way to correct the evil conditions of the slums was to send in middle-class women as missionaries bringing the knowledge of proper child-rearing practices. As one delegate suggested, however, privileged mothers should not give the patronizing impression that they were coming down to the level of the mothers of the slums but instead project the attitude that they were standing together with these less fortunate mothers. In assuming the role of missionaries going into city slums, most members of the congress clearly envisaged themselves as moral crusaders taking light into the savage world of the poor. They could see little of value in the family life of what one delegate called the "Submerged World."[20] The "missionaries" of the National Congress of Mothers believed they should teach the mothers of the slums not only scientific household management but also the latest child-rearing theories, so that these women could gain the love and respect of their children and ensure they would grow up to be good citizens. Clearly, few members of the congress evinced much understanding or appreciation of the economic difficulties of family life in the slums, for they believed that as long as poor mothers were taught essentially middle-class child-rearing methods, they would become better mothers and housekeepers.

Delegates to the inaugural meeting of the National Congress of Mothers, moreover, were convinced that women in the slums would be only too grateful to learn proper methods of bringing up their children, if only their more knowledgeable social betters would recognize their duty to aid the poor. As one delegate expressed it,

> The great trouble in our large cities, and one which leads to anarchism, socialism, or any other bad *ism,* is that the mothers lose the hold they have upon their children, and the child ceases to obey or respect her. The boy who scoffs at mother's authority will soon defy the law of the land. . . . These mothers are willing to learn how to cultivate respect for themselves in their children, but they do not know how of themselves. They need to be told of a better way to make a child obedient than slapping the child on the hand or scream-

20. Lucy S. Bainbridge, "Mothers of the Submerged World-Day Nurseries," *The Work and Words of the National Congress of Mothers,* 47–55.

ing at it. These mothers have the habit of frightening and lying to their children.[21]

Thus, the motives of the National Congress of Mothers delegates—who strove to educate the mothers of poor families in the new theories of child rearing—were far from purely humanitarian. They were working in the traditions of nineteenth-century charitable workers and sought as much to prevent what they saw as the consequences of the breakdown of family life among poor families as to improve the living conditions of these families: "Some people say that the first need of the submerged world is better tenements," argued the same delegate in 1897. "But it seems to me that we must first elevate the woman herself, and then she will be capable of using a better tenement. The woman, the mother, must be helped by other women."[22]

The National Congress of Mothers—while promoting new ideas about the nature of childhood and the importance of the proper rearing of poor children, as well as their own role in these efforts—was still working within the traditionally defined boundaries of woman's role. Whereas it emphasized the centrality of the well-informed mother in the upbringing of children, this group did not seek actively to enlarge the role of the mother outside the home. The aim of the congress was rather to preserve and build on the nineteenth-century idea of separate spheres in which the woman's sphere was her family and home. By creating a nationwide organization of mothers, the National Congress of Mothers sought not to encroach on the male sphere or demand women's rights but to bolster and enhance woman's traditional role as mother of a family. As the draft of its code of rules suggests, "The object of this association shall be to promote conference on the part of parents concerning questions most vital to the welfare of their children, the manifest interest of the home, and in general, the elevation of mankind."[23] It aimed to do this by holding annual conferences to which would be invited all those interested in the cause of children, particularly members of parents' clubs. It also established a board of managers to carry out the work of the congress between annual conferences and to promote the foundation of local branches.[24] As its work moved beyond the education

21. Ibid., 51.
22. Ibid., 49.
23. Minutes of the Board of Managers of the National Congress of Mothers, April 15, 1897, folder 1, NCM Papers.
24. On the organization of the National Congress of Mothers, see minutes, March 30,

of middle-class mothers and sought to elevate the mothers and children of the slums, the congress became involved in campaigning for welfare reforms. Since many of these initiatives required legislative reform, women were brought into the political sphere, even though involvement in the political arena was not their primary motivation. The congress always maintained that its primary purpose was to preserve the traditional role of women in the home and for this reason refused to endorse women's suffrage, but its activities almost inevitably brought its members out of the home and into the public sphere.[25] Thus, it fell very much within the tradition of women's reform organizations in the United States discussed earlier.

The National Congress of Mothers was not associated with the securing of the pioneer Juvenile Court Law in Illinois but quickly became interested in the newly established court. Although the congress did not establish any formal bodies to promote the spread of juvenile courts and probation until January 1903, the organization seems to have been active in such work early on; certainly, some of its local branches had been involved since about 1900.[26] The person most connected with this work within the congress was Hannah Kent Schoff. She not only led the work of the congress in this field for many years but was also—as leader of the Pennsylvania Congress of Mothers—instrumental in securing a juvenile court law in her home state.

Hannah Kent was born on June 3, 1853, in Upper Darby, Pennsylvania, the oldest of the five children of Thomas and Fanny Kent. Her father was a woolen manufacturer and a native of England. Her mother, who was born in Bridgewater, Massachusetts, and graduated from Bridgewater Normal School, was a descendant of Solomon Leonard, one of the original proprietors of Bridgewater. Hannah was first educated by tutors and at a private school in Philadelphia and later at a church school in Waltham, Massachusetts. Yet like many of her generation, she was not college educated. On October 23, 1873, she married Frederic Schoff, a Massachusetts engineer, and

1897, and April 15, 1897, folder 1, NCM Papers; minutes, May 23, 1901, and June 30–July 1, 1902, folder 2, NCM Papers. This is also discussed by Skocpol, *Protecting Soldiers and Mothers*, 336.

25. On women's suffrage, see Minutes of the Executive Board Meeting, February 25, 1918, folder 6, NCM Papers.

26. "The Board deems it desirable, since the Congress is doing so much for delinquent, defective and dependent children, to form a Committee to supervise this department of work," minutes of executive board meeting, January 14, 1903, folder 2, NCM Papers; "National Congress of Mothers, 1897–1907," 7; *Twenty Years' Work for Child-Welfare by the National Congress of Mothers and Parent-Teacher Associations* (Washington, D.C., 1917), 19, 21.

after a few years the couple moved to Philadelphia. Between 1874 and 1894 the couple had seven children.[27] In 1897, representing the women's New Century Club of Philadelphia, Mrs. Schoff attended the first meeting of the National Congress of Mothers. She immediately rose to prominence within the new movement, first as program manager and then as vice president, from 1899 to 1902. In 1899 she founded the Pennsylvania Congress of Mothers and became its first president, a position she held until 1902, when she succeeded Mrs. Birney as president of the National Congress of Mothers.[28]

Mrs. Schoff's involvement in the agitation for the adoption of juvenile courts in the United States and the rhetoric she employed in promoting the cause clearly reflect the aims and ideals of the National Congress of Mothers. She argued that it was both a woman's place and her duty to help in the care, protection, and treatment of unfortunate, friendless, and erring children and in the drafting of those laws needed to protect the interests of all children. For Mrs. Schoff believed that what she called "mother thought" regarding the welfare of children was missing in individual homes and states and in the nation as a whole.[29] It was, however, the case of one little girl, which appeared in the Philadelphia newspapers in May 1899, that apparently prompted Mrs. Schoff to take action on behalf of children who got into trouble with the law.

The case concerned an eight-year-old girl sentenced to the House of Refuge on a charge of arson. To Mrs. Schoff, such treatment appeared both unjust and unwise, since to house such a young child in the House of Refuge seemed tantamount to giving the child an education in evil. Mrs. Schoff remonstrated with the judge and made investigations into the methods of judicial procedure for children in Pennsylvania, but the results of her inquiries served only to intensify the feeling she had that injustice and wrong were being committed in the name of justice. Large numbers of children were to be found in the Philadelphia county prison, from two to three thousand children were passing through the police stations of Philadelphia every month, and all were greatly in need of intelligent direction and guidance. Throughout Pennsylvania, children were confined to county prisons

27. Biographical details taken from James, James, and Boyer, *Notable American Women*, 3:237–39.

28. *Twenty Years' Work for Child Welfare*, 20; James, James, and Boyer, *Notable American Women*, 3:237–39.

29. Hannah Kent Schoff, "Pennsylvania's Unfortunate Children: What the State Is Doing for Them," *Charities* 11 (November 7, 1903): 425.

for trifling offenses and subjected to influences that could not fail but to confirm evil habits. As Mrs. Schoff concluded,

> Such were the conditions in Pennsylvania in 1900. Erring children standing at the bar of justice with their eternal future hanging in the balance! Children with infinite possibilities for good or for evil, victims of environment, neglect or bad homes, yet each one a child of the God who said, "It is not the will of your Father in heaven that one of these little ones should perish." Society ignores them. The churches giving millions to missions, yet blind, unconscious of the need at their very doors. No mother thought for these little ones; only the cold legal procedure of the criminal court.[30]

Hannah Schoff was not alone in her indignation at the treatment of dependent and delinquent children by the law. Women from the New Century Club and the Pennsylvania Congress of Mothers, as well as a number of individual women who were connected with other aspects of child welfare, quickly joined Mrs. Schoff.[31] They formed a committee to investigate what other states were doing for their problem children and eventually decided that the recently passed Illinois Juvenile Court Law represented the best solution. Mrs. Schoff and her colleagues then lobbied the governor and various other political leaders in Pennsylvania on behalf of a juvenile court law based on the Illinois model. The governor and other politicians soon gave their support, and Mrs. Schoff's committee employed a lawyer to draft the bills for the Pennsylvania legislature. Although the measures did eventually pass, becoming law in June 1901, they met with considerable opposition, especially from the vested interests of existing child-saving institutions.[32]

The resulting Pennsylvania Juvenile Court Law mandated a separate time and place for the trial of children's cases; forbade the detention of children in police stations or prisons, providing instead for a house of detention for

30. Hannah Kent Schoff, "A Campaign for Childhood," in Samuel J. Barrows, ed., *Children's Courts in the United States: Their Origins, Development and Results* (Washington, D.C., 1904), 133–35; Hannah Kent Schoff, *The Wayward Child: A Study of the Causes of Crime* (Indianapolis, 1915), introduction.

31. Schoff, "A Campaign for Childhood," 136–37; Schoff, *The Wayward Child*, introduction.

32. Schoff, "A Campaign for Childhood," 136–38; "Pennsylvania," *Charities* 7 (August 3, 1901): 105; *Charities* 7 (December 21, 1901): 562.

children awaiting trial; specified that probation officers were to be appointed by the court but not paid by the public treasury; and established a Board of Visitors composed of men and women to visit all children's institutions. As a result, a child in trouble with the law was now to be kept separate from adult criminals at all points in the judicial process.[33] Moreover, the child was not to be treated as a criminal but as a child in need of treatment. The main purpose of the juvenile court hearing would be to decide what was in the best interests of the child. As Mrs. Schoff noted, "In the Juvenile Court the child who steals, the truant, the runaway, and the vagrant child are considered as children needing treatment. It is more important to prevent continuance in wrongdoing than to punish. It is necessary to consider children individually rather than en masse. Punishment that does not reason from cause to effect usually avails nothing."[34]

The principles of the juvenile court therefore reflected the influence of the child study movement, most especially its emphasis on the individual child and the need to carefully study and guide the child's development.[35] By insisting also on the separation of young offenders from the more hardened, adult offenders at all stages of the judicial process, the juvenile court system recognized the need to protect impressionable children from evil influences. In many ways it reflected new attitudes toward childhood and resulted from the important role women played in promoting the proper nurture of children in their formative years.

The National Congress of Mothers, under the leadership of Mrs. Schoff, was heavily involved in the promotion of the juvenile court idea, both within the United States and internationally. In advocating the establishment of juvenile court systems, Mrs. Schoff was concerned principally with espousing the ideas of others. She was not a great innovator or pioneer who contributed to the development of the juvenile court. Nor was she very sophisticated in analyzing the causes of juvenile delinquency, for she saw it in terms of a failure of the child's home rather than as a result of extraneous factors.[36] The National Congress of Mothers, with its emphasis on the edu-

33. Schoff, "A Campaign for Childhood," 137; *Charities* 7 (December 21, 1901): 562.

34. Mrs. Frederic Schoff, "The Place and Work of the Juvenile Court and Probation System," *Proceedings of the First International Congress for the Welfare of the Child: Held Under the Auspices of the National Congress of Mothers, Washington, D.C., March 10–17, 1908* (Washington, D.C., 1908), 233.

35. See, for instance, Hall, "Some Practical Results of Child Study," 165–71.

36. Schoff, "The Place and Work of the Juvenile Court and Probation System," 242–44; "National Congress of Mothers, 1897–1907," 7.

cation of parents and the proper rearing of children, saw the juvenile court and especially the probation system as a means to extend these concerns to the children of the slums. The juvenile court thus fit well into the purposes of the National Congress of Mothers. Consequently, that organization proved an important lobbyist in promoting the juvenile court idea.

To Mrs. Schoff, it was the incontrovertible duty of middle-class women to improve the conditions that threatened to produce criminality in children. As mothers of all children, not just their own, it was the responsibility of women to secure a means of saving these children from lives of criminality.[37] Thus, in the rhetoric of the National Congress of Mothers, Mrs. Schoff clearly articulated the concerns of many other women reformers with the question of the treatment of dependent and delinquent children by the law:

> The Congress saw what to the mother heart seemed gross neglect of dependent, orphan and erring children. It saw children in prisons and jails in every State; it saw children associated with criminals in all court procedure; it saw no discrimination between the offenses of children and adults and no adequate provision for helping them. To put mother-love and mother-thought into the solution of these conditions and to ask Divine guidance in the great work of guarding and guiding little children was one of the objects to which the Congress pledged itself.[38]

In the hands of the National Congress of Mothers, the juvenile court was very much a maternalist reform, for it emphasized "mother-love" as central to the thinking surrounding both the juvenile court and the concept of probation. Indeed, the congress's involvement in the juvenile court movement possibly reveals maternalist reform at its most straightforward and conservative. In the words of Hannah Schoff,

> The Juvenile Court's great opportunity is to strengthen and improve the home. In the long run and finally, the home is the place for the child. Until the Juvenile Court and probation came into being there was no organized way of reaching weak, poor homes to benefit them. The only possibility was to take a child away for a time.

37. Schoff, "A Campaign for Childhood," 136; Schoff, "Pennsylvania's Unfortunate Children," 425–28.
38. *Twenty Years' Work for Child-Welfare,* 9.

How much greater the system which recognizes that a home and father and mother are better for children, and when homes need help to give it to them. This is one of the strongest and best possibilities of the Juvenile Court.[39]

The National Congress of Mothers was, however, only one among a number of women's organizations involved in campaigning for the establishment of juvenile courts in the United States, and the vast majority of these organizations used maternalist rhetoric to a greater or lesser degree. The outrage felt by Mrs. Schoff and her associates in the National Congress of Mothers at the treatment of children in trouble with the law reflected the response of many other middle-class women confronted with the conditions in which many poor children were forced to live in the cities of late nineteenth-century America. Clearly, the lives of these children did not conform to middle-class ideals of childhood. The women's reaction was one of moral outrage and humanitarian concern, but it also encompassed a certain fear that if something was not done to improve conditions and to check the creation of lawbreakers at the first downward step in childhood, they would develop into criminals who would pose a threat to society.[40] Ideals of educated motherhood and traditions of female activism, as well as the new emphasis placed on child nurture, made it very natural for women to become concerned about these problem children.

It was not only the local branches of high profile national women's organizations that were involved in the agitation for juvenile court legislation in the first years of the twentieth century. Local women's clubs were also instrumental in securing such laws in their own states. Many of these women's clubs, although affiliated with their state federations of women's clubs and often with the General Federation of Women's Clubs, were not controlled by these bodies in quite the same way as branches of national organizations like the National Congress of Mothers were.[41] They therefore enjoyed a large degree of autonomy. As far as can be ascertained, the women's associations that lobbied for juvenile court laws in Missouri and Wisconsin seem to have been influenced more by local conditions and their geographic proximity to Chicago than by their relationship with the federation. Nonetheless, they both proudly announced the passage of

39. Schoff, "The Place and Work of the Juvenile Court and Probation System," 244.
40. Schoff, "A Campaign for Childhood," 136.
41. This organizational point is made by Skocpol, *Protecting Soldiers and Mothers*, 329–34.

their juvenile court laws in GFWC publications and at its biennial meetings.[42]

Missouri and Wisconsin were among the first states to adopt legislation similar to the Illinois Juvenile Court Law. In Missouri the leadership for this reform came from the Humanity Club of Saint Louis. This was an informal association of women whose main purpose seems to have been to aid in securing legislation that would remedy existing evils in the public institutions of Saint Louis. The women of the Humanity Club visited the city jail and were horrified to discover the conditions in which children were housed. Their first action was to raise funds to pay an agent of the Humane Society "to look after the boys in jail." Members of the Humanity Club also investigated how other states dealt with children in trouble with the law and determined that the Illinois Juvenile Court Law was better for Missouri than the more limited Massachusetts probation law. Having decided on legislation, the women reformers lost their nerve and limited themselves to pushing for a juvenile probation law only, fearing that in attempting too much they would lose everything. Although the Saint Louis reformers were hoping to emulate the Chicago Juvenile Court, they apparently were concerned that opposition would be too strong to allow the passage of such a measure in Missouri. These fears proved justified. Even the probation bill was opposed by legislative representatives from Kansas City and Saint Joseph and had to be framed to apply to Saint Louis only, although it is unclear exactly why this opposition occurred.[43]

Whether because it was a women's measure or for some other reason, enforcement of the probation law met with opposition from the judge of the Court of Criminal Correction. He refused to recognize both the use of probation as a method of treating juvenile offenders and the probation officers funded by the women's club and the Humane Society. Other judges did, however, avail themselves of the probation law, and their application of it prepared the way for the passing of a juvenile court law in the winter of 1902–3. This law had much wider support than the earlier measure. The Missouri Conference of Charities, judges of the police court and the circuit

42. For instance, "Reports of States: Missouri," *Records of Sixth Biennial,* 1902, p. 132, Convention Records (Proceedings—Reports) 1900/06/04–1902/05/08, GFWC Papers; "Juvenile Courts and Probation Laws," *Proceedings of the Seventh Biennial of the General Federation of Women's Clubs* (1904), 124, GFWC Papers.

43. Charlotte C. Eliot, "Missouri: The Change Wrought by the Juvenile Probation System in St. Louis," in Barrows, ed., *Children's Courts in the United States,* 162–63; "Missouri," *Club Woman* 7 (December 1900): 87.

courts, and the women of the Humanity Club all endorsed the law. Judge Tuthill of the Chicago Juvenile Court also addressed the Missouri Conference of Charities in the autumn of 1902.[44] His visit suggests that the women reformers in Missouri were not sufficiently influential to secure viable legislation for the protection of dependent and delinquent children without the help of men in positions of power. Indeed, the Missouri law continued to meet with both opposition and questions as to its constitutionality, even though it was soon put into operation, bringing juvenile courts based on the Chicago model to Saint Louis and Kansas City.

In Wisconsin, too, it was women reformers who spearheaded the drive for a Milwaukee juvenile court. The movement was led by middle-class women possessing previous experience in philanthropic work with children: Mrs. Annabelle Cook Whitcombe, head of the boys' club; Miss Marion Ogden, a frequent visitor to children in jail; and Mrs. Kathryn Van Wyck, head of the Milwaukee Associated Charities. These women were personal acquaintances of Jane Addams and Louise deKoven Bowen of Chicago and had traveled to that city on a number of occasions to see the juvenile court in operation.[45] They also had frequent discussions on legal strategies with Judge Tuthill and virtually adopted the provisions of the Illinois law as it stood. They persuaded a number of the Chicago reformers who had been instrumental in securing the juvenile court there to testify before the legislature in Madison on the law's effectiveness and constitutionality. As a result of the agitation of these women, together with the endorsement of the *Milwaukee Sentinel* and the Chicago Juvenile Court reformers, a juvenile court law passed the Wisconsin legislature in 1901 and became operative in July 1902.[46]

Close parallels clearly existed between the establishment of the juvenile courts in Missouri and Wisconsin and those in Chicago and Philadelphia, but there were also some differences. Although women reformers in Saint Louis and Milwaukee led the juvenile court movements in these two states, the fact that they knew of the existence and practicality of the Chicago Ju-

44. Eliot, "Missouri: The Change Wrought by the Juvenile Probation System in St. Louis," 163–64; "Juvenile Courts for Missouri," *Juvenile Record* 4 (January 1903): 10; "Comments upon Summary Statement" and "Juvenile Court and Probation Laws," *Proceedings of the Seventh Biennial of the General Federation of Women's Clubs* (1904), 74, 124–25, GFWC Papers.

45. Schlossman, *Love and the American Delinquent,* 136–37.

46. Ibid.; Bert Hall, "Wisconsin: History of the Juvenile Court of Milwaukee," in Barrows, ed., *Children's Courts in the United States,* 144–46. It is unclear whether other progressive reformers in Wisconsin, such as Robert La Follette, were involved in this agitation.

venile Court gave them a model on which to base their legislation. The
Chicago reformers lent their support in securing juvenile court legislation in
these states, and this seems to have been a fairly important factor in per-
suading the legislatures to pass the bills. Certainly, the maternalist rhetoric
of the women reformers, together with the legal expertise provided by the
judges of the Chicago Juvenile Court, were enough to convince the male
legislators in Missouri and Wisconsin of the expediency of passing these
laws. A number of other states followed the examples of Missouri and Wisconsin, beginning by initiating their own reforms of how children were
treated by the law and then asking the Chicago reformers for help and advice.

As the demand for juvenile court legislation became more widespread,
national women's organizations became more active in the movement.
Thus, in January 1903 the National Congress of Mothers established a
committee on juvenile courts and probation, and the Industrial Committee
of the GFWC sent out a leaflet in May 1903 urging its member clubs to agitate for juvenile courts and probation laws where they did not already exist.[47] The involvement of these national organizations in pressing for the extension of juvenile court laws suggests that the cause of delinquent children
clearly appealed to women. For the National Congress of Mothers, this issue was clearly part of their maternalist agenda. For the GFWC, whose maternalism was not quite so overt, agitation for juvenile court legislation still
seemed appropriate work for women's clubs. It appears, though, that the
National Congress of Mothers was consistently more vigorous in its agitation for the juvenile courts than was the federation. This may well have
been due to Mrs. Schoff, who, as president of the National Congress of
Mothers, was personally an ardent supporter of juvenile courts.

The GFWC was established in New York in April 1890. It was the brain-
child of Mrs. Jane Cunningham Croly, who had founded Sorosis in 1868
and had for some time sought a national forum for women's clubs.[48] The
purpose of the GFWC, according to its constitution, was "to bring into
communication with each other the various women's clubs throughout the

47. Minutes of executive board meeting, January 14, 1903, folder 2, NCM Papers; "Report
of the Industrial Committee of the GFWC," Seventh Biennial, 1904, Convention Records (Proceedings — Reports), 1904/05/17–1904/05/27, GFWC Papers.
48. Skocpol, *Protecting Soldiers and Mothers*, 329; Karen J. Blair, *The Clubwoman as Feminist: True Womanhood Redefined, 1868–1914* (New York, 1980), 93–95; Mary I. Wood, *The
History of the General Federation of Women's Clubs for the First Twenty-two Years of Its Organization* (New York, 1912).

world, that they may compare methods of work and become mutually help-ful."[49] Initially, it seems that Mrs. Croly had intended the new organization to be a means to bring together literary clubs in a national association and to promote cultural programs, but the GFWC quickly became involved in civic work and social reform. At the time of its launch, the GFWC attracted delegates from sixty clubs, but this number grew rapidly until, in 1910, the federation boasted one million members, in local clubs and state federations across the United States affiliated to the GFWC.[50]

It is difficult to ascertain the general tenor of an organization the size of the GFWC. It embraced both the conservatism of the National Congress of Mothers, which at one time was loosely affiliated with the GFWC, and the more radical notions of the suffragists. If it is to be judged by the policy statements of its presidents and national committees, it may be described as a "traditional maternalist" organization. Although it included among its members numerous women like Jane Addams and Florence Kelley, with backgrounds in the social sciences and settlement house work, most of its leaders seem to have been elite women, prominent in their local clubs and state federations, who espoused a traditional maternalist agenda.[51] Thus at the 1892 biennial convention, Mrs. J. M. Logan could assert, "We recog-nize that homemaking, the training of children, the maintenance of social purity, and the uplifting of public sentiment are paramount duties, and we believe that for these duties women's clubs are especially helpful."[52] Simi-larly the GFWC's historian, in noting the transition of the federation's in-terests from purely cultural matters to the welfare of the community, quoted Mrs. Mary Mumford:

> The attention of the women seems to have been turned first toward the needs of children, and in many towns they brought to lagging school boards a knowledge of the newer thought in education. They

49. "Constitution of the GFWC: Article II: Object," vol. 2, 0101–02–1/4, Board of Direc-tors (minutes), GFWC Papers.

50. Wood, *The History of the General Federation of Women's Clubs*, 294; Skocpol, *Pro-tecting Soldiers and Mothers*, 329.

51. Wood, *The History of the General Federation of Women's Clubs*; Blair, *The Club-woman as Feminist*, 93–115, though Blair uses the term "municipal housekeeping" rather than "maternalism"; Skocpol, *Protecting Soldiers and Mothers*, 331–33. The involvement of Jane Addams, Florence Kelley, and the National Congress of Mothers may be traced in the pro-ceedings of the biennials.

52. Mrs. J. M. Logan, "Educational Influence of Women's Clubs," May 13, 1892, Conven-tion Records (Addresses and Papers), 1890–94, vol. 3, pp. 115–20, GFWC Papers.

advocated manual training (tool work for boys, sewing and cooking for girls), while their encouragement of kindergarten gave a valuable impulse to that foundation principle of child training.

Such important work was not begun to be lightly set aside. The great movement toward municipal housecleaning and housekeeping is to find a steady propelling force in the women's club.[53]

The GFWC was formed to coordinate the activities of and to offer advice and encouragement to the local clubs. As Mrs. Charlotte Emerson Brown, the first president of the federation, observed at the 1892 convention, "What the local club is to its individual members the General Federation is to local clubs. The Federation is the local club two hundred times multiplied. What the local club does for a hundred women the Federation is doing for twenty thousand."[54]

The GFWC continued to grow nationally and by the mid-1890s was being used as a model for the formation of state and regional federations. Although this at first caused a certain amount of uneasiness among leaders of the GFWC, who feared that local federations would divert their potentially national membership, these fears quickly proved unfounded. Most state federations quickly affiliated with the GFWC, as did a number of national women's clubs. Indeed, as Karen Blair has observed, these state and local federations often strengthened the GFWC at the expense of local autonomy. The state federations gave reports of their work to the GFWC and at the same time adopted the policies suggested by its board of directors and various committees. However, it is unclear just how much the GFWC controlled the work of local clubs and state federations. Whereas the GFWC certainly strengthened the hand of some groups by giving them a national forum, most local clubs seem to have exercised a high degree of autonomy. Thus, although the GFWC gave the appearance of being highly structured, with three tiers of organization at national, state, and local levels, in practice it probably exercised a fairly loose control over its constituent members.[55]

The GFWC did not, however, welcome all women's clubs into its fold, de-

53. Wood, *The History of the General Federation of Women's Clubs,* 72.

54. Speech at the Chicago Biennial, 1892, Presidents' Papers, Charlotte Emerson Brown (Speeches) 1892/05, GFWC Papers.

55. Skocpol, *Protecting Soldiers and Mothers,* 328–31; Blair, *The Clubwoman as Feminist,* 96–97. Notices of the affiliation of various clubs and state federations may be found in issues of the GFWC's magazine, variously published as *Woman's Cycle, Homemaker, New Cycle, Club Woman,* and *Federation Bulletin* during the period under discussion.

spite its claim to represent all women. A very public row broke out in 1900 when an African-American women's club—the New Era Club of Massachusetts—applied for and was granted membership in the GFWC. The Georgia State Federation objected strongly to this action, and in seeking to placate them, the GFWC president, Mrs. Lowe, had to admit she had not been aware that the New Era Club was a colored woman's club when she had accepted its request for membership. The offer of membership was withdrawn on a technicality, but this precipitated a passionate debate, both among board members and in the GFWC's magazine. It was not until 1902 that a compromise was reached, allowing African-American women's clubs to secure membership only when their state federations had already admitted them to membership.[56] Thus, the GFWC's aim of inclusiveness was limited in practice. There had earlier been some doubt as to whether Jewish and Catholic clubs should be admitted, although debate was quickly resolved in favor of these clubs. Over questions of class, too, the GFWC was somewhat ambivalent. Being essentially an organization for middle-class white women's clubs, it seems to have made no great effort to recruit organizations representing the interests of poor women.[57] Here, the GFWC only reflected the composition of its member clubs.

The most public aspect of the GFWC was its biennial conventions, held in different cities across the country. These were huge and elaborate affairs to which delegates from constituent clubs and federations were invited to discuss federation policy, to report on their activities, and to enjoy carefully organized social events and entertainments. In between these biennial conventions, the elected national officers held regular meetings, which were probably where most of the real business was conducted. The GFWC also ran a national headquarters in Washington, D.C., and maintained several standing committees and subcommittees to formulate various aspects of the federation's work. There were, at various times, committees on civics, art, child labor, legislation, library extension, forestry, pure food, and public

56. This row may be followed in Minutes of the Board Meeting, June 4, 1900, June 7, 1900, November 9, 1900, and November 10, 1900. Those for 1901 and 1902 are missing. Board of Directors (minutes), vol. 2, GFWC Papers. It was also waged in the pages of *Club Woman*. See, for instance, *Club Woman* 9 (March 1902), for the compromise reached. Also detailed in Blair, *The Clubwoman as Feminist*, 108–10.

57. Minutes of the Directors' Meeting, October 16, 1894, vol. 2, Board of Directors (minutes), GFWC Papers. Jewish women's organizations regularly reported their activities in *Club Woman*. The issue of class is discussed in Blair, *The Clubwoman as Feminist*, 110. However, the GFWC clearly saw itself as representing the interests of all women. See, for instance, Wood, *The History of the General Federation of Women's Clubs*, 105.

health, among others. The GFWC thus reflected more than a purely maternalist stance in its interests.

By the early twentieth century the GFWC was pursuing work in areas not traditionally encompassed by women's sphere and arguably not justifiable as such. For instance, as early as the 1898 biennial, the GFWC adopted resolutions that could easily be described as maternalist—resolutions demanding restrictions on child labor, maximum hours legislation for women workers, and adequate provision for school facilities. At the same time, though, it demanded a postal savings bank for the benefit of small savers and passed a resolution expressing sorrow at, but support for, the war against Spain. Such matters clearly went beyond the traditional area of women's influence and into the world of economics—albeit mostly the household economy—and politics.[58] By the time of its 1910 convention, the president of the GFWC was claiming that the city was only a larger home and therefore the legitimate province of women's activism. This statement was, however, still framed in a fairly conservative manner, linking it with women's traditional role: "We have no platform unless it is the care of women and children, and the home, the latter meaning the four walls of the city, as well as the four walls of brick and mortar."[59]

By 1914 the GFWC had gone so far as to claim political equality for women and men:

> *Whereas,* the question of the political equality of men and women is today a vital problem under discussion throughout the civilized world, therefore,
> *Resolved,* that the General Federation of Women's Clubs give the cause of political equality for men and women its moral support by recording its earnest belief in the principles of political equality regardless of sex.[60]

Thus, although the GFWC was much slower to endorse the struggle for suffrage than a number of other women's organizations, in comparison to

58. Wood, *The History of the General Federation of Women's Clubs,* 109–11.
59. Ibid., 250.
60. Twelfth Biennial Convention, Chicago, 1914, folder 3—Resolutions and Legislation (Resolutions) 1911–16, Resolutions and Legislation, GFWC Papers. For an earlier attempt to endorse suffrage, see "The Question," *New Cycle* 8 (July 1894): 1–2, and the reply by Mrs. Henrotin, president of the GFWC, "Record of the Clubs," 19–22.

the National Congress of Mothers, which did not endorse political equality for women before the passing of the federal suffrage amendment, the GFWC was much more willing to embrace a larger sphere for women. Indeed, it seems likely that the GFWC would have pushed for suffrage much earlier if not for the presence of conservative groups under its broad umbrella. Arguably, however, by the time the GFWC did endorse the struggle for the vote, this position was no longer seen as quite the radical departure it might have been in the nineteenth century.[61]

The involvement of the GFWC in the agitation to secure juvenile court legislation in every state was clearly within the tradition of women's activism. It is therefore surprising that it was not until 1903 that the GFWC began to take an active part in encouraging its member clubs to agitate for juvenile court legislation. Discussions of such questions as the restriction of child labor, the improvement of educational facilities, and the spread of kindergartens had been prominent at the biennial conventions and testified to the interest of the GFWC, more or less since its establishment, in matters relating to child welfare. The question of juvenile delinquency and what to do about it seems initially to have been of marginal interest. It is, of course, possible that the matter was discussed during the meetings of some of the standing committees. Certainly, state federations reported the passing of juvenile court legislation in their states, at both the biennial meetings and in the *Club Woman*.[62] Until 1903, however, initiatives to secure juvenile court legislation seem to have been predominantly locally based.

In May 1903 the Industrial Committee of the GFWC issued a leaflet with various recommendations to clubs. Among these recommendations was one suggesting that the clubs "agitate for juvenile courts and probation officers wherever these do not exist." The committee also sent out a circular in November 1903 to ascertain how far its recommendations had been adopted.[63] This new interest in pushing for juvenile court legislation in every state

---

61. On this question, see Paula Baker, "The Domestication of Politics: Women and American Political Society, 1780–1920," *American Historical Review* 89 (1984): 620–47.

62. It is, in fact, more than likely that juvenile court legislation was a subject in meetings of some of the standing committees, since some club women who had been involved in the agitation for the Illinois Juvenile Court Law were involved in these committees. For instance, Ellen Henrotin was president of the GFWC from 1894–98 and afterward was still prominent in the organization. Lucy Flower was chairman of the Philanthropy Committee. Minutes of these committees are not available among the papers of the GFWC in Washington, D.C.

63. "Report of the Industrial Committee of the GFWC," Seventh Biennial, 1904, Convention Records (Proceedings—Reports), 1904/05/17–1904/05/27, GFWC Papers.

came at a time when various other bodies were taking similar steps. The National Congress of Mothers established its own committee on the subject in January 1903, but it was not until January 1904 that the National Conference of Charities and Correction made a concerted effort to press for juvenile court legislation.[64]

It is also clear that the GFWC acted with a number of other women's organizations in its efforts to push for juvenile court legislation. Hannah Kent Schoff was chair of the GFWC's Committee on Legislation in 1904, at a time when she was also president of the National Congress of Mothers, which was then affiliated with the GFWC. Thus it would appear that the latter organization was an essential part of a women's reform network that embraced conservative organizations such as the National Congress of Mothers and more "progressive" women such as those from the settlement house movement.[65] Whereas these groups remained independent of GFWC control and often acted from rather different motivations, the GFWC could serve as a forum in which various different women reformers could meet.

Since the GFWC campaign for juvenile court legislation in every state was the work of a coalition of reformers, it is rather difficult to ascertain whether the GFWC itself had a particular stance on women's involvement in pushing for such legislation. Through its various publications, however, it is clear that leaders of the GFWC thought club women should become involved in such work. One such publication noted,

> If women's clubs are at all concerned in the civic welfare of the community, their relation to the Juvenile Court movement is inevitable. . . .
>   The women's club is the natural patroness of the Children's Court. Wherever there is a Court already established the club should be allied to its organization, holding it to the highest possible standard of

64. Although Judge Ben Lindsey first attended the National Conference of Charities and Correction in 1902, it was not until 1903 that he formally gave a paper on the Denver Juvenile Court and not until 1905 that he presented his first report as chairman of the subcommittee on juvenile courts. See Ben B. Lindsey, "The Reformation of Juvenile Delinquents Through the Juvenile Courts," *PNCCC* (1903), 206–22; Ben B. Lindsey, "Recent Progress of the Juvenile Court Movement," *PNCCC* (1905), 150–55. According to the "Report of the Industrial Committee of the GFWC," eight states had reported having promoted juvenile courts and probation with varying degrees of success.

65. See the "Report of the Committee on Legislation to the General Federation of Women's Clubs," 122–27, and "Greetings from the National Congress of Mothers," 13, in which Mrs. Schoff urges the cooperation of the two organizations in the work for mothers and childhood; both are found in Seventh Biennial, 1904, Convention Records (Proceedings—Reports), 1904/05/17–1904/05/27. Florence Kelley had been chair of the Industrial Committee in 1902, and Jane Addams addressed the biennials on several occasions.

excellence; wherever a Court is yet to be created, there the women's club should be the pioneer in its creation.[66]

In 1904 the Legislative Committee made a clear commitment to pushing for juvenile court legislation:

> RESOLVED, that we further the establishment of the Juvenile Court and probation system in every state as the foundation of an adequate system of child care.
>
> RESOLVED, that for the probation work we recognize the necessity for intelligent, individual care over each child, and that in the further-ance of the probation system we recommend only such persons shall be employed as probation officers as have been fitted by maturity and study of child nature and its development to deal wisely with each child at the critical moment of his life.[67]

While the above resolution may well have been drawn up by Mrs. Schoff as chairman of the Legislative Committee, its adoption by the GFWC's board of directors suggests that it reflects their views on the matter.

Beyond the passing of resolutions exhorting local women's clubs and state federations to agitate for juvenile court legislation in their states, the role of the GFWC in the juvenile court movement is not very clear. Unlike the National Congress of Mothers, which became actively involved in local cam-paigns to secure this reform, the GFWC seems to have had a more distant in-volvement. This was largely because of the very nature of the organization. Its aim since its founding had been to coordinate the work of local women's clubs, providing them with the necessary encouragement and support. Thus, agitation for such reforms as the passage of juvenile court legislation was car-ried out by local clubs and state federations, while the GFWC formulated the policies to be pursued and occasionally provided clubs with model legislation. Nonetheless, the encouragement and exhortation given by the GFWC seems to have had a profound effect, motivating women's clubs to pursue juvenile court reform. Appeals such as that given in the report of the Civic Committee to the eighth biennial convention in 1906 clearly show the importance at-

66. Kate Cassatt MacKnight, "The Relation of the Woman's Club to the Juvenile Court," *A Civic Primer,* folder 1, Program Records, 1904–6, (Pamphlets) Civic Committee, Program Records, GFWC Papers.

67. Board of Directors, May 26, 1904, vol. 6, p. 13, May 26, 1904–June 7, 1906, Board Records of GFWC, GFWC Papers.

tached to juvenile court reform among the leadership of the GFWC. They also reveal the extent to which maternalist rhetoric pervaded efforts to persuade women's clubs to agitate for such legislation:

> Probably few of the forms of modern philanthropy appeal to us more than the juvenile court, and the overseeing of naughty children (many of them more sinned against than sinning) by probation officers, selected for their efficiency. The club women in many of our states are co-operating heartily in this work. . . .
>
> After all, nothing will repay us so much as the protection, care, and training of our children, who are to take upon their shoulders the government of our country after we have passed hence, and this part of the work of a civic committee we commend particularly to your careful and prayerful consideration.[68]

Clearly the Civic Committee believed that attempts to secure juvenile court legislation were in women's province, and it was their duty as mothers to ensure that all children be properly protected and cared for—if necessary, by the state.

The securing of juvenile court laws in those states in which the GFWC had members remained a concern for some years. Although it was never as central to the presentations before the biennial conventions as were more high-profile campaigns for child welfare such as the demands for child labor restriction, it was nonetheless part of the reform agenda of the GFWC for much of the first decade of the twentieth century. The rhetoric the GFWC employed in pushing for this reform was never as sentimental as that used by some other national women's organizations, like the National Congress of Mothers, but the GFWC still framed its appeal in maternalist terms. The reports presented by the state federations at GFWC biennial conventions and published in the pages of the *Club Woman* are ample testimony to the efficacy of both the rhetoric and the appeal of juvenile court reform to women's clubs.

A decade after the passing of the first juvenile court law in Illinois, twenty-two other states had secured similar legislation, often modeled on the Illinois law. Not all of these laws were purely the result of agitation by individual women or women's organizations, but it was unusual for a state to pass a juvenile court law without at least the active support of local

68. Report of Civic Committee, pp. 198–99, Eighth Biennial, 1906, Convention Records (Proceedings—Reports) 1906/05/30–1906/06/07, GFWC Papers.

women. Women's concerns were very often at the heart of agitation for this reform, and they were frequently conveyed in maternalist rhetoric. This usually remained true whether the women reformers involved were traditional maternalists or the more social-science oriented "professional maternalists."

Women reformers were an essential part of the juvenile court movement. At a local level they often took the initiative in agitating for the passage of legislation that would change how the law and the courts dealt with dependent and delinquent children. In their localities they were frequently part of a coalition of reformers that included women's clubs and settlement houses but sometimes also agencies that were more male dominated. Male reformers were also involved in the juvenile court movement, though usually for different reasons and using different methods from those of female reformers. It was not, however, just local initiatives that played a part in securing this reform. Long before the juvenile court movement was formalized in the International Juvenile Court Association in 1907, the Chicago women reformers and national women's organizations had been acting as publicists for the movement. They played a significant role in providing information, support, and model laws for other female reformers wishing to establish juvenile courts in their localities. Some of the female pioneers in this field, notably Julia Lathrop and Hannah Kent Schoff, played an active role in securing legislation in other states by giving speeches, providing information, and even testifying before state legislatures.

Middle-class women and their organizations were at the heart of the campaign to secure a juvenile court law in every state. That they very often succeeded is testimony to both the strength of the women's reform network in the United States and the appeal of this reform. Through such organizations as the GFWC, reforms legislated in other states quickly came to the attention of women around the country through publications and conventions. The endorsement of such a reform as the establishment of juvenile courts by a national women's organization was a significant factor in encouraging local women's groups to pursue similar reforms in their own localities, for both the GFWC and the National Congress of Mothers framed their work within traditional concepts of the role of women. Clearly, child welfare reform fit easily into this framework. Indeed, the fact that the National Congress of Mothers was among the foremost advocates of juvenile court legislation is testimony to how well this particular reform fitted into the maternalist agenda of this conservative women's organization—not all child welfare reforms were so quickly embraced by the National Congress of Mothers. Thus, although neither the National Congress of Mothers nor the GFWC had been instrumental in shaping the new methods of dealing with children who got into trouble with the law, they played an important part in ensuring the spread of the idea.

4

The Spread of the Juvenile Court Idea, II

The Masculine Influence

Every fortnight on a Saturday morning, a large number of boys would crowd into the courtroom in Denver, Colorado. They were greeted by County Court Judge Ben B. Lindsey, who proceeded to address them with a speech full of homilies and anecdotes designed to illustrate a particular subject of interest to the boys. The session ended with each of the boys presenting his report to the judge, who inspected it and, if it was a good report, congratulated the boy before the whole assembly. If the report was bad, however, the judge commiserated with him, showing disappointment rather than anger—the aim of this being to hurt the boy's pride and thus encourage him to do better. This was report day at the Denver Juvenile Court, and it represented the pivot of Lindsey's method of dealing with juvenile offenders—a personal, child-centered approach that aimed to help the child through "character building." It rested on some of the same principles as the Chicago Juvenile Court but in a number of respects differed quite markedly. Rather than emerging from the female tradition of reform as the Chicago court had, the Denver court was more a reflection of an alternative, quite separate masculine tradition of reform. The Denver Juvenile Court was, moreover, very much an expression of the personality of Judge Lindsey himself. For although Lindsey has often been portrayed as the archetypal juvenile court reformer, his methods were far from typical. Indeed, Lindsey's methods were rarely transplanted to other courts. Whereas anecdotes about "Lindsey's boys" captured the public's imagination, it was usually the Illinois Juvenile Court Law that was adopted in other states.

Nonetheless, Lindsey epitomizes an alternative conception of juvenile court reform that, as the juvenile court idea spread, also had its advocates.

This chapter explores the masculine influence in the juvenile court movement. Clearly, male reformers had been involved, though often fairly marginally, in those states where women were the dominant influence in finding new methods of dealing with children in trouble with the law. In these states, male reformers had played only supporting roles while female concerns shaped the reform. In some states, however, the most notable being Colorado, masculine concerns dominated. Like women reformers, male juvenile court reformers were influenced in part by their gender consciousness; certainly, a sense that the traditional masculine role was under threat may be identified in the writings and actions of some male reformers.[1] Possibly more important in influencing their actions was their conception of the "proper" behavior of children, by which they usually meant boys.

Identifying the ideal of manhood in the late nineteenth century is, ironically, more problematic than identifying the ideal of womanhood. This is partly because such ideals were less clear-cut for men but also because the examination of cultural constructions of gender has been pursued more rigorously by historians of women than by those of men.[2] Thus, the very concern of historians of women to correct the absence of women's experience from "traditional history" has made them more willing to devise new paradigms that use gender as a category of analysis. No such absence of men from traditional history exists, and gender has consequently been of less concern in looking at the experience of men in history.[3] The emergence of the new men's history in recent years has begun to address the issue of gender consciousness and its relationship to men's actions, but this field is still

1. The idea that traditional conceptions of masculinity were under threat in the late nineteenth century may be found in, for instance, Joe L. Dubbert, "Progressivism and the Masculinity Crisis," in Elizabeth H. Pleck and Joseph H. Pleck, eds., *The American Man* (Englewood Cliffs, N.J., 1980), 303–20; Peter Filene, *Him/Her/Self: Sex Roles in America,* 2d ed. (Baltimore, 1986). For a view suggesting some limitations of this position, see Clyde Griffen, "Reconstructing Masculinity from the Evangelical Revival to the Waning of Progressivism: A Speculative Synthesis," in Mark C. Carnes and Clyde Griffen, eds., *Meanings for Manhood: Constructions of Masculinity in Victorian America* (Chicago, 1990), 183–204.

2. On this point, see E. Anthony Rotundo, "Learning About Manhood: Gender Ideals and the Middle-Class Family in Nineteenth-Century America," in J. A. Mangan and James Walvin, eds., *Manliness and Morality: Middle-Class Masculinity in Britain and America, 1800–1940* (Manchester, 1987), 35–51; Griffen, "Reconstructing Masculinity," 183–204.

3. Nancy F. Cott, "On Men's History and Women's History," in Carnes and Griffen, eds., *Meanings for Manhood,* 205–11; Rotundo, "Learning About Manhood," 35–36.

very much in its infancy.[4] Indeed, relatively little work has been done on the influence of male gender consciousness on men's involvement in reform. Nonetheless it is clear that the male tradition of reform in the nineteenth century was quite distinct from the female tradition.

In many senses the male tradition of reform may be identified by how it differs from the female tradition. The social, economic, and ideological factors that, in the early nineteenth century, had played such an important part in reshaping women's position in society had an equally important influence in reshaping men's position. Rigid patterns of gender differentiation were constructed as home and work were counterpoised. The masculine sphere of work was defined in terms of independent wage labor and its relationship to the market economy. Thus, middle-class white men construed the male role as characterized by economic independence, men being the sole representatives of the family in the wage economy.[5] Men were also the occupants of the public sphere of politics, again defining their role in contrast to that of women. For universal white male suffrage had been achieved during the Jacksonian Era, and the rise of mass political parties occurred alongside an increase in political participation among the male electorate.[6]

The growth of the electorate and mass political parties did not, however, accompany a growth in the apparatus of the state to ensure any kind of social or economic equality. The antebellum period saw widespread debate about the direction the American economy should take and the role government should adopt. Gradually, national and local governments retreated from involvement in market relations or the regulation of social behavior.[7] Male political culture, as it came to be defined by the late nineteenth century, precluded government interference in many aspects of the economic and social life of the nation. Indeed, as a number of historians

4. A review of the current concerns of historians of men appears in "Looking Toward Future Research," in Carnes and Griffen, eds., *Meanings for Manhood*, 179–81, and more recently in E. Anthony Rotundo, *American Manhood: Transformations in Masculinity from the Revolution to the Modern Era* (New York, 1993), 1–9.

5. This transformation is discussed in Amy Dru Stanley, "Home Life and the Morality of the Market," in Melvyn Stokes and Stephen Conway, eds., *The Market Revolution in America: Social, Political, and Religious Expressions, c. 1800–1880* (Charlottesville, 1996), 74–96, and Charles Sellers, *The Market Revolution: Jacksonian America, 1815–1846* (New York, 1991), 237–68, though both are more concerned about the effects of this transformation on women.

6. Sellers, *Market Revolution*, 199–201, 362–63. This is also discussed by Paula Baker in "The Domestication of Politics: Women and American Political Society, 1780–1920," *American Historical Review* 89 (1984): 620–47.

7. Baker, "The Domestication of Politics," 620–47.

have observed, male politics became defined strictly as electoral and party politics, and economics as governed exclusively by the tenets of laissez-faire.[8]

Despite this dominant political culture, some groups of middle-class men believed that proper masculine behavior involved a duty of social ameliora-tion. Thus, they became involved in reform movements throughout the nineteenth century, as long as these did not extend the boundaries of the state beyond certain limited functions. Instead, it was women reformers, prompted by their own gender consciousness, who began to see the possi-bilities of using the government to improve conditions for certain portions of society. By the beginning of the twentieth century, women had shown themselves to be much more willing to use the state to accomplish their re-form agenda than were men.[9] By the early twentieth century, however, some men were beginning to realize that classic individualism—in many senses the epitome of manliness—would have to give way to regulation and coop-eration in the face of the overwhelming problems created by industrializa-tion and urbanization.[10]

The male tradition of reform was consequently bound up with a particu-lar notion of manliness and was limited to certain aspects of national life. In the antebellum period, it was widely accepted that middle-class men would be involved in reform. Male reformers were leaders in many of the great re-form crusades that developed as a result of the Second Great Awakening— among them abolitionism, the demand for public education, and the cre-ation of public reformatory and philanthropic institutions. Many of these were led by clergymen or those closely associated with the church, but often also by those who sought the fulfillment of republican and democratic ideals generated by the American Revolution. Such reform movements epit-omized a certain construction of manliness, which, as the historian Clyde Griffen has suggested, "believed devoutly that economic life must be gov-erned by moral values, that individual and collective righteousness ought to be sustained by public policy, and that the gentler virtues should be applied

8. Rotundo, *American Manhood*, 271–74; Arnaldo Testi, "The Gender of Reform Politics: Theodore Roosevelt and the Culture of Masculinity," *Journal of American History* 81 (March 1995): 1509–33; Theda Skocpol, *Protecting Soldiers and Mothers: The Political Origins of So-cial Policy in the United States* (Cambridge, Mass., 1992).

9. Testi, "The Gender of Reform Politics," 1509–33; Paula Baker, *The Moral Framework of Public Life: Gender, Politics and the State in Rural New York, 1870–1930* (New York, 1991); Maureen A. Flanagan, "Gender and Urban Political Reform: The City Club and the Woman's City Club of Chicago in the Progressive Era," *American Historical Review* 95 (Octo-ber 1990): 1032–50.

10. Filene, *Him/Her/Self*, 75–78; Testi, "The Gender of Reform Politics," 1509–33. This, of course, gave rise to what is generally referred to as the Progressive Movement.

wherever possible in human relationships."[11] By the 1850s, however, such values had already become widely associated with women. After the Civil War, the northern urban middle-classes insisted increasingly on a construction of masculinity that emphasized the contrast between the gender spheres, making it progressively more difficult for middle-class men to be involved in reform movements of the kind with which they had been associated before the Civil War. Indeed, men involved in reform activity were often characterized as effeminate.[12]

The climate of the Gilded Age did not readily lend itself to the success of any kind of social reform movement. Social Darwinism had a profound influence on the thought of the period, and its emphasis on "Survival of the Fittest" made it very difficult to justify any kind of social reform. Even the Protestant churches lost their evangelical zeal for reform. In a climate where classical individualism was dominant, especially in legislative bodies and the judiciary, it proved extremely difficult to secure any social welfare legislation. Indeed, as Theda Skocpol has argued, attempts to secure social welfare measures that would aid working men consistently failed until the 1930s.[13] On the other hand, reform programs focused on mothers and children and advocated by female reformers were consistently more successful.

In a number of ways, by the late nineteenth century, masculinity had become problematic. The profound social and economic changes produced by rapid industrialization and urbanization in the decades after the Civil War forced many middle-class men to redefine their masculinity. Manly achievement, determined by economic independence, no longer seemed possible for many middle-class men in an age of large corporations, when these men were either employees or independent entrepreneurs who found it difficult to compete. As several historians have suggested, many middle-class men also felt increasingly threatened in public life, where female values were winning recognition and male behavior was under scrutiny.[14]

The competing discourses constructed by male reformers involved in the

11. Griffen, "Reconstructing Masculinity," 187. Some aspects of these reform movements are discussed in Sellers, *Market Revolution,* 202–68. Also in Paul Boyer, *Urban Masses and Moral Order in America, 1820–1920* (Cambridge, Mass., 1978); David J. Rothman, *The Discovery of the Asylum: Social Order and Disorder in the New Republic* (Boston, 1990; first published, 1971).

12. Griffen, "Reconstructing Masculinity," 189–92; Rotundo, *American Manhood,* 247–83.

13. Skocpol, *Protecting Soldiers and Mothers,* 153–310; Richard Hofstadter, *Social Darwinism in American Thought,* rev. ed. (Boston, 1955; first published, 1944).

14. Griffen, "Reconstructing Masculinity," 183–204; Susan Curtis, "The Son of Man and

juvenile court movement make clear that not all middle-class men reacted
to the apparent assault on their conception of masculinity in the same way.
On the one hand, men who played little part in the initial shaping of the juvenile court idea but who actively supported the initiatives of the women reformers often adopted the discourse of maternalism. On the other hand, a
minority of male juvenile court reformers who sought to reassert an older
tradition of masculine reform addressed juvenile delinquency in terms different from those adopted by maternalist women reformers. This latter reaction is clearly illustrated by Judge Ben Lindsey.

Benjamin Barr Lindsey was born on November 25, 1869, in Jackson,
Tennessee, the son of a telegraph operator who had served as a captain in
the Confederate army. The Colorado gold rush and an offer to the elder
Lindsey of a job in Denver led the whole family to move to Colorado in
1879. Much of Lindsey's youth was marked by disruption, as the family's
declining fortunes caused him to move between his parents in Denver and
his grandparents in Jackson. At the age of eighteen, the suicide of his father
forced Ben and his younger brother, Chal, to go to work to support the family. Ben Lindsey secured a job in a lawyer's office in Denver and in 1894 was
admitted to the bar. Soon afterward he entered into partnership with Frederick A. Parks.

The two young lawyers were soon involved in politics. Parks ran for the
state senate and won as a Silver Republican. Lindsey, on the other hand,
worked for the "fusion" ticket of Democrats and Silver Republicans and
helped to secure the election of Charles S. Thomas as governor. As a re-
ward, Lindsey was appointed public administrator of Arapahoe County. He
continued to be active in politics and in 1900 was again rewarded for his
support of the Democratic governor when, as the result of the elevation of
county court judge Robert W. Steele to the Supreme Court, Lindsey was appointed to fill the vacancy. Thus, on January 1, 1901, at the age of thirty-
one, Lindsey assumed his duties as county court judge in Denver. He developed this post into that of juvenile court judge.[15]

Colorado already had in place a framework of legislation that would al-

---

God the Father: The Social Gospel and Victorian Masculinity," in Carnes and Griffen, eds.,
Meanings for Manhood, 67–68.

15. Lindsey has received a fair amount of attention from historians: Charles Larsen, *The
Good Fight: The Life and Times of Ben B. Lindsey* (Chicago, 1972); Frances Anne Huber,
"The Progressive Career of Ben B. Lindsey, 1900–1920" (Ph.D. diss., University of Michigan,
1963); Marjorie Hornbein, "The Story of Judge Ben Lindsey," *Southern California Quarterly*
55 (1973): 469–82; D'Ann Campbell, "Judge Ben Lindsey and the Juvenile Court Movement,
1901–1904," *Arizona and the West* (Spring 1976): 5–20; Elizabeth J. Clapp, "The Personal

low Lindsey to establish his juvenile court. The state also possessed a net-work of reformers, male and female, concerned about the condition of chil-dren in the slums of Denver. Moreover, Lindsey's predecessor, together with other district judges, had already begun to set aside one afternoon a week especially for children's cases, clearly in the hope that doing so would pro-tect the children from contamination by adult criminals.[16]

Lindsey himself dated his first interest in wayward children from the time when he was appointed, while still a fledgling lawyer, to defend some bur-glars. He found these "burglars" to be two boys who, housed in the Denver jail, passed the time gambling with hardened criminals. In various accounts, written some time after the juvenile court was well established, Lindsey claimed this to be the formative experience that laid the foundation for his interest in children. In an account written in 1925 he observed, "As I look back upon my experiences, I think it must have been some of the impres-sions, conscious or unconscious, that came to me in that experience of de-fending young criminals that really enlisted my interest in what afterwards was to become the Juvenile Court. Of course I could only see the whole sub-ject vaguely then, as compared to the vision that came to me in after years. I had been very much interested in the change made in that school law and I remember I had some conferences and correspondence with Senator Stuart upon it."[17]

It seems likely that Lindsey claimed this early interest in the School Law and the plight of children before the criminal courts with the benefit of hindsight. There is little evidence to suggest that he took any active interest in changing the way children were treated by the courts before he became county court judge. Indeed, his own reaction to what he later called the Tony Costello case suggests little realization of what it meant to the children and their families.[18]

It was the Tony Costello case itself that proved the judge's real spur to ac-

Touch? Ben Lindsey and the Denver Juvenile Court," *Mid-America* 75 (April–July 1993): 197–221. Biographical details are taken from Ben B. Lindsey and Rube Borough, *The Danger-ous Life* (New York, 1974; first published, London, 1931), chaps. 1–3.

16. *The Problem of the Children and How the State of Colorado Cares for Them*, (Denver, 1904), 33; *Second Biennial Report of the State Board of Charities and Correction of Colorado*, 1894, pp. 34–44.

17. Extract from speech presented to Friends of the Denver Juvenile and Family Court in Commemoration of twenty-five years of the court, February 1925, 3, box 277, folder 7, Ben B. Lindsey Papers, Manuscript Division, Library of Congress (hereafter BBL Papers).

18. Lindsey always used false names in relating stories about his work with children—as, for instance, in the case of Tony Costello. This maintained confidentiality and protected the children involved.

tion, and it occurred soon after he became county court judge. One day Lindsey was presiding over a matter concerning the ownership of some mortgaged furniture when he was interrupted by the assistant district attorney, who asked him to quickly dispose of a larceny case. He agreed to do so, and a boy was brought in and arraigned before the court. The clerk read the indictment, and a railroad detective gave his testimony. The boy had nothing to say in his defense, and since the case was clear, Lindsey found him guilty and sentenced him to a term in the state reform school. He then returned to the previous case but was almost immediately interrupted by a woman's loud and unrelenting screams, which forced him to adjourn the court and retreat to his chambers. The woman screaming was the boy's mother, inconsolable at having her son taken away from her.

Lindsey, shaken at the experience, telephoned the district attorney and asked if he could suspend sentence. The district attorney was doubtful as to the legality of this, but Lindsey took responsibility for the boy, whom he returned to his mother. Lindsey then went to the boy's home in the Italian quarter, found it poverty-stricken, and talked to the boy and his mother. He found, as he explained, that the boy was not a criminal, not even a bad boy, but a boy trying to help his family. Tony was given a lecture on the need to obey the law, put "on probation," and ordered to report to Lindsey at regular intervals. The incident, Lindsey noted, set him thinking about the question of punishing children as if they were adults and maiming their young lives. "It was an outrage against childhood, against society, against justice, decency and common sense," wrote Lindsey later. "I began to search the statutes for the laws in the matter, to frequent the jails in order to see how the children were treated there, to compile statistics of the cost to the county of these trials and the cost to society of this way of making criminals of little children. And the deeper I went into the matter, the more astounded I became."[19]

It would appear from this account that Lindsey's adoption of the cause of children before the law came from a fairly sudden conversion rather than a long-term, growing awareness of the problem. The case of Tony Costello and the realization it brought of the conditions in which many children who appeared before the courts lived prompted Lindsey to attempt to ameliorate the system. His response seems to have been more a reaction to necessity than part of a philosophy about the nature of childhood. Rather than seeking new legislation to address this problem, Lindsey chose to adapt existing laws.

19. Ben B. Lindsey and Harvey J. O'Higgins, *The Beast* (New York, 1910), 79–85.

Prompted by the Costello case and other similar incidents, Lindsey began to investigate the conditions of childhood in Denver. He found boys in the jail locked up with men of the "vilest immorality," taking lessons in what Lindsey called the "high school of vice." He also discovered that many hardened criminals were graduates of the system. In an attempt to do something to help these children, he searched the statutes of Colorado and discovered a clause in the School Law of 1899 that pronounced children in trouble to be not criminals but juvenile disorderly persons and, as such, wards of the state to be corrected by the state in its capacity as *parens patriae*. In effect, this meant that the state was to act as the parent of all children in its care, working in the child's best interests rather than punishing him as a criminal. Technically, the law applied only to children who violated the School Law by playing truant, but it could be construed to apply to all children who violated any criminal law. Lindsey was able to persuade the district attorney to file all complaints against children under this law in Lindsey's court.[20] The School Law provided the basis on which Lindsey established his juvenile court, but the legality of this interpretation was somewhat dubious, and its operation depended very much on the cooperation of the district attorney and other court officials.[21]

The Denver Juvenile Court was therefore established on an informal basis, using a law that, while it could be construed to apply to all children who violated the law itself, was obviously not intended to be interpreted this way. Hence, the court's use of it was on doubtful legal grounds. Lindsey exploited the School Law further by asking the school board to provide truant officers to act as probation officers in the court, although Lindsey usually fulfilled this function himself.[22] The court relied heavily on the cooperation of court officials and the school board, as well as on teachers from whom Lindsey requested a report on his probationers every two weeks.[23] Thus, while much of the credit for the establishment of the Denver juvenile court must go to Lindsey, his work was heavily dependent on the cooperation of others, and it is significant that when he discovered the existence of the Illi-

20. Ibid., 85–87.

21. Lindsey himself acknowledged his dependence on the friendly cooperation of court officials: letter to Hon. R. L. Chambers, June 21, 1902, box 83, folder 2, BBL Papers.

22. Lindsey and O'Higgins, *The Beast*, 87–88; letter to T. D. Hurley, January 1, 1904, box 7, folder 1, BBL Papers.

23. Lindsey sent letters to teachers asking for a report on the conduct of particular boys to be sent every two weeks. See, for instance, letter to Miss Ames, February 16, 1901, box 80, BBL Papers.

nois Juvenile Court Law in early 1902, he quickly realized the necessity for more concrete legislation on which to base his own court.[24]

Lindsey's court developed gradually using the School Law. A child under sixteen found guilty of any offense was charged with being a juvenile disorderly person under section 4 of the School Law of 1899. In extreme cases the boy would be sentenced to the state industrial school at Golden and his sentence suspended during good behavior. Lindsey would then keep track of the boy by asking him to attend school regularly and bring to the court a report from his teacher detailing his record for attendance and deportment. On report day Lindsey would receive these reports and speak on some topic of interest to the boys. Lindsey used his own methods to influence the children's behavior: "We always treat the boys soundly & endeavor to impress upon them the consequences sure to result from their waywardness & by tactful appeals to their pride and better nature win them over to a different & proper course of conduct."[25] In more extreme cases Lindsey would talk individually with the boy, in a "companionable discussion" designed to reach the boy's confidence and bring out the good in him.[26] He operated by no hard and fast rules, but as he noted, "The method of reaching them & getting them started on the right track sometimes differs & must depend on a sort of instinct and by the history or facts in the case."[27]

Until the passing of the juvenile court laws of 1903 and subsequent years, the Denver Juvenile Court was heavily dependent on Lindsey's own instincts. It did not have the systematic investigation of a child's home surroundings on which the Chicago Juvenile Court prided itself. Its emphasis was on the regular attendance of probationers at school or, if beyond school age, on the securing of a permanent job. More significantly, though, it placed considerable importance on the influence of the judge on disorderly children, most of whom were boys.

Lindsey's motives in seeking an improvement in the treatment of children before the law were somewhat ambivalent. While he shared some of the same concerns as the women juvenile court reformers in Chicago, his perspective was also influenced by his gender consciousness. On the face of it, Lindsey's motives seem entirely humanitarian; he was anxious simply to get children out of the clutches of the police and to keep them away from the reform school. On closer inspection, however, it is clear that like the women

24. Letter to Crawford Hill, July 21, 1902, box 83, folder 3, BBL Papers.
25. Manuscript letter, unaddressed, box 84, folder 5, BBL Papers.
26. Ibid.
27. Ibid.

reformers of Chicago, he was motivated by a fear that if these children were not properly treated and educated for proper citizenship when they were children, they would present a danger to society when they had become more and more hardened by a life of criminality. Like the women of Chicago, Lindsey was concerned that the family was breaking down under the pressures of city life and that parents were not taking proper care of their children: "The country life with its wholesomeness, its sweetness and its beauty, nearer to God and all that's good and true in nature, is no longer for the great masses of the children of this nation. . . . It is the city with its teeming masses that is abolishing the home and building up a new condition of life that our forefathers knew not of. It is the children of the city, the children of the toiling masses, who must sooner or later handle and solve the new problems new conditions present."[28] It therefore behooved the state and its representatives to guide these children along the right paths. Lindsey further argued that love and understanding would achieve more with these children than harsh treatment: "Love, kindness, gentleness and patience mixed with a certain amount of firmness will do more for a boy than all the cursings, abuse, nagging or chastisements at home, or the swearing, threatening, cuffing and sweating of the police station or workhouse."[29]

In this attitude toward childhood and family, Lindsey was echoing those accepted ideas about the nature of the family and the threats to it from the new urban environment that had prompted the women of Chicago to seek a solution to the problem of children who lived in the slums. In other respects Lindsey's ideas were out of sympathy with the thinking at that time about child rearing and suggested a more masculine view of family life. Instead of accepting that it was the woman's role to bring up children and prepare them for later life, Lindsey seems to have believed that a father's influence was of greater importance in a boy's upbringing. In this he was reflecting older ideas about child rearing that gave the father the dominant role. Such ideas had been largely superseded by the late nineteenth century as more and more fathers worked outside the home and were absent much of the day. Social thinking and child-rearing literature of the time reflected this, stressing the primary importance of the mother's role in bringing up children and downplaying the role of the father.[30]

It is possible that Lindsey's emphasis on the importance of a father's in-

28. Speech delivered at Trinity Church, January 11, 1903, "Our City Children," pp. 1–3, box 277, folder 3, BBL Papers.

29. Ibid., 12.

30. John Demos, *Past, Present, and Personal: The Family and the Life Course in American*

fluence in the home resulted mainly from personal experience. Lindsey's father was often absent during the boy's childhood and committed suicide when young Lindsey was only eighteen, forcing him to take on family responsibilities at an early age.[31] Formative in Lindsey's development was his own experience of a boyhood without a father's influence. He believed that the despair he felt in early manhood might have been avoided had his father been a real presence at that time in his life. Lindsey's attitude toward family life was, in many respects, dominated by the idea that a father's influence was of the greatest importance in a boy's upbringing. He may also have been reflecting anxieties among some middle-class men that because of the increasing distance in relationships between fathers and sons and the growing dominance of the mother, young men were growing up without proper male role models. Thus, Lindsey considered that the mother's contribution should be confined to the early years of a child's life:

> If you could read the hundreds of letters we have in this court from mothers who are unable to do anything with their boys when they arrived at a different age and a different period and they were "up against" the proposition of the boy running out nights with the wild boys of the neighborhood and getting into mischief, and eventually into crime, in which they have voluntarily expressed their gratitude to the officers of this court for the help and assistance they have received, and even the redemption of their boys from a life of crime, which, in spite of all their knowledge and ability and in spite of the fact that nine-tenths of these boys had received a little more spanking and a few more "lickings" than most any other boys, I think you would concede that the juvenile court does do something about one end of this important problem.[32]

A home without a father's influence was likely to produce children who would not be good citizens. "How many despairing cries I have heard from mothers who have been deserted by miserable husbands," he observed, "that they were unable to look after the boy when he arrives at this age,

History (New York, 1986), 41–47; Peter N. Stearns, *Be a Man: Males in Modern Society* (New York, 1979), 49, 96–98; Rotundo, *American Manhood*, 26–28.

31. Lindsey and Borough, *The Dangerous Life*, chaps. 1–3.

32. Letter to Perry Clay, November 17, 1904, p. 1, box 3, folder 3, BBL Papers; Joe L. Dubbert, *A Man's Place: Masculinity in Transition* (Englewood Cliffs, N.J., 1979), 140–44.

because there was no home and no father's care."[33] It was up to fathers, whether they came from poor families or prosperous ones, to make companions of their boys and give time to their needs. It was also important that both parents get to know their children: "The great majority of boys who go wrong do so because their mothers or fathers do not know them," wrote Lindsey. "Even for his serious faults I could never frame an indictment against the American boy; but there might well be an indictment against careless mothers and fathers."[34]

Thus it was that Lindsey blamed many of the misdemeanors of the children who came before his court on their parents and the failure of their homes, but he seems to have had little sympathy for the reasons why such homes failed. He did not, however, see parental failure as a reason for removing a child from his home, unless the circumstances were very extreme, for he believed the home to be the best place for the child in most circumstances. Instead, he relied on the child himself to develop character enough to resist the temptations of a life of criminality and to keep on the path of good citizenship. To reinforce the child's own efforts to reform himself, Lindsey sought means to ensure that the child's environment was as favorable as possible.

Lindsey seems to have been ambivalent in his thinking about the essential nature of childhood. His ideas about children and the factors affecting their behavior developed over time, as a result of both his experience in the juvenile court and the fight he had to preserve his position as juvenile court judge. Also affecting Lindsey was his own growing awareness of more theoretical works on the nature of childhood and adolescence. Some of Lindsey's later writing on the "boy question" is clearly influenced by the work of the psychologist G. Stanley Hall, although it seems likely that, as Lindsey noted himself, he was unaware of Hall's work until the publication of the psychologist's major study on *Adolescence* in 1904. In this sense Lindsey was again out of step with the female juvenile court reformers, who seem to have been more directly influenced by Hall's ideas.[35]

In the earliest days of the juvenile court, Lindsey seems to have believed

33. Letter to Perry Clay, November 17, 1904, 2, box 3, folder 3, BBL Papers.
34. Ben B. Lindsey, "My Experience with Boys," *Ladies Home Journal* (October 1906), box 260, folder 4, BBL Papers; letter to Perry Clay, November 17, 1904, 3, box 3, folder 3, BBL Papers; letter to John S. Phillips, November 20, 1905, box 5, folder 6, BBL Papers.
35. Lindsey corresponded with Hall about his work. See, for instance, letter to Rev. G. Stanley Hall, September 20, 1904, box 2, folder 6, BBL Papers. In this letter Lindsey stated, "I wish to say that the methods I have employed here have simply grown up as the result of my obser-

that the child was basically good; it was his environment that made him criminal. This meant a boy could be reformed through appeals to his better nature. "It is astonishing how much good there is in some boys apparently of criminal tendencies," he wrote, "if you can reach the boy in the right way. They are more often the creatures of environment than real criminals."[36] Many of the boys merely needed to overcome the disadvantages of their upbringing and home environment in order to become good citizens. It was this faith in the basic goodness of "boy nature" that prompted Lindsey to treat children in his court with as much patience and love as possible. Lindsey believed that wayward youth could not be brought to truth and light through force and violence, hate and despair; a real cure could only be achieved through a change in the human heart, through love, and because the boy was taught to do right because it was right, not because he was afraid of being caught.[37]

Much of the language employed by Lindsey in describing boy nature is evangelical and suggests he was influenced by such forces as the Social Gospel movement, which tried to apply the tenets of Christianity to society as a whole. Together with the principle of individual salvation, Social Gospellers sought to use the doctrine of social redemption through the application of Jesus' teaching to solve everyday problems.[38] Social Gospel ministers may also have done much to help redefine Christianity in a more masculine way. As Susan Curtis has observed, the Social Gospel was in part a reaction against the feminization of Protestantism that had been occurring since the Second Great Awakening. The Jesus of the Social Gospel was a "man's man." As Walter Rauschenbusch, an exponent of the Social Gospel,

---

vations and experience, and I have up to this time purposely refrained from consulting or studying any sociological works for fear I might embibe some theory, preferring to work things out from what seemed to me the practical standpoint, and after an experience of four years I am glad I have taken this course, but I shall now devote myself to more study along this line." Hall's major work to which Lindsey referred was G. Stanley Hall, *Adolescence: Its Psychology and Its Relations to Physiology, Anthropology, Sociology, Sex, Crime, Religion and Education*, vols. 1 and 2 (reprint, 1920; first published, 1904). On Hall's influence on other juvenile court reformers, see David J. Rothman, *Conscience and Convenience: The Asylum and Its Alternatives in Progressive America* (Boston, 1980), 207–11.

36. Letter to William C. Sprague, April 19, 1902, box 82, folder 4, BBL Papers.

37. Ben B. Lindsey, introduction to Lilburn Merrill, *Winning the Boy* (1908), 5–10.

38. The Social Gospel Movement is described by, among other historians, Charles H. Hopkins, *The Rise of the Social Gospel in American Protestantism, 1865–1915* (New Haven, 1940); Eric F. Goldman, *Rendezvous with Destiny: A History of Modern American Reform* (New York, 1956; first published, 1952), 83–85.

insisted, "there was nothing mushy, nothing sweetly effeminate about Jesus."[39] Thus, ministers of the Social Gospel and their followers, in a reaction against individualism, redirected both Protestantism and manliness toward social reform. As Susan Curtis has noted, "The social gospel was not, however, a new expression of feminized religion. The men who came to the movement wrestled with the meaning of manhood and the legacy of their fathers. They articulated a gospel that transformed the domestic concerns of their reforms into expressions of manly endeavor."[40] It is quite possible that this more masculine concept of Protestantism as well as its emphasis on social reform appealed to Lindsey.

Lindsey applied the tenets of the Social Gospel by putting a great emphasis on the individual child and, by loving him and treating him with kindness and patience, bringing about his salvation. This more active Protestantism also involved a belief that human conduct was shaped by environmental factors. Here again, this view is clearly stated in Lindsey's writings on boy nature and his campaigns to protect the children of Denver from what he saw as bad influences. Thus, Lindsey was prompted by his belief that if the boys who came to his court showing criminal tendencies were given a chance and encouraged to overcome the handicaps created by their environment, they would develop into good citizens. They needed merely to be taught the right direction: "Our purpose is by this system to implant within wayward children results of purity, truth, honor, and righteousness," Lindsey argued, "so that there may be a soul awakening, as it were."[41]

Although the Social Gospel may well have been one influence in shaping Lindsey's more masculine conception of juvenile court reform, there are other, clearer indications that Lindsey was affected in his methods by his perceptions of proper masculine behavior. In this respect, it is significant that the vast majority of the juvenile offenders who came before Lindsey's court were boys. Indeed, Lindsey had an entirely different attitude toward the girls who appeared before him and frequently asked his female assistants to deal with them. This can be explained, in part, by the fact that many girls were brought before the juvenile court for what was euphemistically called "immorality," and it was felt that a woman could deal with such cases more delicately. But Lindsey displayed a good deal of ambiva-

39. Curtis, "The Son of Man and God the Father," 72.
40. Griffen, "Reconstructing Masculinity," 194–95; Curtis, "The Son of Man and God the Father," 72.
41. Letter to T. D. Hurley, January 1, 1904, box 87, folder 1, BBL Papers.

lence even toward those female offenders who had committed offenses similar to those of the boys.[42]

Lindsey's perception of the nature of childhood and the proper behavior of children was very different from that of the female juvenile court reformers. In addition to believing that fathers had an essential role to play in the rearing of their sons, Lindsey maintained that the development of character was central to the creation of upright citizens. As he noted, "What we want to impress upon our boys is that we are learning more and more in America every day that which counts most is character and manhood, and that all American boys have equal chances to become useful and respected citizens if they are faithful, industrious and honest."[43]

"Character" was defined in terms that were quintessentially masculine. It emphasized self-help and individualism but also implied courage, honor, loyalty, independence, boldness, self-control, a sense of duty, and even an impulse toward the defense of the family.[44] Lindsey was not alone in extolling such masculine qualities. Many middle-class men, concerned about what they perceived as the increasing "feminization" of all aspects of their public and private lives, sought to construct an ideal of manhood that reflected these virtues. The public figure who did most to popularize this construction of masculinity was Theodore Roosevelt. Concern that boys develop these masculine virtues was behind the creation of such organizations for middle-class boys as the boy scouts and its forerunner, the YMCA.[45] Lindsey clearly admired and sought to emulate Roosevelt, of-

42. *Report of Hon. Ben B. Lindsey, Chairman of Committee on Juvenile Courts: Before the International Congress on the Welfare of the Child. Held Under the Auspices of the Mothers' Congress at Washington, D.C., April 22–27, 1914,* 8; *The Problem of the Children and How the State of Colorado Cares for Them,* 71. The way in which female offenders were treated in the juvenile courts is discussed by Steven Schlossman and Stephanie Wallach, "The Crime of Precocious Sexuality: Female Juvenile Delinquency in the Progressive Era," *Harvard Educational Review* 48 (February 1978): 65–94; Mary Odem, "Single Mothers, Delinquent Daughters, and the Juvenile Court in Early Twentieth-Century Los Angeles," *Journal of Social History* 25 (Fall 1991): 27–43.

43. Lindsey, "My Experience with Boys."

44. This list appears in Testi, "The Gender of Reform Politics," 1520. Similar attributes of "character" are also suggested in Lindsey's writings—for instance, Lindsey and O'Higgins, *The Beast,* 145—and in the countless stories of "Lindsey's boys."

45. On Roosevelt, see Testi, "The Gender of Reform Politics," 1513–33; Dubbert, *A Man's Place,* 122–33; Kathleen Dalton, "Why America Loved Teddy Roosevelt: Or, Charisma Is in the Eyes of the Beholders," in Robert J. Brugger, ed., *Our Selves / Our Past: Psychological Approaches to American History* (Baltimore, 1981), 269–91. On youth organizations, see David I. Macleod, *Building Character in the American Boy: The Boy Scouts, YMCA and Their Forerunners, 1870–1920* (Madison, Wis., 1983); Boyer, *Urban Masses and Moral Order,* 108–22; Rotundo, *American Manhood,* 222–46.

ten making reference to Roosevelt in his homilies before the juvenile court.[46]

Lindsey's attitude toward the boy offenders who came before his court was clearly shaped by the importance he placed on character in influencing behavior. Indeed, he often interpreted juvenile delinquency as a matter of weakness on the boy's part, and his approach reflected this.[47] His methods depended very much on the personality of Lindsey himself and his ability to convince boys that it was in their own best interests to do right because it was right, not because they would be punished otherwise.

A clear illustration of Lindsey's methods may be seen in his treatment of those boy offenders whom he considered in need of a spell in the state industrial school at Golden. As one journalist explained, "The method of commitment is all Judge Lindsey's own. He simply gives the boy the warrant and tells him to go out to Golden and lock himself up. Not one boy has betrayed the judge's trust, although the trip furnishes numerous opportunities for escape in a street-car ride across the city to the railroad station, a train ride to the Golden station in the foothills and a half-mile walk to the destination. The superintendent is not even notified to look out for the boy's arrival."[48] Such methods laid Lindsey open to charges by some journalists of hypnotizing the boys—charges Lindsey adamantly denied.[49] To Lindsey, the explanation was much more straightforward: "when I send a boy to the Industrial School, or a young criminal to the reformatory, I tell him that he can run away, if he wants to, but I proceed to convince him that he should not want to,—and so far, they have all been convinced."[50]

Lindsey saw this as a character-building exercise, but it was also an extension of the judge's belief that a child treated with love and kindness and trusted to do his best would do what was asked of him. He believed that boys who had to be committed to the industrial school were weak rather

46. Letter to Jacob Riis, November 17, 1904, box 3, folder 3, BBL Papers; letter to President Roosevelt, December 9, 1904, box 3, folder 4, BBL Papers. Emulation of Roosevelt may also be seen in Lindsey's reference to himself as the "Bull Mouse" during Roosevelt's Bull Moose campaign.

47. This is the gist of many of Lindsey's stories about the boys before his court. See, for instance, Lindsey, "My Experience with Boys"; editorial, *American Primary Teacher* 28 (June 1905), box 312, folder 6, BBL Papers; *The Problem of the Children and How the State of Colorado Cares for Them*, 72–82.

48. Frances M. Bjorkman, "The Children's Court in American City Life," *Review of Reviews* 33 (March 1906): 309.

49. Ben B. Lindsey, "Letter to the Editor: 'Hypnotism and the Juvenile Court,' " *Charities* 14 (August 26, 1905): 1020.

50. Letter to Mrs. Frances Maule, December 27, 1905, box 6, folder 2, BBL Papers.

than vicious and that the industrial school would teach them strength of character. In order to impress on the boy that the judge had no doubt the boy would overcome his weakness, Lindsey trusted him to get himself to the industrial school and made it obvious that he would not make any effort to enforce the commitment. He made it equally clear that failure to deliver himself to the authorities at Golden would be interpreted as a sign of weakness. Thus Lindsey appealed to the boy's pride and sense of honor.

There was another reason why Lindsey allowed these boys to arrive on their own. By allowing a boy to travel to Golden unaccompanied by any officer of the law, the judge did not make it obvious where he was going, and the boy was able to maintain his self-respect. One of the boys Lindsey treated in this way observed that had he been shackled and accompanied to Golden, he would have hated the judge and the person who took him there and would have tried his best to escape. Instead, since he was sent alone, people had no idea where he was going and did not stare at him, and so he was not ashamed.[51] Moreover, by making the boy feel that he alone was responsible for his condition, it ensured he did not hate the judge who had sent him to the school and regarded him instead as a friend. In this way, on his release from the reform school, the boy would not feel that hatred toward the state that often prompted further offenses.[52]

This use of what Lindsey called "chains unseen" clearly rested on an assumption of a sense of honor and pride in the boys he dealt with—characteristics that contributed to the middle-class construction of masculinity. Like a number of other leaders working with boys in the late nineteenth and early twentieth centuries, Lindsey imposed his own belief about proper male behavior on working-class boys.[53] He achieved considerable success, although he was not without his critics.[54]

Such methods relied heavily on the judge's personality and his ability to convince young offenders that they should do right because it was right and not because they would get into trouble otherwise. It also placed great em-

51. Description of a "former inmate" called "The Honor of a Boy," undated, box 225, folder 7, BBL Papers.

52. Ben B. Lindsey, "Additional Reports on Methods and Results," in Samuel J. Barrows, ed., *Children's Courts in the United States: Their Origin, Development and Results* (Washington, D.C., 1904), 116.

53. The most obvious parallel was with William R. George and his experiment with the boy gangs of New York in the George Junior Republic. Jack M. Holl, *Juvenile Reform in the Progressive Era: William R. George and the Junior Republic Movement* (Ithaca, 1971); William R. George, *The Junior Republic* (1912; first published, 1909).

54. *Eel Martin's Record,* republished from *Clay's Review* (June 18, 1910), is only one example of the criticism Lindsey faced for his methods.

phasis on the boy's strength of character and his sense of loyalty to the judge. These methods clearly could be neither institutionalized nor embodied in legislation but relied instead on Lindsey's personality and the support he received for his work.

As his efforts became known to the general public of Denver, Lindsey received a good deal of public support. This came particularly from the Denver Woman's Club and from those who were themselves involved in the work, such as the truancy officers. In the 1901 elections for county court judge, Lindsey was endorsed by the club: "Many ladies of the Woman's Club, and the County truancy officers, endorse Judge Lindsey's active and efficient work in dealing with truants and bad boys, and the splendid results he has accomplished in this direction."[55] Lindsey also received a stream of letters from other county court judges and district attorneys in Colorado expressing an interest in his methods, asking how they could do similar work, and inquiring about the legal basis on which he ran his juvenile court.[56] By the middle of 1902, however, Lindsey was having some doubts as to whether the law could continue to be construed in this way. He began to gather support to agitate for legislation that would give full legal sanction to the court in Denver as well as enable other counties to establish similar courts.[57]

It seems likely that one of the factors prompting Lindsey to believe it was necessary to place the juvenile court on a firmer legal basis was his discovery in January 1902 of the Illinois Juvenile Court Law.[58] As a result, Lindsey began a correspondence with Timothy D. Hurley, editor of the *Juvenile Record* and one of those interested in the promotion of the Chicago Juvenile Court and the juvenile court idea throughout the country. This correspondence also involved Lindsey in the nationwide reform community and secured for him an invitation to the National Conference of Charities and Correction held in Detroit in May 1902. Thus Lindsey became aware of other juvenile courts already established in other states, and it is probable that this influenced him to seek legislation in Colorado. Although he was

55. Notice entitled "Vote for Judge Ben B. Lindsey for County Judge," 1901 election, box 82, folder 1, BBL Papers; letter to Emma C. Lentz, March 22, 1902, box 62, folder 3, BBL Papers.

56. As in, for instance, letter from Jesse C. Wiley, August 11, 1902, box 1, folder 1, BBL Papers; letter from P. B. Jackson, August 28, 1902, box 1, folder 1, BBL Papers.

57. See, for instance, letter to Hon. R. L. Chambers, June 21, 1902, box 83, folder 2, BBL Papers.

58. Letter to T. D. Hurley, January 17, 1902, box 82, folder 1, BBL Papers, notes Lindsey's discovery of the Chicago Juvenile Court.

very insistent that his own methods were working well and that the Illinois system was in no sense a superior one, he realized by mid-1902 that legislation was required: "Our 'school law' (compulsory education act) was passed the same year, and while we have, by a very elastic but doubtful construction, twisted it into a 'Juvenile Court Act' as much as possible, it is very imperative that the next legislature shall make it certain and substantial."[59]

Lindsey initiated the campaign for legislation, but he was heavily dependent on the support of the women's clubs, the Charity Organization Society, and the churches. Many of these agencies had been involved in work to improve the condition of children in the state for some time, so they were a natural constituency to call on for support.[60] Lindsey also received encouragement and support from the Colorado County Judges Association and was able to draw on their legal expertise in framing the necessary legislation.[61] Moreover, the fact that other states, especially Illinois, already had tried and tested juvenile court laws on their statute books helped immensely. In some cases these laws had had their constitutionality tested. Thus Lindsey had few of the concerns about the legality of such a law that had affected the Chicago women.[62] The Colorado legislature had proved itself willing to pass social welfare legislation in the past, most obviously the School Law of 1899, and the fact that other states had already passed juvenile court measures made Lindsey's aim to regularize his court through law considerably easier to achieve than it was in other states.

Lindsey employed very different tactics in his campaign from those used by the women reformers elsewhere. As a man he did not have to justify his own role in the public sphere of reform, and the fact that he had been run-

59. Letter to Crawford Hill, July 21, 1902, box 83, folder 3, BBL Papers; "Report to the State Association of County Court Judges of Colorado," undated, box 284, folder 6, BBL Papers.

60. George Creel and Ben B. Lindsey, *Measuring Up to Equal Suffrage* (New York, 1913), 2–8. Here Lindsey notes, " 'Colorado has the sanest, the most humane, the most progressive, most scientific laws relating to the child to be found on any statute books in the world.' And of these laws which drew such praise from impartial sociologists, not one but has come into operation since Colorado's adoption of equal suffrage in 1893" (3). Letter from Mrs. Izetta George, February 21, 1901, box 80, file for 1901, BBL Papers; letter to Mrs. Emma Lentz, March 22, 1902, box 82, folder 3, BBL Papers.

61. "Preparing a New Code of Laws: County Judges Will Meet in Denver December Six," *Denver Republican,* clipping, December 1, 1902, box 260, folder 5, BBL Papers; "Judges Speak for New Juvenile Law," (Denver) *Times,* February 4, 1903, Newspaper and Magazine Clippings, vol. 1, BBL Papers.

62. Letter to T. D. Hurley, September 20, 1902, box 84, folder 1, BBL Papers; letter to Mrs. Lucy Flower, July 29, 1902, box 83, folder 3, BBL Papers.

ning the juvenile court on an informal basis for some time made circumstances rather different. Nonetheless, he still had to convince many
conservative elements in Colorado that such legislation was required, and
to overcome the resistance of those who had a vested interest in the status
quo. Lindsey proved himself to be a natural publicist. Even before recognizing the need for legislation to place the juvenile court on a more secure legal
footing, the judge had begun to make inquiries into the number of children
held in the county jail, in an attempt to secure a separate detention room for
children. Hoping to protect children from the evil influences of the saloons
and wine rooms in Denver, he had also instigated a campaign against these
establishments. In order to achieve maximum publicity and thus force the
county fire and police board to do something about the conditions for children in the county jail and the saloons, Lindsey invited journalists and
members of the fire and police board, together with prominent churchmen,
to a session of his court at which several of Lindsey's probationers told of
the horrors they had experienced in jail. This resulted in headline news that
created widespread revulsion at the treatment of such children in the jail
and produced public support for the legislation Judge Lindsey was trying to
secure, as well as further public awareness of the juvenile court.[63] Such publicity stunts, however, were not Lindsey's only method of agitating for the
legislation he wished passed.

He also sought to gain the support of more conservative elements by
pointing out the financial savings to the state of his system. Thus, in August
1902 he appealed to B. F. Montgomery, an influential Denver citizen, to
read the report Lindsey had prepared on the juvenile court: "The report of
the juvenile division, while very lengthy, I nevertheless consider of great importance, and I think you will so consider it if you find time to read it, especially that part relating to expenses to the state and county, and the facts
shown by statistics concerning juvenile delinquents, who eventually become
charges upon the state as convicts or paupers and vagabonds."

Lindsey consistently used this argument to appeal to conservative opinion in his attempts to secure legislation to protect children.[64] Although
women reformers occasionally made the same point, it was not one they
emphasized. In an echo of the arguments used by the women reformers,
however, Lindsey contended that while the financial savings to the state of

63. Lindsey and O'Higgins, *The Beast*, 101–10; several letters, dated May 1902, congratu-
lating Lindsey on his stand before the fire and police board, box 83, folder 1, BBL Papers.
64. Letter to Hon. B. F. Montgomery, August 5, 1902, box 83, folder 4, BBL Papers; letter
to Crawford Hill, December 1, 1902, box 83, folder 3, BBL Papers.

his methods were great, the unquantifiable savings to the state and to society of children who would become better citizens were even greater. Above all, though, Lindsey was finding it difficult to ensure that all child offenders were brought to his court where they could be charged as "juvenile disorderly persons." Since policemen received fees for all arrests, it was in their interest to have these children charged as criminals. So the judge sought legislation ensuring that all children's cases came before the county court and abolishing the fee system for children's cases. This legislation would sanction the work he was already doing and remove any possibility it could be challenged.[65]

The Colorado Juvenile Court Law was very clearly modeled on that of Illinois. In fact, Lindsey asked Timothy Hurley for advice on drawing up the bill.[66] There were some significant differences, however. The Colorado law placed much less emphasis on the influence of the home on the child's formation than did the Illinois law. Lindsey placed the accent on the provision of direct help and assistance to the child rather than on the reformative powers of the home assisted by the support of a probation officer.[67] In this emphasis, Lindsey differed quite sharply from the women who agitated for the Chicago Juvenile Court Law. They were influenced by their own perceptions of women's role and their belief in the importance of the home and the mother's influence in the formation of the child. Lindsey was more child-centered in his approach, believing a child would be reformed by the strength of his own character with the love and encouragement of the juvenile court. This ultimately meant that the Denver Juvenile Court was heavily reliant on the personality of its judge to achieve results with the wayward children who came before it, whereas the Chicago Juvenile Court was more dependent on its probation officers and attempts to improve the child's home environment. It also helps to explain why Lindsey's methods were not successfully copied elsewhere.

65. "Report to the State Association of County Judges of Colorado," undated, box 284, folder 6, BBL Papers; "Preparing a New Code of Laws."

66. Letter to T. D. Hurley, September 20, 1902, box 84, folder 1, BBL Papers; letter to T. D. Hurley, January 1, 1904, box 1, folder 3, BBL Papers.

67. This is apparent in the final section of the law, which stated its philosophy. It echoed the Illinois law but differed significantly in its final lines: "The act is to be liberally construed to the end that its real purpose may be carried out, to-wit, that the care, custody and discipline of a delinquent child shall approximate as nearly as may be that that should be given by its parent, and that, as far as practicable, any delinquent child shall be treated, not as a criminal, but as misdirected and misguided, and needing aid and encouragement, help and assistance." As quoted in "Report to the State Association of County Judges of Colorado," undated, box 284, folder 6, BBL Papers.

The Denver Juvenile Court suggests an alternative version of the juvenile court idea, based on perceptions of masculinity and developing out of a male tradition of reform that was reluctant to use the state for purposes of social welfare. It is significant that the discovery of Illinois's already functioning juvenile court law prompted Lindsey to seek similar legislation in Colorado. That he was heavily dependent on the support of women's agencies to secure this legislation suggests that even in those states where the male influence was dominant, women played an important part in lobbying for social welfare legislation. It is to be doubted that such legislation could have been secured without the active support of women's organizations. As Lindsey himself noted: "We must depend on the women . . . for what they have done for the children of the nation, and for the encouragement, kind words and assistance they have always given me and those of us here in Denver, who have tried, in a poor, feeble way, I fear, to accomplish something in the interest of this great cause."[68]

The difference between Lindsey's approach and that of the Chicago court epitomizes the divergence between the masculine influence on the juvenile court idea and the feminine influence—the former emphasizing the importance of individual character developed through the example of a strong male role model; the latter, the importance of nurture and protection in the child's own home supported by a probation officer, who was often female. It was, however, the feminine model that seems to have been the most pervasive in the early years of the juvenile court movement in the United States. The women's organizations were already agitating for juvenile courts across the country before Lindsey appeared on the national scene. Nor was Lindsey typical of those male juvenile court reformers who did take the initiative in agitating for such reform. Only one other juvenile court judge seems to have attempted to adopt Lindsey's methods to develop character in the boys before his court. This was Judge Willis Brown of Salt Lake City, but his career as a juvenile court judge was short-lived. It ended in widespread recrimination, not least from Lindsey, as several dubious decisions led to scandal that threatened to embroil the whole juvenile court movement.[69]

Lindsey's use of existing legislation construed in such a way as to effectively produce a juvenile court was not entirely atypical. One judge who

68. Letter to Mrs. Sarah Platt Decker, March 19, 1906, box 7, folder 1, BBL Papers; letter to Mrs. Frances E. Platfect, October 10, 1904, box 3, folder 1, BBL Papers; Creel and Lindsey, *Measuring Up to Equal Suffrage*, 3.

69. Steven L. Schlossman and Ronald D. Cohen, "The Music Man in Gary: Willis Brown

also did this was Judge George W. Stubbs of Indianapolis. He was reelected judge of the police court of Indianapolis in October 1901, having previously held the position from October 1893 to October 1895. On assuming office the second time, he was astounded by the number of children brought before him charged with offenses against the law or with violating the city ordinances. The passage of such large numbers of children through the police court suggested to Judge Stubbs that current methods of dealing with these offenders were inadequate. Moreover, further investigation revealed that boys and girls who were arrested were taken to the police stations in the police wagon and lodged in the city prison, where they were liable to be contaminated by evil influences.[70]

Judge Stubbs's first efforts were to secure the cooperation of the chief of police in preventing the detention of children in the city prison. Instead, patrolmen were instructed that when arresting boys and girls under the age of sixteen, they were to take these children to their homes and instruct their parents to bring them to the police court the following Friday at two o'clock, when Judge Stubbs heard children's cases. However, the judge was still only able to deal with the children as adults and to punish them as adults might be punished. Although he had established separate hearings for children's cases and was able, through the cooperation of the police, to ensure that children were not associated with adult offenders while awaiting trial, his methods of dealing with the boys and girls who came before him were not very different from those of the criminal court.

While Judge Stubbs was experimenting with the treatment of juvenile offenders in Indianapolis, he learned of the work being carried out in Chicago. In August 1902, accompanied by William M. Hersdell of the Indianapolis *News* and Judge James Collins, Stubbs spent three days in Chicago watching the proceedings of the juvenile court and gathering information that might help in dealing with the problem in Indianapolis. On his return, Stubbs determined that he must have better quarters than his official chambers to work out his plans for handling juvenile offenders, and he had a room in the police station set up as a courtroom. Out of this he developed

---

and Child-Saving in the Progressive Era," *Societas* 7 (1977): 1–17; Ben B. Lindsey, "Ex-Judge Willis Brown Objectionable: Statement by Judge Lindsey of Denver Regarding Willis Brown," *Juvenile Court Record* 8 (October 1907): 14–15, 17.

70. Hon. George W. Stubbs, "The Mission of the Juvenile Court of Indianapolis," in Barrows, ed., *Children's Courts in the United States*, 149; James A. Collins, "The Juvenile Court Movement in Indiana," *Indiana Magazine of History* 28 (March 1932): 1.

further an embryonic juvenile court based on the Chicago model, but one without any legislative sanction.[71]

Others interested in the problem of how the law treated dependent and delinquent children soon became aware of Judge Stubbs's work. Among these men and women were Timothy Nicholson and Amos Butler of the State Board of Charities, as well as other judges, such as James Collins and Fremont Alford, and club women, most notably Mrs. Helen Rogers, who later became chief probation officer for Indianapolis, and Mrs. Julia Goodhart.[72] They realized that Judge Stubbs's work with these children should be secure and children's cases should be dealt with uniformly, and so there was a need to coordinate the various laws relating to the welfare of children and to place all children under the jurisdiction of one court. Thus, like Lindsey's court, the rather uncertain legal grounding of the Indianapolis Juvenile Court and the need to bring more uniformity to the treatment of children in trouble with the law prompted the campaign to secure juvenile court legislation.

Although Judge Stubbs was prominent in the agitation for legislation, he was aided by other judges, members of the State Board of Charities, and various charity workers, several of them women.[73] The judges and various others met in the Union Trust Building and took steps to urge the enactment of a senate bill, prepared by Senator Thompson, which covered every phase of the problem of dependent and delinquent children as considered necessary by the reformers. The bill met with some opposition in the legislature from those unwilling to have the state pay the salary of the additional officer required for the new children's court. There also may have been opposition from those who had a vested interest in the existing system by which the state subsidized the various private child-saving institutions and for whom the introduction of probation seemed to offer an unwelcome alternative to custodial sentences. Nevertheless, the bill passed the legislature and was approved by the governor on March 10, 1903.[74]

The Indiana Juvenile Court Law had largely originated in the initiative of one man who created, on dubious legal ground, an embryo juvenile court that survived for more than a year without challenge. He was motivated in part by humanitarian considerations but also by the fear that if these chil-

71. Collins, "The Juvenile Court Movement in Indiana," 2–3.
72. Ibid., 3–4; Stubbs, "The Mission of the Juvenile Court of Indianapolis," 149.
73. Collins, "The Juvenile Court Movement in Indiana," 4.
74. "Changes in Indianapolis Jurisdiction over Children," *Juvenile Court Record* 4 (January 1903): 5; Collins, "The Juvenile Court Movement in Indiana," 4.

dren were allowed to continue on what was considered to be their downward path, they would grow into vicious adults. A little attention at the
right time, however, would make good adults of them. Like Lindsey, Stubbs
had great faith in the basic goodness of children: "The sweetest flower with
which God has blessed the world is a little child, and if the juvenile court
can do anything to preserve its sweetness and purity, the establishment of
such tribunals will be more than justified." However, he warned, if these
children were not set on the right paths when they were young, they would
later be a danger to society: "Let the boys of our country become corrupted
and their manliness destroyed, the hope of a nation poisoned at its fountain
head, and the abomination of desolation spoken of by Daniel will be upon
us."[75]

Stubbs, like Lindsey also laid great emphasis on the personal touch—the
personal relationship between the judge and the boy before him—as well as
the close relationship between the boy and his probation officer. Yet he utilized none of Lindsey's methods to develop character in the boy offenders
and was quite prepared to have women as probation officers. Clearly, Stubbs
did not consider the provision of a strong male role model to be quite as important as Lindsey considered it. He did, however, have a rather unusual,
and perhaps superficial, understanding of one of the main causes of delinquency among boys—cigarettes: "Cigarettes lead to craps, craps lead to
playing the horse races, horse races lead to larceny, larceny leads to burglary, and burglary leads to the State prison. I can say more than that. Out
of the great number of boys that came before me last year, the majority of
them smoked cigarettes, and when you find a boy that is a cigarette fiend,
he is the hardest of all to reform."[76]

The origins of the Indianapolis Juvenile Court clearly show some parallels with the origins of the Denver Juvenile Court, insofar as both courts
were the result of the initiative of their judges in introducing new methods
of dealing with the children who came before them and in operating an embryo juvenile court on dubious legal grounds. In this sense, that initiative reflected the male tradition of reform, with its reluctance to seek social welfare legislation. Although judges in Chicago also operated informal juvenile
courts before legislation was achieved, these were generally the result of requests to hold separate court sessions for children by women reformers. In

75. George W. Stubbs, "The Mission of the Juvenile Court," *Proceedings of the National
Conference of Charities and Correction* (1904), 350, 357; "Changes in Indianapolis Jurisdiction over Children," 5.
76. "Indianapolis Juvenile Court," *Juvenile Record* 5 (June 1904): 10.

emphasizing the personal touch of the judge, Judge Stubbs also paralleled Lindsey's methods. Yet Stubbs also stressed the importance of the probation officer, and in Indianapolis the chief probation officer was a woman.[77] Thus, while the male judicial influence was undoubtedly instrumental in securing both the informal juvenile court in Indianapolis and juvenile court legislation, the feminine influence was still of some importance in lobbying for the legislation and in the administration of the court after legislation was secured.

Thus, in a number of states the establishment of a juvenile court was the result of male initiatives. In states where this influence was dominant, certain characteristics differentiated the reform process from that found in states where the female influence was predominant. For instance, where men began a juvenile court, they did so using existing legislation construed in a novel way to allow children before the courts to be treated differently from adult criminals. They were usually able to do so because, as in the cases of Lindsey and Stubbs, the male reformers in question were themselves judges and therefore in a position to manipulate existing laws, though their activities very often depended on the cooperation of court officials. Such methods were uncertain, however, and once they had discovered the existence of juvenile court legislation in other states, they quickly lobbied to get similar laws adopted. It is highly significant that male reformers proved themselves more reluctant to seek new legislation than their female counterparts. Moreover, they were often dependent on the support of women to get the legislation passed.

Another factor that characterized the male influence in the early days of the juvenile court movement was the emphasis placed by certain male reformers on the personal touch of the judge. Their concern was to provide a male role model exhibiting the masculine virtues of honesty and character as a way of reforming the boy offender in their courts. For this reason, too, Lindsey in particular saw the role of the probation officer in quite a different light from that of the women reformers. He did not believe that the main function of probation officers should be to offer nurture and guidance to their juvenile charges, as the women reformers believed, but that the officers themselves should be good examples of upright and manly behavior. This suggests that Lindsey had a quite different view of the reasons for juvenile delinquency. In many senses his theory was much less sophisticated

---

77. Lindsey refused to employ women as probation officers in the early days of his juvenile court. Letter to Mrs. Izetta George, April 1, 1902, box 82, folder 4, BBL Papers; letter from Izetta George, April 2, 1902, box 82, folder 3, BBL Papers.

than that of some of the women reformers, for Lindsey often attributed the offenses of the boys before his court to a simple weakness in character.

Lindsey's methods and his emphasis on character-building and the personal touch set him apart from the maternalist reformers, for this emphasis suggested a more masculine approach to the problem of how to deal with wayward children. It was not Lindsey's methods, however, that proved most influential in the juvenile court movement. Although he was an able publicist, and the stories of "Lindsey's boys" captured the public imagination, it was usually the Illinois Juvenile Court Law that was adopted in other states. Nor was Lindsey typical of male juvenile court reformers. While men were involved in the early establishment of juvenile courts, they did so usually in a supportive capacity, acting on the initiative of female reformers rather than as the initiators of reform themselves.

5

The Juvenile Court Movement

By 1909, ten years after the passage of the first juvenile court law in Illinois, twenty-two other states had enacted similar laws. Some of these, as we have seen, were the result of local initiatives, using the Chicago Juvenile Court as a model, but many others grew from conscious agitation by the juvenile court movement. Until 1907, no separate formal organization had been founded with the specific purpose of spreading the juvenile court message. Instead this was undertaken by such groups as the National Congress of Mothers and the General Federation of Women's Clubs as well as by the individual efforts of those involved in establishing the Chicago and Denver courts. Although these groups and individuals often cooperated, it was not until the formation of the International Juvenile Court Association in September 1907 that they deliberately set out to work together to achieve a juvenile court law in every state.[1] The remarkable success of the movement is illustrated by the fact that by 1920, all but three states had some form of juvenile court legislation.[2]

This chapter explores the deliberate efforts made by informal coalitions of reformers and later by the formal organizations they created to achieve a juvenile court law in every state. It examines the way in which the three broad traditions of reform identified in earlier chapters—the traditional maternalists, the female social science tradition of the professional mater-

---

1. "Certificate of Incorporation of the International Juvenile Court Association in Illinois," September 13, 1907, box 226, folder 6, Ben B. Lindsey Papers, Manuscript Division, Library of Congress (hereafter BBL Papers).
2. Herbert H. Lou, *Juvenile Courts in the United States* (Chapel Hill, 1927), 24; Grace Abbott, *The Child and the State*, 2 vols. (Chicago, 1938), 2:332.

nalists, and the male philanthropic tradition—came together to work for
the common goal of protecting children in trouble with the law. The juvenile court movement brought together male and female reformers, often
with markedly different ideas on what the priorities of the movement
should be. This chapter therefore considers how these priorities were contested and resolved to produce a set of aims on which reformers from all
three traditions could agree. It also suggests that as the juvenile court movement developed, a new factor, emphasizing the legal and professional aspects of this new system of juvenile justice, began to enter the discussion.
This new discourse developed less out of a particular social construction of
"proper" gender behavior, either male or female, than out of evolving constructions of expertise. Thus, while the male reform tradition epitomized by
Judge Lindsey and the female "maternalist" tradition continued to be
prominent, a parallel discourse that emphasized professional expertise became increasingly apparent. Yet, even this approach remained gendered.
Women reformers continued to stress their expertise as social scientists, and
male reformers, judges, and lawyers highlighted their legal skill.[3]

Central to this chapter is an exploration of the relationship between
Judge Ben Lindsey and the women reformers. Lindsey was a highly effective
publicist and thus tended to dominate the juvenile court movement. This
should not, however, obscure the fact that it was the Illinois Juvenile Court
Law that the vast majority of states, including Colorado, used as their
model for legislation. Although it might appear that Lindsey had captured
the agenda of the juvenile court movement, this was not in fact the case.
Maternalist reformers, female social scientists, and male legal experts all ensured that their concerns influenced developments, even if Lindsey was the
focus of public attention. In fact, Ben Lindsey did not become involved in
the juvenile court movement outside Denver until he attended the National
Conference of Charities and Correction held in Detroit in May 1902.[4] Previously the initiative had been taken by others, most obviously by some of
those involved in securing the Chicago Juvenile Court.

3. Kathryn Kish Sklar, "Two Political Cultures in the Progressive Era: The National Con-
sumers' League and the American Association for Labor Legislation," in Linda K. Kerber, Alice Kessler-Harris, and Kathryn Kish Sklar, eds., U.S. History as Women's History: New Feminist Essays (Chapel Hill, 1995), 36–62; Maureen A. Flanagan, "Gender and Urban Political
Reform: The City Club and the Woman's City Club of Chicago in the Progressive Era," American Historical Review 95 (October 1990): 1032–75.

4. "Minutes and Discussion," Proceedings of the National Conference of Charities and
Correction (hereafter PNCCC) (1902), 423–25; letter from Joseph P. Byers of the National
Conference of Charities and Correction, March 15, 1902, box 82, folder 3, BBL Papers.

The Illinois Juvenile Court Law was, at first, only applied in Chicago, where informal methods had foreshadowed the passing of the law. Reports of the working of the Chicago court, and its difficulties implementing the law, soon publicized the aims of the juvenile court outside Chicago. Other counties within Illinois quickly established their own juvenile courts, despite the problems they had securing suitable probation officers. In these early days the Illinois Conference of Charities and Correction and the Chicago press served as forums where the difficulties of administering the newly established juvenile court could be discussed. What was perhaps more important, these forums publicized the existence of the Chicago court.[5]

In late 1899, Timothy D. Hurley, president of the Catholic Visitation and Aid Society and chief probation officer of the Chicago Juvenile Court, began publishing the *Juvenile Record*.[6] This seems to have been initially a purely local paper representing both the Chicago court and the Visitation and Aid Society, but it soon became national in scope. Even from its earliest days, the *Juvenile Record* clearly aimed to present a favorable picture of the Chicago Juvenile Court. Articles about the operation of the court, the benevolent nature of its work with children, and the good results it was achieving made up the majority of articles in the early issues. There were also editorials calling for amendments to the Juvenile Court Law that would make clearer the duties of probation officers and the role of child-saving agencies. Although the *Juvenile Record* was in part the result of Hurley's own desire for self-promotion, it also served a useful purpose by advertising the Chicago Juvenile Court.[7]

Timothy Hurley had been involved on the edges of the campaign to secure a juvenile court law in Illinois—although he accorded himself a much larger part in the agitation than seems to have been the reality.[8] His main concern, as head of the Visitation and Aid Society, seems to have been to protect the interests of child-saving agencies in the new system for dealing

5. *Proceedings of the Illinois Conference of Charities and Correction* (1899) and (1900); *Chicago Tribune*, June 17, 1899, June 22, 1899, June 26, 1899, July 1, 1899, July 6, 1899.

6. The *Juvenile Record* was also published under the title *Juvenile Court Record;* the two names were apparently used interchangeably.

7. See, for instance, "Child Saving Conference," *Juvenile Record* 2 (November 1900): 3–4; "One Day in the Juvenile Court," *Juvenile Record* 2 (November 1900): 7–8; "Second Day in the Juvenile Court," *Juvenile Record* 2 (December 1900): 18–19.

8. See, for instance, "Origin of the Juvenile Court Law," *Juvenile Record* 3 (June 1902): 6–8; Timothy D. Hurley, *Juvenile Courts and What They Have Accomplished* (Chicago, 1904).

with dependent and delinquent children. He also wished to ensure that Catholic children, in particular, who were removed from their families would only be placed in families or institutions run by their coreligionists.[9] Thus, in 1891 Hurley had sponsored an unsuccessful bill to protect the interests of child-saving agencies, and in the agitation for the 1899 Juvenile Court Law, this had been his prominent concern. It was, no doubt, his position as head of one of the leading Catholic child-saving agencies in Chicago, as well as his involvement in the juvenile court movement, which led the mayor to appoint him as an assistant in the city law department and thence, as chief probation officer. He does not seem to have acted as an informal probation officer before the law was passed.[10]

Hurley was, nonetheless, an important publicist of the juvenile court idea. In promoting the juvenile courts, he echoed much of the rhetoric utilized by the women reformers. He emphasized the importance of the parents' role in bringing up their children to be good citizens: "But the state demands as a necessity for the wholesomeness and healthy growth of the child as well as for the protection of every other person under its jurisdiction, that the parent shall bring up the child in environments and under circumstances that will make it a good law-abiding citizen." In certain circumstances, though, the state had to step in: "The natural parent is allowed to retain the custody and control of his child, not as an absolute right of the parent, but rather as a trustee. When the natural parent violates his trust, in any way, then the State steps in and supplies the place of the natural parent."[11]

Thus, Hurley recognized that the state had an important role to play in ensuring that all children received proper parental guidance: "The whole trend and spirit of the act is that the state, acting through the Juvenile Court, exercises that tender solicitude and care over its neglected, dependent and delinquent wards that a wise and loving parent would exercise with reference to his own children under similar circumstances."[12] Moreover, he stressed the importance of probation as being the keystone to the

9. "Origin of the Juvenile Court Law," 6–7; letter from T. D. Hurley, January 1, 1903, box 1, folder 3, BBL Papers.

10. Hurley, *Juvenile Courts and What They Have Accomplished,* 15–24; "Origin of the Juvenile Court Law," 7; T. D. Hurley, "Juvenile Court Report," *Proceedings of the Illinois Conference of Charities* (1900), 30–33.

11. "Juvenile Courts and What They Have Accomplished: What the Juvenile Court Is," *Juvenile Record* 3 (June 1902): 4; T. D. Hurley, "Discussion," *Proceedings of the Illinois Conference of Charities* (1900), 30.

12. Timothy D. Hurley, "History of the Illinois Juvenile Court Law: Continued," *Juvenile Court Record* 8 (September 1907): 18.

juvenile court system: "The probation system is the cord upon which the pearls of the Juvenile Court are strung. It is the keynote of a beautiful harmony. Without it the Juvenile Court would not exist."[13] However, he was less willing to acknowledge the leading role women had played in shaping the juvenile court and was, at times, frustrated by their continued involvement in the running of the Chicago Juvenile Court. While promoting an essentially maternalist reform, Hurley was clearly ambivalent about whether the court should act as the mother or the father of the erring children before it. He displayed none of the confident masculinity of Judge Lindsey or the fatherliness of Judge Tuthill.[14] Yet, it was the Chicago model of the juvenile court, as shaped by women reformers, that Hurley sought to promote through the *Juvenile Record.*

As a number of cities became interested in the Chicago Juvenile Court and sought to introduce their own form of juvenile courts, the Chicago reformers began to mobilize themselves to provide advice and information about the court. It was at this point that Hurley's *Juvenile Record* came into its own. It not only publicized the workings of the Chicago court but also printed details of the Illinois Juvenile Court Law and the various amendments to it. The *Juvenile Record* also gave accounts of how the Chicago reformers had secured their legislation, and soon the paper began to advocate the establishment of juvenile courts in every state in the Union.[15] At first, Hurley's editorials suggested that states might wish to adopt only certain parts of the Illinois law—a separate court for children's cases, the appointment of probation officers, the recognition of child-saving societies, or a law preventing children from being confined in prisons.[16] It was not long, however, before the *Juvenile Record* was advocating the adoption of the juvenile court legislation in its entirety throughout the Union, with only minor concessions to suit local conditions.[17]

13. Hurley, *Juvenile Courts and What They Have Accomplished,* 14.

14. Hurley, *Juvenile Courts and What They Have Accomplished,* plays down the role of women reformers, promoting that of Hurley and the bar association. On Hurley's frustration with the women reformers, see letter from T. D. Hurley, June 13, 1905, box 4, folder 1, BBL Papers; letter to Paul Kellogg, June 15, 1905, box 4, folder 1, BBL Papers. On Judge Tuthill, see Richard S. Tuthill, "The Juvenile Court Law in Cook County," *Proceedings of the Illinois Conference of Charities* (1900), 10–16.

15. See, for instance, "Probation System, Juvenile Court," *Juvenile Record* 2 (April 1901): 9; "What the Juvenile Court Record Has Accomplished," *Juvenile Record* 5 (January 1904), 8; "Chicago's Juvenile Court," *Juvenile Record* 4 (December 1903): 5.

16. "Juvenile Court Laws in Sister States," *Juvenile Record* 2 (June 1901): 15.

17. "Juvenile Court Laws Adopted in Other States," *Juvenile Record* 3 (June 1902): 11; "Spread of Juvenile Court Sentiment," *Juvenile Record* 4 (April 1903): 6; "Objects of the Juvenile Court Record," *Juvenile Record* 4 (September 1903): 1. The headline "We advocate the establishment of a juvenile court in every state in the Union," also appeared on the front page of every issue of the *Juvenile Record,* as well as on its letterhead.

Hurley was not the only Chicago reformer to become involved in spreading the "gospel" of the juvenile courts. Judge Tuthill and later Judge Mack were in great demand to address various legislatures on the legal aspects of the juvenile courts. Harvey B. Hurd, a member of the Chicago Bar Association and one of those involved in drawing up the Illinois juvenile court bill, also addressed a large number of audiences interested in securing such legislation for their state or locality. Whereas the women reformers of Chicago were not as prominent as the men in campaigning for juvenile court legislation in other parts of the country—at least in terms of addressing legislatures and public meetings—they nonetheless took on an important role in spreading the idea by addressing women's clubs and various national women's associations.[18]

The Chicago Juvenile Court reformers and the *Juvenile Record* played a significant part in the early dissemination of the idea of the juvenile court. They also influenced the establishment of juvenile courts in other states, not so much by directly lobbying for legislation in these states but by giving assistance to those within the state already agitating for this reform. The Chicago reformers made addresses urging the importance of the juvenile court and gave help through reports and information showing how the Chicago Juvenile Court worked.[19] It was with the arrival on the national scene of Judge Lindsey that the campaign to secure a juvenile court in every state became more aggressive and ceased to rely only on local initiatives.

Until early 1902, Lindsey's efforts to help children in trouble with the law had been confined to Colorado; he seems to have been unaware of the existence of the Chicago Juvenile Court. With his discovery of the *Juvenile Record* and the Chicago court, however, Lindsey became involved in the Chicago reformers' efforts to spread the idea of the juvenile court. Lindsey contributed to the *Juvenile Record* articles full of anecdotes about the Denver Juvenile Court and his own part in setting the boys who came before him on the path to good citizenship.[20] He soon became the greatest publicist

18. "Hon. Harvey B. Hurd Addresses the National Congress of Mothers," *Juvenile Record* 2 (June 1901): 15–19; "Something Accomplished," *Juvenile Record* 6 (May 1905): 8; "Works in the Cause of Humanity: Miss Julia Lathrop of Chicago," undated clipping, box 1, scrapbook 3, Lucy Flower and Coues Family Scrapbooks, Manuscript Division, Chicago Historical Society.

19. Editorial, *Juvenile Record* 4 (January 1903): 6; "Something Accomplished," 8.

20. "The World's Opinion," *Juvenile Record* 3 (January 1902): 5; letter to T. D. Hurley, January 17, 1902, box 82, folder 1, BBL Papers; Ben B. Lindsey, "Denver Juvenile Court," *Juvenile Record* 3 (February 1902): 9–10; "Denver Has a Youthful Juvenile Court Officer," *Juvenile Record* 4 (January 1903): 9.

of the juvenile courts. At first, like the Chicago reformers, he confined himself to only giving answers to inquiries about his own methods, but he later took the initiative in pushing for juvenile court legislation in other states.

In promoting the juvenile court idea, Lindsey drew on his own experiences and emphasized his own methods. Although he acknowledged that Illinois had secured a juvenile court law before Colorado, he insisted that his court in Denver had been created at about the same time, albeit without the sanction of legislation. He also espoused his own version of the juvenile court idea, with its emphasis on the "personal touch" and the individual child. As he had done in Denver, he asserted the masculine influence on the juvenile court movement, stressing both the importance of developing character in boy offenders and his belief that a good many juvenile offenses were more the result of weakness of character than criminality. As he noted, the Juvenile Court Law

> has awakened the State to see with clearer vision that the child is not to be *reformed,* but to be *formed;* that it has every advantage while character is plastic, in the golden period of adolescence, to redeem a possible offender of the future to good citizenship before he has really become an offender at all. This should be accomplished as a wise and loving parent would accomplish it, not with leniency on the one hand or brutality on the other, but with charity, patience, interest, and what is most important of all, a firmness that commands respect, love, and obedience, and does not produce hate or ill-will.[21]

It seems likely that Lindsey became interested in the promotion of the juvenile court idea at the urging of Hurley and some of the other Chicago reformers.[22] However, it was Lindsey's attendance at the National Conference of Charities and Correction at Detroit in May 1902 that marked the beginning of his career as a publicist outside Denver. Although he had no official place on the program, Lindsey was involved in discussions in the children's section at the conference and explained his work with boys in the juvenile court of Denver. He also began his efforts to promote the idea that other

21. *The Problem of the Children and How the State of Colorado Cares for Them* (Denver, 1904), 30; Report of Ben B. Lindsey, Chairman of the Committee on Juvenile Courts, undated, box 279, folder 4, BBL Papers; letter to T. D. Hurley, January 17, 1902, box 82, folder 1, BBL Papers.

22. Letter from T. D. Hurley, February 25, 1902, box 82, folder 2, BBL Papers; letter from Richard S. Tuthill, February 20, 1902, box 82, folder 2, BBL Papers.

states should secure juvenile court legislation: "Before I leave this conference," he announced, "I desire to impress upon the delegates the necessity
of earnest work in your respective states to have your legislatures next winter enact the proper laws to establish juvenile courts."[23] He clearly made numerous less-formal contacts during the conference, for on his return from
Detroit he received many letters asking about his methods from people who
claimed his acquaintance at the conference.[24]

On his return to Denver, Lindsey prepared a report on the work of the
Denver Juvenile Court that was published by the *Denver Republican*. This
was, in part, for local use—to help secure a juvenile court law in Colorado—but he also mailed copies to reformers and educators all over the
country, among them Judge Tuthill, Mrs. Lucy Flower, Booker T. Washington, and others involved in charitable work. In his covering letter to Mrs.
Flower, he noted, "we will send them all over the United States to legislators, governors and others, to help along the good work of our friend Hurley, Judge Tuthill and others in getting juvenile courts established in every
state in the Union."[25] He also gave a lecture to the Kansas Society for the
Friendless, in the autumn of 1902, that was full of anecdotes and stories of
his personal involvement in the reformation of boys. This approach was to
become the trademark of the many speeches and addresses he gave in the
next few years in the cause of the juvenile courts.

Lindsey continued to receive requests about his methods and calls for him
to address meetings of various kinds on the merits of the juvenile courts. In
June 1903 he was asked to contribute to a report for the International
Prison Congress, and around the same time he made his first speech before
the National Conference of Charities and Correction, in Atlanta. Later in
that year he also began writing articles for *Charities,* a magazine published
in New York by the Charity Organization Society that circulated among
many of those involved in charitable work in the United States.[26] Thus he

23. "Discussion," *PNCCC* (1902), 423–25, 436, 541.

24. See, for instance, letter from Rev. Edward A. Fredenhagen of the Kansas Society for the
Friendless, July 24, 1902, box 1, folder 1, BBL Papers; letter to Alexander Aird of Canada, August, 4, 1902, box 83, folder 4, BBL Papers.

25. Letter to Mrs. Lucy Flower, July 29, 1902, box 83, folder 3, BBL Papers. Letters from
Judge Richard Tuthill, August 6, 1902, Booker T. Washington, August 6, 1902, and G. S.
Robinson of the Board of Control of State Institutions of Iowa, January 6, 1902, box 1, folder
1, BBL Papers.

26. Letter from Samuel J. Barrows, June 17, 1903, box 1, folder 5, BBL Papers; Ben B. Lindsey, "The Reformation of Juvenile Delinquents Through the Juvenile Courts," *PNCCC* (1903),
206–30; Ben B. Lindsey, "Some Experiences in the Juvenile Court of Denver," *Charities* 11
(November 7, 1903): 403–13.

quickly became established as one of the leaders and publicists in the juvenile court movement.

By mid-1903 a number of different organizations and individuals were working, quite separately, to spread the juvenile court idea. The National Congress of Mothers under the leadership of Mrs. Hannah Kent Schoff had been working in the cause for some time, though the organization only formalized its efforts with the establishment of a committee to work on behalf of defective, dependent, and delinquent children in January 1903. Mrs. Schoff was a member of the committee, and so were Lucy Flower and Hastings H. Hart, from the Chicago court.[27] Similarly, in May 1903 the Industrial Committee of the GFWC mailed a circular to its constituent clubs and federations recommending that they work to secure a juvenile court law in their own states. Both these national women's organizations tended at first to confine their efforts to urging local women's clubs—their natural constituents—to take up juvenile court work.[28] Like the *Juvenile Record,* however, the publications of these groups offered help and advice to women's associations seeking juvenile court legislation and soon adopted policies urging the adoption of juvenile courts in every state. Using the discourse of maternalism to push their cause, these women's organizations played an important role in disseminating the juvenile court idea and in securing legislation in many states.

As the national women's organizations became more involved in promoting juvenile courts, some of their leaders became more visible in the wider juvenile court movement. The most prominent of these leaders was Mrs. Schoff. Like Ben Lindsey, she was an able publicist. She contributed an article to the November 1903 special edition of *Charities,* which focused on juvenile court reform and included Lindsey's article, as well as pieces by some of the Chicago reformers.[29] In preparation for the World's Fair at Saint Louis in early 1904, she had begun to organize an exhibit on the juvenile courts. However, when she heard that Lindsey was to organize one, she at first deferred to him, though the eventual exhibit included contributions from the National Congress of Mothers and the Chicago court as well as

---

27. Minutes of the Executive Board Meeting, January 14, 1903, National Congress of Mothers, May 1900–November 1909, folder 2, National Congress of Parents and Teachers Records, Special Collections, University of Illinois at Chicago (hereafter NCM Papers).

28. "Report of the Industrial Committee of the GFWC," Seventh Biennial, 1904, Convention Records (Proceedings—Reports), 1904/05/17–1904/05/27, General Federation of Women's Clubs Papers, Archives of the General Federation of Women's Clubs, Washington, D.C.

29. *Charities* 11 (November 7, 1903).

from Lindsey. It was believed that the exhibit at the World's Fair would be the most effective method of spreading the gospel of child saving that had yet been devised. It covered all aspects of the work of the juvenile courts and included photographs, charts, and model laws. It is difficult to tell exactly how effective this exhibit was, although it is likely to have reached an audience that might not previously have been particularly concerned with the problem of delinquent children. Clearly, advocates of the juvenile court had expected the exhibit to do much to aid their cause.[30]

By autumn 1904, the juvenile court movement remained without formal organization, but the various strands were cooperating. Mrs. Schoff tried to involve Lindsey in her efforts to promote the juvenile courts through the National Congress of Mothers, and both Lindsey and various of the Chicago reformers were active in a number of the congress's initiatives. Similarly, Lindsey invited several of the women reformers, notably Lucy Flower and Julia Lathrop, to visit his court. He also appealed to them for their support when he had to run for reelection as judge in the face of fierce political opposition.[31]

It would appear that there was little tension, at least overtly, between male and female reformers involved in the movement. They agreed that the juvenile court, within the legal framework established by the Illinois law, should be promoted as a desirable reform to be adopted throughout the United States. Until a considerable number of states had established their own juvenile courts, the main concern of reformers was simply to promote the idea of the juvenile court. This inevitably meant that juvenile court laws were not the same in every state, since they had to be adapted to suit local needs.

In promoting reform, men and women utilized gendered discourses. The women reformers emphasized the importance of women's role both in promoting the welfare of the child and in protecting and nurturing children who clearly did not conform to standards of proper childlike behavior. Lindsey, on the other hand, through anecdotes about "his boys," empha-

30. Letter from Mrs. Hannah Kent Schoff, January 18, 1904, box 87, folder 2, BBL Papers; "Juvenile Courts Should Exhibit," *Juvenile Record* 5 (February 1904): 9; "The Problem of the Children," *Juvenile Record* 5 (November 1904): 3; letter to S. C. Morgan, February 4, 1904, box 87, folder 3, BBL Papers.

31. Letter from Mrs. Schoff, April 28, 1904, box 2, folder 1, BBL Papers; letter from Julia Lathrop, February 24, 1904, box 87, folder 4, BBL Papers; letter to Julia Lathrop, March 19, 1904, box 88, folder 2, BBL Papers; *Report of Hon. Ben B. Lindsey, Chairman of Committee on Juvenile Courts: Before the International Congress on the Welfare of the Child. Held Under the Auspices of the Mothers' Congress at Washington, D.C., April 22–27, 1914.*

sized the way in which the juvenile court helped them to overcome the weakness in character that had caused their offenses. The dominant discourse, however, was one that echoed the maternalists but was increasingly wrapped in the legal language of *parens patriae*—the insistence that the state should act as the parent of all children.[32] In fact the legal discourse of *parens patriae* was little different from the maternalist vision, for both were willing to use the state to achieve their objectives—the protection of all children.

While women reformers were undoubtedly a key factor in spreading the juvenile court idea at a local level, the most visible part of the juvenile court movement in 1904 was led by male reformers, with Lindsey as their acknowledged leader. The movement also had a quasi-institutional form as the National Conference of Charities and Correction's juvenile court subcommittee, to which Lindsey was appointed chairman. It included among its members Timothy Hurley and many juvenile court judges, among them Robert Wilkin of the Brooklyn Juvenile Court and Richard Tuthill and Julian Mack of the Chicago court. The size of the subcommittee and the difficulties of communication resulting from the great distances between the various committee members meant that much of the work devolved on Lindsey and Hurley. This was not, strictly speaking, the foundation of a formal, independent, juvenile court movement, for it was subsumed within the National Conference of Charities and Correction. It is, however, a mark of faith in the efficacy of the juvenile court as a solution to the problem of dependent and delinquent children that so many juvenile court judges should have been prepared to help in the dissemination of information about juvenile courts. The committee undertook a national campaign of propaganda, addressing it to every state legislature that did not already have a juvenile court law and to many other individuals and organizations. Among the material prepared for their campaign was a pamphlet Lindsey compiled entitled "The Problem of the Children," which gave a detailed account of the work of the Denver Juvenile Court, its activities, and how the Juvenile Court Law was secured.[33]

The committee sent a circular to the press in every city in the United

32. Judge Julian Mack of the Chicago Juvenile Court was most prominent in developing the concept of *parens patriae* as the legal basis of the juvenile court, though it had existed for some time. Julian W. Mack, "The Juvenile Court, the Judge and the Probation Officer," *PNCCC* (1906), 123–31; Julian W. Mack, "The Juvenile Court," *Harvard Law Review* 23 (1909): 104–22; Harvey B. Hurd, "Juvenile Court Law: Minimum Principles Which Should Be Stood For," *Charities* 13 (January 7, 1905): 327–28.

33. Letter from Judge Robert Wilkin, July 2, 1904, box 1, folder 5, BBL Papers; "A Juvenile

States and Canada, as well as to philanthropic, educational, and religious journals, urging the establishment in all states of juvenile court laws that should be uniform in principle and application so far as possible. It also urged the adoption of detention homes, contributory delinquency laws for adults, and the replacement of jails with schools for juvenile offenders. The aim of the committee was, as Lindsey expressed it, "To encourage personal, practical, active work and earnest effort to bring about correction, as far as possible, through aid, help, encouragement, proper firmness and assistance, rather than punishment, fear, hate and degradation."[34]

As well as waging a propaganda campaign, Lindsey sought the endorsement of the juvenile courts by various national figures. To this end, he wrote President Roosevelt's secretary asking if he would bring a booklet on the juvenile court of Denver to the president's attention and urge him to consider the question of a juvenile court in the District of Columbia. He also sought the endorsement of Cardinal Gibbons of Baltimore and Jacob Riis, a reformer in his own right and a friend of the president.[35] Lindsey was rewarded when, in his annual message to Congress in December 1904, President Roosevelt praised the work of the juvenile courts and urged the establishment of a juvenile court in the District of Columbia: "In the vital matter of taking care of children, much advantage could be gained by a careful study of what has been accomplished in such States as Illinois and Colorado by the juvenile courts. The work of the juvenile courts is really a work of character-building . . . by profiting . . . [from] the experiences of the different states and cities in these matters, it would be easy to provide a good code for the District of Columbia."[36]

Although it was not until 1906 that a juvenile court law was passed in the District of Columbia, several states approved such legislation in the winter session of 1904–5. Public awareness of the juvenile courts, particularly among those individuals involved in charitable work, and among women's organizations, was becoming very high. Lindsey and some of the other juvenile court reformers also began to receive requests about the juvenile

Court for Every City," *Juvenile Record* 5 (November 1904): 4–5, 9; Ben B. Lindsey, "Recent Progress of the Juvenile Court Movement," *PNCCC* (1905), 150–55.

34. Lindsey, "Recent Progress of the Juvenile Court Movement," 150.

35. Letter to Hon. William Loeb, secretary to the president, September 27, 1904, box 2, folder 6, BBL Papers; letter to Cardinal Gibbons, September 27, 1904, box 2, folder 6, BBL Papers; letter to Jacob Riis, November 17, 1904, box 3, folder 3, BBL Papers.

36. As quoted in Joseph M. Hawes, *Children in Urban Society: Juvenile Delinquency in Nineteenth-Century America* (New York, 1971), 248.

courts from abroad, most notably England and Australia.[37] By 1906, however, several of those involved in the juvenile court movement were beginning to feel that the National Conference of Charities and Correction did
not give the juvenile courts sufficient recognition but was submerged in
other work for children undertaken by the conference.[38] Calls for a national
juvenile court committee separate from any other national organization
seem to have come first from those who had not been involved in establishing the pioneer juvenile courts, but the idea was soon adopted by Timothy
Hurley and later taken up by Lindsey. Throughout 1906 and early 1907, as
Lindsey, the Chicago reformers, and Mrs. Schoff continued to lecture
throughout the United States in the cause of the juvenile courts, moves were
made to establish a formal juvenile court committee.[39]

I lurley tried to organize a conference of juvenile court workers, with addresses to be given by President Roosevelt and Jacob Riis, among others,
but this effort was not successful. The idea of a national juvenile court committee was not abandoned, however. Lindsey, working with Timothy Hurley and Julia Lathrop, took up the idea and gradually began to put together
a formal organization. Although Lindsey seems to have taken the leadership
of the nascent organization, Julia Lathrop was active in its founding, and it
was centered around Hull House. Unlike the earlier subcommittee within
the National Conference of Charities and Correction, this new organization
sought to include representatives of the many agencies involved in the wider
juvenile court movement. Thus, women's organizations were represented by
Mrs. Hannah Schoff of the National Congress of Mothers and Mrs. Sarah
Platt Decker, president of the GFWC; the Chicago women reformers by
Jane Addams and Louise deKoven Bowen; and juvenile court judges and
probation officers by, among others, Henry Thurston, Helen Rogers, Judge
Tuthill, and Bernard Flexner.[40] The list of directors of the new organization

37. Letter from E. J. Forbes, Sydney, Australia, July 10, 1905, box 4, folder 3, BBL Papers;
letter from Miss N. Adler, London, England, July 30, 1905, box 4, folder 3, BBL Papers; Lindsey, "Recent Progress of the Juvenile Court Movement," 150–55; "The Year in the Juvenile
Courts," Charities 14 (July 1, 1905): 873–74.

38. Letter to Julia Lathrop, August 7, 1905, box 4, folder 4, BBL Papers; letter from Edward T. Devine, October 11, 1905, box 5, folder 5, BBL Papers.

39. Letter to Prof. Thurston from Edward Frost of Milwaukee, January 2, 1906, box 6,
folder 3, BBL Papers; letter from Paul Kellogg of Charities, August 16, 1905, box 4, folder 5,
BBL Papers; letter from C. W. Hadden of Milwaukee to Mr. Thurston, January 3, 1906, box 6,
folder 3, BBL Papers; letter from Hurley to Lindsey, January 27, 1906, box 6, folder 3, BBL Papers; minutes of a meeting held at Hull House, June 9, 1906, box 7, folder 5, BBL Papers.

40. Letter from T. D. Hurley, January 27, 1906, box 6, folder 3, BBL Papers; letter from Ed-

reflected the wide range of reformers who were interested in the juvenile court movement.

Hull House was chosen as the venue for the first gathering of the Juvenile Court Committee, as the national organization was initially called. This is perhaps unsurprising, for not only was it fairly central, but the Chicago Juvenile Court was acknowledged as the pioneer court and, next to Lindsey's own, the most famous. The choice of Hull House as the venue for the first meeting testifies to the important part the women of this settlement played in both establishing the Chicago Juvenile Court and continuing to foster the juvenile court idea.[41] The new organization held its inaugural meeting on January 4, 1907, and at this time Lindsey was authorized to correspond with other societies interested in juvenile court work and to suggest the forming of an international juvenile court society.[42]

The International Juvenile Court Association was incorporated on September 13, 1907, with Lindsey as president. Its aim was to function as a clearinghouse for information concerning juvenile courts. To this end, it established a central bureau with a paid secretary and assistant who sent out copies of model laws and other details of how juvenile courts should be established and administered. Its work concentrated on securing juvenile courts and the essential agencies that should accompany them in every state.[43] As Lindsey wrote in a letter to William R. George, "It was believed at the various meetings that much good could be done by such an international society, especially in the next few years, while the juvenile court is in its formative period, and so much needs to be done in the way of propaganda and educational work, in getting the law securely and firmly established in the States and building up a system of effective work for the protection of the child-life of the community."[44]

In many respects the association was a highly successful organization, for many states adopted some type of juvenile court legislation during the next few years. However, it seems to have developed financial difficulties, and

---

ward M. Frost, November 26, 1906, box 7, folder 4, BBL Papers; List of Directors of the International Juvenile Court Society, undated, box 311, folder 1, BBL Papers.

41. Letter from Julia Lathrop, May 7, 1906, box 7, folder 4, BBL Papers; letter to Judge Mack, May 28, 1906, box 7, folder 4, BBL Papers.

42. Minutes of meeting at Hull House, January 4, 1907, box 9, folder 1, BBL Papers; letter to William R. George, May 6, 1907, box 9, folder 4, BBL Papers.

43. "Memorandum of Work for the International Juvenile Court Society," undated, box 226, folder 1, BBL Papers; "Certificate of Incorporation of the International Juvenile Court Association in Illinois," September 13, 1907, box 226, folder 6, BBL Papers; "International Juvenile Court Society," Charities 19 (December 7, 1907): 1149.

44. Letter to William R. George, May 6, 1907, box 9, folder 4, BBL Papers.

much of its work devolved on Lindsey and the Chicago reformers. They continued to answer inquiries from within the United States and around the world about juvenile courts and to address meetings of all kinds to press for the introduction of juvenile court legislation. Various journals also published articles about the juvenile courts. Some of these were folksy in character, describing the human side of the juvenile court; some emphasized the legal aspects of the courts; and others pointed out that the juvenile courts were more economical than the criminal justice system, with its expensive criminal courts and reformatory institutions.[45]

With the development of a formal organization to spread the juvenile court idea, and as more and more states began to adopt juvenile court legislation, some leaders of the movement began to look closer at the minimum principles necessary to constitute a juvenile court. In the early stages of the movement, most of the juvenile court reformers had been prepared to accept the model established by the Chicago reformers. As the Chicago court itself developed and sought to resolve some of the problems it encountered, and as other states developed their own courts, the leading reformers sought a clarification of the principles on which the juvenile court rested. They also looked beyond the juvenile court at some of the wider implications of reform. As they did so, the gendered discourses that had been so important in the early years of reform became less prominent, and "experts," both male and female, grew increasingly central to the movement. In some cases these experts were the professional maternalists of the settlement houses, but other experts, most notably judges and lawyers, became a more obvious component of the movement. Unlike Judge Lindsey and some of the women reformers, these legal experts used the language of their profession in advocating reform, rather than a specifically gendered discourse.

Lawyers had, by necessity, become involved on the edges of the juvenile court movement. In Chicago, the women reformers had turned to the bar association to help them frame the legislation needed to place their reform initiatives on a legal basis. In other states, too, women reformers instigated reform but required legal advice to draw up legislation. In some areas, as we have seen, judges played a more central part by operating informal juvenile

---

45. "Statement Regarding the International Juvenile Court Association," undated, box 280, folder 2, BBL Papers; Frederic Almy, "The Economics of the Juvenile Court," *Charities* 13 (January 7, 1905): 337–39; Charles P. Henderson, "Juvenile Court: Problems of Administration," *Charities* 13 (January 7, 1905): 340–43; Hastings H. Hart, "Distinctive Features of the Juvenile Court," *Annals of the American Academy of Political and Social Science* 36 (1910): 57–60; Bernard Flexner, "The Juvenile Court—Its Legal Aspects," *Annals of the American Academy of Political and Social Science* 36 (1910): 49–56.

courts without the immediate sanction of legislation.[46] Lawyers also helped the juvenile court reformers when the constitutionality of their reform was questioned, and legal experts were instrumental in drawing up model laws to encourage states to institute a juvenile court. Juvenile court judges were themselves an important part of the movement, testifying to the efficacy of the reform and their own belief in its superiority over other systems of dealing with wayward children.[47]

Lawyers were keen to maintain their own role in the juvenile court system. Thus they insisted that juvenile court judges be legally trained. Some demanded that attorneys be present in the courtroom to protect the legal interests of the child. This latter battle was, however, soon lost, since the juvenile court itself was based on the idea that it would protect the best interests of the child. Behind the concept of *parens patriae,* which lawyers used to justify the juvenile court, was the idea that the state, as represented by the juvenile court, served as the parent and thus acted on the child's behalf.[48]

Lawyers in the juvenile court movement did not act from purely humanitarian motives any more than did their fellow reformers. Their insistence on correct legal frameworks for juvenile court legislation and on the need for juvenile court judges to have legal training reflects the increasing professionalization of the legal profession and suggests they were concerned with maintaining their own role in this new system of justice.[49] Like other middle-class reformers, however, they were concerned that if children were treated as criminals at a young age, they would be set on the road to crimi-

46. See, for instance, "Chicago's Juvenile Court," *Juvenile Record* 4 (December 1903): 5; Helen Page Bates, "Digest of Statutes Relating to Juvenile Courts and Probation Systems," *Charities* 13 (January 7, 1905): 329–37. The most obvious examples of juvenile courts operating without the formal sanction of law are Denver and Indianapolis, though Judge Tuthill also ran a separate court session for children in Chicago before the Juvenile Court Law was passed.

47. Letter from Mrs. Schoff, November 17, 1904, box 3, folder 3, BBL Papers; letter from T. D. Hurley, January 1, 1903, box 1, folder 3, BBL Papers; Report of the Chicago Bar Association Committee on Juvenile Courts, 1899, Manuscript Collections, Chicago Historical Association; Hastings H. Hart, "Report of Committee," *PNCCC* (1906), 87. Lawyers were not as influential in shaping the original juvenile court as some historians have suggested. See, for instance, Robert M. Mennel, *Thorns and Thistles: Juvenile Delinquents in the United States, 1825–1940* (Hanover, N.H., 1973), 134–39; David J. Rothman, *Conscience and Convenience: The Asylum and Its Alternatives in Progressive America* (Boston, 1980), 236–60.

48. Julian W. Mack, "The Juvenile Court," *Juvenile Record* 9 (February 1908): 5–9; Bernard Flexner, "A Decade of the Juvenile Court," *PNCCC* (1910), 105–16; Hurd, "Juvenile Court Law: Minimum Principles Which Should Be Stood For," 327–28; Edward Lindsey, "The Juvenile Court from a Lawyer's Standpoint," *Annals of the American Academy of Political and Social Science* 52 (1914): 140–48; T. D. Hurley, "Necessity for the Lawyer in the Juvenile Court," *PNCCC* (1905), 172–77.

49. Robert H. Wiebe, *The Search for Order, 1877–1920* (New York, 1967), 116–17.

nality. To many judges, the increasing number of children in the police and criminal courts was likely to have an unsettling and detrimental effect on society if no action were taken. As one juvenile court judge put it,

> To save children from lifelong consequences of childish errors, to check their feet at the very entrance of the downward road and to set them upon the gently graded pathway leading to usefulness and happiness, to let them expiate a fault at their own homes under the surveillance of kindly probation officers, and to accomplish these ends without the publicity that tends to blast later attempts at welldoing, as well as to save young souls from the taint of contact with matured criminals, these were the purposes sought to be accomplished in the establishment of juvenile courts of Buffalo.[50]

Hastings H. Hart—who, although neither an attorney nor a juvenile court judge himself, had helped to frame the pioneer law in Illinois—phrased it even more succinctly:

> Protected, he [the child] will become a contributor to the wealth, prosperity, morality and good government of the state; neglected, he will become a burden upon his fellowmen, a destroyer instead of producer, an enemy to society. An enlightened self-interest therefore unites with altruism in the juvenile court.[51]

Thus, lawyers connected with the juvenile courts, like the women reformers, reflected the concern of their class: that juvenile delinquency was a symptom of wider social breakdown.

By the end of the first decade after the passing of the Illinois law, a number of juvenile court judges had become vocal supporters of the juvenile court idea. In doing so, very few of them took Lindsey's line of asserting the importance of "masculine values" in reforming boy offenders, though several noted that juvenile court judges should be chosen for their understanding and sympathy for children.[52] Many worked in juvenile courts through which large numbers of children passed, and these judges clearly did not have the resources to exercise the kind of personal touch Lindsey empha-

---

50. Hon. Thomas Murphy, "History of the Juvenile Court of Buffalo," in Samuel J. Barrows, ed., *Children's Courts in the United States: Their Origin, Development and Results* (Washington, D.C., 1904), 10.

51. "The Juvenile Court as a Non-criminal Institution," in Hastings H. Hart, ed., *Preventive Treatment of Neglected Children* (New York, 1910), 253.

52. Julian W. Mack, "Juvenile Courts as Part of the School System of the Country,"

sized, even if they had agreed that it was an essential part of the juvenile justice system. Significantly, in testifying to the efficacy of the juvenile court system and in asserting the necessary factors to establish such courts, the juvenile court judges demanded the components that had shaped the Chicago Juvenile Court—probation, separate hearings for children, and chancery procedures based on the principle of *parens patriae*. These were essentially the principles that had been pioneered by the Chicago women reformers. Their insistence on these elements testified to the continued influence of their work in the juvenile court movement.[53]

The formal Juvenile Court Association and the publicists—including juvenile court judges and other experts—did not, however, represent the whole of the juvenile court movement. Although those who led the campaign at the national level to secure juvenile court legislation in every state were the most public aspect of the movement, they were only a small part of it. Clearly, in order to achieve legislation in nearly every state by 1920, a great deal of support had to exist at state and local levels—both to create the demand for reform and to lead the movement itself. The juvenile court movement sought to increase public awareness of the juvenile courts as a more humane and effective way of dealing with problem children and, by increasing public awareness, to create a demand in the states for juvenile court legislation. In most states, however, the movement does not seem to have actually taken the initiative for reform. The exception to this was, perhaps, the District of Columbia, which, because it was governed directly by the U.S. Congress, had a unique position in the United States. In the majority of states, once the public was aware of the Chicago and Denver juvenile courts, the initiative for reform came from many different groups and individuals.

In some states, agitation for reform sprung from local branches of national organizations. It was at this level that the National Congress of Mothers, through its local affiliates, came into its own. Mrs. Schoff made it her business to rouse support for juvenile courts within the National Congress of Mothers and asked various national leaders to address the congress.[54] She also produced a number of pamphlets outlining the necessity of

---

PNCCC (1908), 369–83; editorial, *Survey* 23 (February 5, 1910): 593–95; Harvey H. Baker, "Procedure of the Boston Juvenile Court," *Survey* 23 (February 5, 1910): 643–52.

53. Hurd, "Juvenile Court Law: Minimum Principles Which Should Be Stood For," 327–28; "International Juvenile Court Society," *Charities* 19 (December 7, 1907): 1149.

54. Letter from Mrs. Schoff, April 28, 1904, box 2, folder 1, BBL Papers; letter from Mrs. Schoff to Edward Frost, November 19, 1906, box 8, folder 4, BBL Papers; letter from the president of the Connecticut Congress of Mothers, Frances Sheldon Bolton, January 31, 1903, box 1, folder 3, BBL Papers; *Report of Hon. Ben B. Lindsey, Chairman of Committee on Juvenile*

juvenile courts and the role women should play in both securing and help-ing to administer them. The National Congress of Mothers and Mrs. Schoff seem to have been essential to the establishment of juvenile courts in a num-ber of states, beyond merely Mrs. Schoff's home state of Pennsylvania.[55]

Other women's organizations also agitated for juvenile court legislation, es-pecially local women's clubs that, like the Chicago Woman's Club, had fairly widespread interests but were particularly concerned about the welfare of chil-dren in the slums of the cities. Many clubs operated within a maternalist framework and justified their demands for juvenile courts with this discourse. Although their connection to the GFWC was not always clear, it is likely that a substantial number were loosely affiliated to it.[56] Settlement houses in the large cities of the United States also played their part, though none was as prominent as Hull House. Women were very much in evidence in the juvenile court movement, and their involvement in agitating for or securing juvenile court legislation was used by the leaders of the National American Woman Suffrage Association as an argument in favor of giving women the vote. In fact, one of their leaders wrote to Lindsey asking for his endorsement in May 1904: "I therefore write to ask whether you will just send a few lines of en-dorsement, saying that you believe that a constituency of voting women, the mothers of families, would have the greatest determining power in favor of the prevention of crime among children than any other factor you know of."[57] Al-though it is likely that the vast majority of women who agitated for the juve-nile courts were not doing so as a way of winning the vote—and certainly this was not the aim of the National Congress of Mothers—their involvement in reform movements for the welfare of children was seen by those fighting for woman's suffrage as a powerful factor supporting their arguments.[58]

Courts: *Before the International Congress on the Welfare of the Child. Held Under the Aus-pices of the Mothers' Congress at Washington, D.C., April 22–27, 1914;* "Hon. Harvey B. Hurd Addresses the National Congress of Mothers," *Juvenile Record* 2 (June 1901):15–19.

55. Mrs. Frederic Schoff, "The Place and Work of the Juvenile Court and Probation Sys-tem," *Proceedings of the First International Congress for the Welfare of the Child: Held Under the Auspices of the National Congress of Mothers, Washington, D.C., March 10–17, 1908* (Washington, D.C., 1908), 229–44; *Twenty Years' Work for Child Welfare,* pamphlet, NCM Papers.

56. This work may be followed in the publications of the General Federation of Women's Clubs—*Club Woman* and the *Federation Bulletin*—and in the reports of the biennials.

57. Letter from Kate M. Gordon, May 30, 1904, box 2, folder 2, BBL Papers; article in *Fed-eration Bulletin* 2 (June 1905): 292–96; George Creel and Ben B. Lindsey, *Measuring Up to Equal Suffrage* (New York, 1913).

58. This has been commented on by a number of historians: Aileen Kraditor, *The Ideas of the Woman Suffrage Movement, 1890–1920* (New York & London, 1965); Paula Baker, "The

The juvenile court movement was, in many respects, concerned with the preservation of the home and, as such, was a matter that concerned women. As we have seen, however, male reformers were also active, especially at the national level, where they tended to dominate the movement. Men were also involved locally as judges, as members of State Boards of Charities, and occasionally as superintendents of state institutions or other philanthropic associations and child-saving agencies. It was customary for a coalition of male and female organizations to work together, often with the help of national leaders, to secure a juvenile court law in their state.

In many cases a particular reform movement followed one of the paradigms established for the Chicago or Denver courts. There were, though, a very small minority of cases where the paradigms established for the juvenile courts simply do not apply. This tended to occur where there were strong vested interests preventing the establishment of a juvenile court system along the lines of the Chicago model. Often in these cases a modified version was eventually established. Here, since other concerns were more to the forefront, the gender consciousness of the reformers was less apparent. Nonetheless, an examination of these exceptions helps illustrate how social constructions of proper gender behavior influenced reform. For in those places where the gender consciousness of reformers was not a dominant factor in influencing the shape reform took, the juvenile court system was constructed in a rather different way.

New York City and Massachusetts are prime examples. Massachusetts had introduced probation as part of its justice system earlier in the century, and an 1891 law made the appointment of probation officers mandatory. Following the example set by New York state in 1892, Massachusetts had also provided for the separate trial of juvenile offenders. Indeed, the women reformers in Chicago had noted these initiatives and had used them to claim that Illinois was far behind other states in its methods of dealing with troublesome children.[59] Thus, although in both Massachusetts and New York City some efforts had been made to improve the methods of dealing with children in trouble with the law, there was no change in the idea that underpinned the justice system as regards children: they were still to be treated

---

Domestication of Politics: Women and American Political Society, 1780–1920," *American Historical Review* 89 (1984): 620–47; Molly Ladd-Taylor, *Mother-Work: Women, Child Welfare, and the State, 1890–1930* (Urbana, 1994).

59. Lucy L. Flower, "The Duty of the State to Dependent Children," *Proceedings of the Illinois Conference of Charities and Correction* (1896), 14–15; Mrs. James Patton, *Proceedings of the Illinois Conference of Charities and Correction* (1897), 61–63.

as adult criminals and governed by all the formalities of the criminal law. This is what the juvenile court system changed, for not only did the Illinois Juvenile Court Law introduce probation and separate court hearings for children, it also ceased to treat children as criminals, seeing them instead as children in need of help.

Although it had provided some of the original inspiration for the Chicago court, New York City was slow to adopt the Chicago model. Much of this may be explained by the fact that by the late nineteenth century, New York City had in place some well-established non-institutional methods of dealing with children in trouble. It also had a large number of state and privately run institutions for the incarceration of delinquent children.[60] Prominent among child-saving agencies was the New York Society for the Prevention of Cruelty to Children. This organization was founded in 1875 by Elbridge Gerry in answer to a call by a woman missionary searching for an agency to help a child who was being cruelly treated by her parents. The only organization able to help was the Society for the Prevention of Cruelty to Animals, of which Gerry was counsel. As a result of this case, Gerry established the Society for the Prevention of Cruelty to Children, which was soon known as the Gerry Society. The society became very influential, both in its efforts to secure legislation against such problems as child-begging and the presence of children in saloons and dance halls and also in its aggressive child-saving techniques, which it often carried out regardless of the wishes of the child's parents. By the end of the nineteenth century, the society, a private corporation, had become so influential that it was able to control the reception, care, and disposition of destitute, neglected, and wayward children in New York.[61] It was therefore a force to be reckoned with in any attempts to change the methods of dealing with problem children, and it tended to be a fairly conservative force.

In 1892 the New York legislature passed a statute prohibiting "the detention of children in station houses, prisons, courts, vehicles, etc. in company with adults." It also insisted on the trial of all children's cases in rooms apart from those in which adults were tried.[62] The law appears to have re-

60. Hawes, *Children in Urban Society*, chaps. 3, 6; Walter I. Trattner, *Homer Folks: Pioneer in Social Welfare* (New York, 1968), 40–41.

61. Hawes, *Children in Urban Society*, 138–39; Trattner, *Homer Folks: Pioneer in Social Welfare*, 40–41; Ann Vandepol, "Dependent Children, Child Custody, and the Mothers' Pensions: The Transformation of State-Family Relations in the Early Twentieth Century," *Social Problems* 29 (February 1982): 225.

62. "Notes of the Month," *Charities Review* 1 (May 1892): 328; Lou, *Juvenile Courts in the United States*, 16–17.

sulted from agitation by the Gerry Society, for it was very similar to a bill of 1877 sponsored by the society in an attempt to keep children apart from adult offenders before trial. Whereas the new law set a precedent by providing for the trial of juvenile offenders in surroundings separate from those of adults, some reformers wished to secure entirely separate courts for the trial of children's cases. The magistrates' courts, where the majority of children's cases were heard, still allowed children to associate with adult criminals. As one magistrate noted, "Several thousand children are arraigned yearly in the eight Magistrate's courts in the city. The establishment of such a court will save many from following a criminal career. The association of children with criminals, as is now the case, has a bad influence on the minds of the young."[63]

A modified juvenile court system was achieved under New York City's revised charter, which took effect on January 1, 1902. A further act, signed by the governor on April 16, 1902, provided for a special judge for the new court and decreed that all offenses of children under sixteen, except capital offenses, be regarded as misdemeanors. This meant that such cases could finally be dealt with in the children's court without the necessity of going to a higher tribunal. The new act resulted from agitation by several magistrates who had presided over children's cases. The law itself was drawn up by Magistrate Joseph M. Deuel, president of the Board of City Magistrates. He believed that the purpose of the new court was to protect children from exposure to the environment of crime in the criminal courts. He was also concerned that New York lagged behind other cities in their treatment of juvenile delinquents, and it was clearly to some degree a matter of local prestige to secure such a court. As Magistrate Deuel commented, "The new court will be a great improvement over the present system. It will be a model for other cities, and you will find we will have delegations here to see it. It is something that the Magistrates, and, I must admit, I myself, have given much consideration to."[64]

The Gerry Society continued to exercise considerable influence over the new court, being the only child-saving society to have offices in the new children's court building.[65] The new court, however, was not based on

63. Editorial note, *Charities* 7 (August 17, 1901): 151.

64. "New Court for Children: The Governor Signs the Bill Providing for Its Operation," *New York Times,* April 16, 1902, p. 3.

65. Trattner, *Homer Folks: Pioneer in Social Welfare,* 86; editorial note, *Charities* 7 (July 27, 1901): 87; Frances M. Bjorkman, "The Children's Court in American City Life," *Review of Reviews* 33 (1906): 310; "Separate Children's Court: Plan Regarded by Several Magistrates as Impractical—Gerry Society Favors It," *New York Times,* January 30, 1900, p. 3; "For a Children's Court: Old Charities Building Found to Be Suitable and Will Be Remodeled," *New*

chancery procedure and as such was not truly a juvenile court. It remained a criminal court, and children were still charged as criminals and found guilty or not of a particular offense. Adult court procedures remained, with the child represented by an attorney and required to plead guilty or not guilty to the charge. Since the court dealt only with children's cases, however, its supporters claimed that it had a different atmosphere—one designed to protect the interests of the child. One proponent argued, "That is the keynote of the Children's Court. There is none of the atmosphere which prevails in other judicial sessions. There is nothing of the impersonal, nothing of the unprejudiced, of the unfeeling, emotionless. Judge, counsel, witnesses for and against are banded together in one ambition—to save the boys."[66] Nevertheless, the New York Children's Court did not fulfill one important criterion advocated by the juvenile court pioneers: by remaining a criminal court and insisting on the trial of a child for a particular offense, it continued to stigmatize the child and, by convicting him, brand him as a criminal.[67]

More significantly, New York City made no provision for the introduction of a probation system for children. Some magistrates agreed to try parole instead of sending some of the boys to institutions, but this operated on an informal basis and does not appear to have involved the use of probation officers. Rather, the boy placed on parole with a suspended sentence was expected to report directly to the court with a letter from the pastor of his church, announcing that he had been reformed and was leading a religious and honest life, and another from his school or employer, confirming that he was attending school or working.[68] Although there were parallels with Lindsey's early methods and his reliance on his personal influence over boys in trouble with the law, Lindsey operated his probation system on a fairly small scale. New York City judges could hardly have maintained such a personal system, for the numbers of children before their courts were much greater than in Denver.[69] Moreover, it was likely that, in a city the size of

---

York Times, July 19, 1901, p. 5; "New Court for Children: The Governor Signs the Bill Providing for Its Operation," 3.

66. "In the New York Children's Court," *Juvenile Record* 4 (April 1903): 5.

67. Letter to Jacob Riis, November 17, 1904, box 3, folder 3, BBL Papers.

68. "Paroled Boys Examined: Observations of the Results of the Work of the Children's Court," *New York Times*, December 28, 1902, p. 10; "Success of the Children's Court: Results of Merciful System Shown on Parole Day," *New York Times*, February 15, 1903, p. 10.

69. Exactly comparable figures are difficult to obtain, but rough comparisons may be made. For instance, in the first year of the Manhattan and Bronx courts, 7,400 children were arraigned, and the chief probation officer reported 1,204 paroled during the period from September 3, 1902, to December 31, 1903. Lindsey reported 389 cases before his court in the year

Denver, Lindsey was acquainted with a large number of the rectors, teachers, and employers from whom he requested reports. The New York system, on the other hand, operated on a much more haphazard level, with no close supervision of a boy's behavior while he was on parole.

Moves toward creating a formal probation system in New York City were slow, in large part because the Gerry Society did not consider it to be in their interest to introduce a noncustodial method of treating children. When the provisions excluding children from the 1901 probation act were removed in 1903, a stipulation was added allowing the officers of the Gerry Society to serve as probation officers.[70] For several years a probation system operated in the children's court in a fairly haphazard fashion. Probation officers were not paid, but the court was authorized to appoint a police officer, a clerk of the court, or any other discreet person to perform the duties of a probation officer. Several police officers were appointed, as were agents paid by charitable agencies, including a number of women from various church and women's clubs. The chief probation officer, however, was Superintendent E. Fellows Jenkins of the Society for the Prevention of Cruelty to Children, and it was this agency that dominated the appointment of probation officers.[71]

The domination of the probation system by an agency with little commitment to the ideals of probation—which, indeed, saw it less as a means to protect and guide the child than as a method of supervision that carried with it the threat of punishment if the child violated the terms of his suspended sentence—caused several reformers to lobby the governor for a change in the way the system was administered.[72] Interestingly, women reformers do not seem to have been prominently involved in this agitation. Instead, it was dominated by two men already associated with reform efforts of other kinds in the city—Homer Folks, of the State Charities Aid Society, and Lawrence Veiller, who had been prominent in lobbying for tenement house reform in the city. These men were prompted by both their resent-

---

January 1, 1903, to January 1, 1904, of whom 276 were placed on probation. Julius M. Mayer, "The Child of the Large City," in Barrows, ed., *Children's Courts in the United States,* 16–24; E. Fellows Jenkins, "New York Parole Report," *Juvenile Court Record* 5 (January 1904): 6–7; Ben B. Lindsey, "Additional Report on Methods and Results," Barrows, ed., *Children's Courts in the United States,* 47–132.

70. Homer Folks, "Juvenile Probation in New York," *Survey* 23 (February 5, 1910): 667.

71. Ada Eliot, "The American System of Probation Officers," *Proceedings of the Third International Congress for the Welfare and Protection of Children* (1902), 60–61; "Success of the Children's Court: Results of Merciful System Shown on Parole Day," 10; Trattner, *Homer Folks: Pioneer in Social Welfare,* 89–90.

72. "New York Parole Report," *Juvenile Record* 5 (January 1904): 6–7.

ment of the Gerry Society's control of the probation system and their belief that the existing system was inefficient and did little to exercise a restraining influence over children disposed to continue their criminal ways.[73]

In 1905 Folks persuaded the Governor to establish a committee to examine the operation of probation in the state. Folks was appointed to and elected chairman of a commission of fourteen that included Samuel J. Barrows of the New York Prison Association, Frederick Almy of the Buffalo Charity Organization Society, and Lawrence Veiller.[74] The report produced by the commission condemned the probation work practiced in the state as irresponsible and inefficient and concluded that better results would be obtained if the power to appoint probation officers were taken from the magistrates, the chief probation officer in each city were appointed as the result of a competitive examination, and all probation officers were paid.

It was not until 1907, however, that Folks and his fellow reformers were able to secure legislation placing probation work under the supervision of the state in the form of a newly created probation commission, which thus removed probation not only from political influence but also from that of the Society for the Prevention of Cruelty to Children. By so doing, the state was able to secure competent and independent probation officers committed to the ideals of probation. The measures had been virulently opposed by judges of the magistrates' courts; police officers; officers of the Gerry Society, who were fearful of state supervision and in favor of retaining magistrates' control over the appointment of probation officers; and politically appointed probation officers, who saw their own interests threatened by the proposed law. The legislation was, however, supported by the State Charities Aid Association and various other charitable societies who saw it as a means of achieving a more efficient probation system that would put the needs of the children it sought to help before those of the various child-saving agencies.[75]

Although probation in New York still implied a suspension of sentence,

73. We can only speculate as to why women reformers were not a dominant influence here, especially given the presence of both Florence Kelley and Lillian Wald in the city. It could be simply that their involvement is undocumented, though this seems unlikely. Given that a separate court had been established and a rudimentary probation system was in place, women's organizations may have been prepared to allow male reformers with more political clout to take the lead. There is, for instance, no mention of juvenile court reform in Lillian Wald's autobiography: Lillian D. Wald, *The House on Henry Street* (New York, 1915).

74. Folks, "Juvenile Probation in New York," 667; Trattner, *Homer Folks: Pioneer in Social Welfare*, 89–90.

75. Folks, "Juvenile Probation in New York," 667; Trattner, *Homer Folks: Pioneer in Social Welfare*, 89–90.

reformers like Folks succeeded in bringing it more in line with the ideals of probation elsewhere. As Folks argued, "It is the personal influence of the probation officer, going into the child's home, studying the surroundings and influences that are shaping the child's career, discovering the processes which have been exercising an unwholesome influence, and, so far as possible, remedying these conditions—this is the very essence of the probation system." To Folks and his fellow reformers, the political and Gerry Society appointees of the New York Children's Court were not committed to these ideals of probation and so failed to achieve the desired results. The reformers believed that the new system by which probation officers were to be appointed and the fact they would be paid would produce a more committed and efficient probationary force.[76]

Yet New York remained something of an anomaly in its treatment of juvenile offenders, for although in 1909 the legislature changed the law so that a child coming under the jurisdiction of the juvenile court could not be convicted of a crime but would be deemed guilty of juvenile delinquency only, the child could still be convicted of and punished for a particular offense. Unlike the situation in other juvenile courts, the offense remained the central issue, rather than the child and the reasons that had led him to commit the offense. Although in practice the New York City Children's Court operated in a fashion similar to other juvenile courts, the maintenance of juvenile court ideals depended a great deal on the personality of the judge.[77]

The New York case demonstrates that a juvenile court could be instituted without the help of the wider juvenile court movement, but by implication it also suggests how influential that movement was in dictating the shape of juvenile courts elsewhere. The New York Children's Court had been constructed in a piecemeal fashion and by different groups of reformers. Whereas the securing of a separate court for children's cases was achieved relatively easily, this being a fairly conservative measure, probation was more of a struggle, because of the strong, vested interests of the Gerry Society. Significantly, it was largely due to the influence of Homer Folks, who was part of the wider national community of reformers and who became one of the directors of the International Juvenile Court Society, that New

76. Homer Folks, "Juvenile Probation," in Savel Zimand, ed., *Public Health and Welfare, the Citizen's Responsibility: Selected Papers of Homer Folks* (New York, 1958), 55–56.

77. Theodore Roosevelt, "The Court of the Children," *Outlook* 100 (March 2, 1912): 490–92; Franklin Chase Hoyt, "Procedure of the Manhattan Children's Court of the City of New York," in Hart, ed., *Preventive Treatment of Neglected Children*, 329; Franklin Chase Hoyt, *Quicksands of Youth* (New York, 1921), 11–14.

York eventually secured a probation system for children resembling that demanded by the wider juvenile court movement.[78]

The failure of local women reformers to take the initiative in demanding reform may be a major reason why New York City did not fully adopt the juvenile court model. The idea that the juvenile court should serve as the parent of those children before it and act in their best interests—a viewpoint that was advocated by women reformers and that developed out of a maternalist consciousness—was not at the base of the New York Children's Court. The city, with its high rate of juvenile delinquency, adopted some methods of the pioneer juvenile courts but stopped short of complete acceptance of their view that the child should be treated as a child in need of guidance and protection rather than as a criminal in need of punishment. By maintaining its status as a criminal court, the New York Children's Court still effectively convicted children as criminals. Thus, it failed to live up to all the criteria demanded by the women reformers in Chicago.

Massachusetts, like New York, had been among the pioneers in new methods of dealing with child offenders. Some twenty years before Illinois passed its juvenile court law, Massachusetts had already secured two of the main features of a juvenile court—separate hearings for children's cases and a probation system.[79] Proceedings remained those of a criminal court, however, with probation implying the suspension of sentence. With the establishment of juvenile courts in Illinois and Colorado followed by other states, Massachusetts seemed to be falling behind. Then in 1906, the state legislature created the Boston Juvenile Court, probably because of lobbying by the Boston Children's Aid Society and several other child-saving agencies.[80]

The Massachusetts Juvenile Court Law of 1906 differed from the already existing system in that it specifically noted that "proceedings against children under this act shall not be deemed to be criminal proceedings." Despite this provision, court proceedings continued to be against the child

78. Such as the National Conference of Charities and Correction. Folks appears among the directors in List of Directors of the International Juvenile Court Society, box 311, folder 1, BBL Papers.

79. N. S. Timasheff, *One Hundred Years of Probation, 1841–1941. Part One: Probation in the United States, England and the British Commonwealth of Nations* (New York, 1941), 44; Björkman, "The Children's Court in American Life," 311; *Harvey Humphrey Baker: Upbuilder of the Juvenile Court* (Boston, Mass., 1920), 3.

80. Eric C. Schneider, *In the Web of Class: Delinquents and Reformers in Boston, 1810s–1930s* (New York, 1992), 150. It seems likely that women's clubs may also have been involved; the GFWC had a fairly strong presence in the state, and a state federation of women's clubs had existed since 1894.

rather than on behalf of the child, with the purpose of determining the child's guilt or innocence. The new law also included a clause, as the Illinois law had done, allowing for liberal construction of the act.[81] What this effectively meant was that "wayward children" who had not committed a specific offense but who habitually associated with vicious persons and were growing up in surroundings exposing them to immoral or criminal influences liable to lead them into lives of crime could be brought into the court and set on the path to good citizenship. Exact interpretation of this clause was left to the juvenile court judge. It also permitted the juvenile court to deal with cases the criminal court had neither the time nor the expertise to handle.[82]

The establishment of the Boston Juvenile Court underlines the fact that the purpose of juvenile court legislation was not merely to introduce separate court hearings for children or even to introduce a probation system that would guide and protect children after they had appeared in court. Its primary aim was to establish the principle that children should be treated as children and not as criminals to be punished. This meant that the juvenile court should protect young offenders from possible contagion by the crime they would be exposed to in the ordinary courts. It also involved the juvenile court exerting steady pressure, through probation officers, to bring children back into what was regarded by the courts' officers as their normal relation to society—in essence, to get them back to school and to their families. Judge Harvey H. Baker of the Boston court did not entirely disregard the necessity of punishment in dealing with wayward children, but he considered this to be subordinate to the main function of the juvenile court: "The punishments thus administered are always considered by the court as subsidiary and incidental to its main function of putting the child right, and they are not given for retribution or example."[83] Nevertheless the Boston court, like that of New York City, seems to have been more concerned with the offense committed by the child than with the child's welfare, and in this respect fell short of the ideals of either the child-centered approach espoused by Lindsey or the family-centered treatment advocated by the Chicago court.

New York City and Massachusetts do not seem to have been typical of

---

81. Hawes, *Children in Urban Society,* 247.
82. *Harvey Humphrey Baker: Upbuilder of the Juvenile Court,* 28–29.
83. Baker, "Procedure of the Boston Juvenile Court," 650; "Boston Juvenile Court: Boston Juvenile Courts Sets Youngsters Aright by Heart-to-Heart Talks," *Juvenile Record* 8 (April 1907): 7.

the juvenile court movement as a whole. Indeed, the fact they pioneered some features of the juvenile court may well explain why they were slower to adopt the innovations advocated by the juvenile court movement. Despite the best efforts of the movement, however, the juvenile court legislation secured in the various states was far from uniform. Indeed, in 1905 one reformer, seeking to draw up a digest of the laws relating to juvenile courts, noted that no clear definition of what was meant by a juvenile court existed, since this varied from state to state.[84] While many juvenile court laws were based on that of Illinois, a number of these laws had to be adapted so they would not be found unconstitutional in the individual states. In some states, local circumstances and the opposition of certain elements meant that some aspects of the model juvenile court laws had to be dropped. Attempts were made by the national leaders of the juvenile court movement to outline the minimum principles needed to constitute a juvenile court: the appointment of probation officers, the separate trial of children, the provision of a detention home, and the recognition of child-saving agencies. Possibly most important of all was the requirement that the jurisdiction of the juvenile court should be that of a chancery court rather than a criminal court and that it should act in its capacity as *parens patriae*—the ultimate parent of all children of the state. This last principle, however, proved the most difficult to achieve in some states, and it continued to vex the leaders of the national juvenile court movement even after many states had adopted most other principles of the juvenile courts.[85]

In their administration, too, juvenile courts differed considerably. In the South, courts were segregated, with African-American children frequently still treated as criminals and placed less often than white children on probation and more often in (also segregated) juvenile reformatories. The juvenile courts in rural areas often suffered from a lack of resources and probation officers, which meant that the judges of these courts had difficulty carrying out the principles of a juvenile court, if indeed they were at all concerned to do so.[86] Although few judges tried to emulate Lindsey's personal touch, to a large extent the administration of individual juvenile courts depended on

84. Bates, "Digest of Statutes Relating to Juvenile Courts and Probation Systems," 329–37.
85. Hurd, "Juvenile Court Law: Minimum Principles Which Should Be Stood For," 327–28; Bernard Flexner, "Juvenile Court Laws," *Charities* 20 (July 4, 1908): 455–58; Flexner, "A Decade of the Juvenile Court," 106–16; Roosevelt, "The Court of the Children," 490–92.
86. Florence Kelley, "A Burglar Four Years Old in the Memphis Juvenile Court," *Survey* 32 (June 20, 1914): 318–19; Elmer L. Coffeen, "Juvenile Courts and Social Work in the Rural Districts of the Central West," *Annals of the American Academy of Political and Social Science* 27 (1906): 447–50.

the interest of its judge, its officers, and the community it served. In many cases the juvenile courts, because the legislation that established them was so vague, provided little in the way of additional protection or more enlightened methods of dealing with problem children than what had been practiced before. Thus, as the juvenile court idea was spread throughout the United States, the principles behind the original juvenile courts became diluted.

Despite this dilution of its message, the juvenile court movement clearly had a great influence on the way in which dependent and delinquent children were treated by the law in the various states. Moreover, its influence stretched beyond the United States itself to Britain, the Australian colonies, Japan, Canada, and parts of continental Europe. The success of the juvenile court movement was largely due to the efforts of the Denver and Chicago reformers and the membership of the National Congress of Mothers, who acted as evangelists of the juvenile court gospel, but it is also testimony to the fact that the juvenile court offered a solution to the problem of dependent and delinquent children faced by many cities in the United States.

The juvenile court movement was marked by the cooperation of a variety of reformers to achieve a common goal—a juvenile court law in every state of the United States. Although these reformers themselves differed in a number of respects, most came from the middle-class, and this background tended to give them a common perspective on the problem of juvenile delinquency. They feared that if something were not done about the conditions in which these children lived and the way in which the justice system dealt with them, social disintegration was likely to result. To an extent, therefore, the juvenile court movement should be seen in terms of middle-class reformers seeking to impose their values and cultural norms on working-class and immigrant children who did not appear to be conforming to these values. The perspectives of these reformers on how to deal with the problem varied, however, for beneath this broad umbrella, middle-class reformers were fairly diverse in their motives and methods. Whereas a number of factors played a part, gender consciousness, whether male or female, clearly had a significant influence on the outlook of the reformers concerned.

Given the difference in perspective between the male and female reformers, it is not surprising that the juvenile courts varied in how they were established and administered. Although it is not always apparent, debate about the priorities and aims of the juvenile court movement occurred, and compromises had to be reached between the different perspectives. In the initial stages of the juvenile court movement, the female influence was undoubtedly the dominant one, and the Chicago model, shaped as it had been by women reformers, continued to be influential in the establishment of juvenile courts in other states. It was therefore female values that lay at the heart of the juvenile court movement, though these were often overlaid with the more masculine discourse of Judge Lindsey and some of the other male reformers. By the end of the first decade of the juvenile court's history, another discourse had also become prominent: that of the "expert," either male or female, which emphasized professional concerns rather than gendered ones. Moreover, by 1909 reformers had begun to move beyond their immediate concern with establishing juvenile courts and probation systems to focus on the scientific investigation of the causes of juvenile delinquency and ways to prevent it.

6

The Development of the Juvenile Courts

Chicago, A Case Study

Many juvenile court reformers were concerned with not only establishing juvenile courts across the United States but also developing the juvenile court idea and the institution itself. In the first decade or so of its existence, the juvenile court proved itself to be a dynamic institution, adapting to the changing needs of its administrators and the children it sought to protect. Some development of the juvenile court idea took place at the national level, for the community of reformers that constituted the juvenile court movement and the publications and organizations they used to publicize the juvenile court idea also acted as a forum in which ideas about the aims and functions of the juvenile court continued to be debated. Developments also took place at the local level, where juvenile courts evolved to meet the needs of the communities they served. Although juvenile courts were often influenced in their evolution by innovations in other juvenile courts and by changing ideas about the nature of juvenile delinquency, local factors continued to be important.

This chapter explores the development of the juvenile court idea through an examination of the operation of the Chicago Juvenile Court. As the pioneer, the Chicago court frequently faced problems and had to find solutions that, though often only a pragmatic response to a pressing question, were at times truly innovative. The Chicago court maintained its status as a model for other juvenile courts for more than a decade after the passing of the Illinois Juvenile Court Law and thus provides a useful case study through which to investigate trends in the growth of the juvenile court idea. This court also provides an illustration of how the female reformers who had played such a significant role in establishing the juvenile court continued to be influential in its development.

Several years after the opening of the Chicago Juvenile Court on July 1, 1899, a journalist writing for the *Chicago Illustrated Review* observed that it was the women of Chicago who had played the most significant role in both the founding and the development of the court. He did not seem in the least surprised by this, for these women appeared to have been acting in their traditional role as mothers and nurturers in pursuing this reform and as a result were working within a conservative view of the role of women. Thus he wrote, "When the juvenile court system of this city was started it was inspired and sustained by Chicago's women friends who opened their purses and paid the salaries of probation officers in order to keep the work alive until the city government should be compelled, in view of demonstrated results, to give the work municipal standing and basis. And to-day, in this field of collective misfortune, patient women, untiring in faith and devotion, are in a big sense 'mothering' Chicago."[1]

The women of Chicago did more than pay the salaries of probation officers. They had been instrumental in securing the juvenile court bill, and they were not content simply to watch the work of the previous decade fizzle out due to the failure of the law to make any provision for its implementation. Chapter 6 explores how those women reformers who had agitated for the passage of the court law helped to overcome its inadequacies and to ensure the success of the Chicago Juvenile Court. In so doing, this chapter investigates how the two traditions of women reformers, the "traditional maternalists" and the "professional maternalists," continued to work together. For though these two groups often worked from different perspectives, they cooperated to ensure that the juvenile court developed along the lines they had envisaged and was not betrayed by either juvenile court judges or child-saving organizations, who all had their own concerns. In working with male reformers to implement and develop the ideas behind their agitation for a juvenile court, the women reformers continued to be influenced by socially constructed ideals of feminine behavior. However, as the court developed, the female social science tradition, rather than the "maternalist" tradition, was often to the forefront.

The Illinois Juvenile Court Law, more formally entitled "An Act to Regulate the Treatment and Control of Dependent, Neglected and Delinquent

---

1. "Mothering Chicago," *Chicago Illustrated Review* [December 30, 1908?], box 1, folder 1, Ethel Martin Henrotin Papers, Women's History Archive, Schlesinger Library, Radcliffe College.

Children," came into effect on July 1, 1899. It contained comprehensive definitions of dependent, neglected, and delinquent children, and it conferred on county and circuit courts original jurisdiction concerning such children. The act provided that in counties with a population of more than fifty thousand, the circuit court judges should designate one of their number to deal with cases covered by the law, and children's cases coming before a justice of the peace or police magistrate should be immediately transferred to the judge so designated. Thus, separate courts for children were finally a legal reality. The law did not, however, create a new court. Rather, in order that its existence be constitutional, the juvenile court remained a division of the circuit court. Moreover, referral of children's cases to the juvenile court could not be mandated. In this respect the law had to be permissive rather than compulsory and as a result did not entirely deal with the lack of uniformity in the treatment of children by the courts, for it still allowed children to be tried in other courts.

The law also provided for the separate detention of children while their cases were pending and prohibited the committal of children under twelve to a common jail or police station. It also recognized all child-saving organizations approved by the State Board of Charities, gave validity to their contracts in reference to the surrendering of children by their parents and the adoption of children, and provided for a system of supervision by the State Board of Charities over children placed in homes throughout the state, thus making legitimate the role of these child-saving agencies in the juvenile justice system. The law further provided for the appointment by the court of probation officers and outlined their duties: to investigate as required by the court; to be present in the court to represent the interests of the child; and to take charge of any child before and after trial, as directed by the court. Thus, a probation system became a formal part of the juvenile justice machinery in Illinois. The law also laid down the procedure by which a child was to be brought before the court, with the aim of avoiding arrest and therefore the stigma of criminal charges. Of perhaps most significance was the act's final clause, which embodied the spirit of the law and recognized the state's obligation to the child. Although it emphasized the importance of the family, this clause gave judges considerable discretion in their handling of children.[2]

2. "An Act to Regulate the Treatment and Control of Dependent, Neglected and Delinquent Children," July 1, 1899, as outlined in the Report of the Chicago Bar Association Committee on Juvenile Courts, Chicago, October 28, 1899, 5–6, typescript, Manuscript Division, Chicago Historical Society. The final clause is quoted in Chapter 2, above.

Recognizing the role of the state as parent of all children—in legal terms, *parens patriae*—the law embodied the fundamental idea, which the women reformers had been agitating for, that the state must step in and exercise guardianship over a child found under such adverse social or individual circumstances that might lead to crime. It also aimed to keep children separate from adult offenders at all stages of the judicial process, so the children would not be corrupted by exposure to hardened criminals. Moreover, the juvenile courts were to be chancery courts rather than criminal ones. This meant they were to look after the best interests of the children and to find them dependent or delinquent rather than criminal. In some respects, the juvenile court law only formalized existing practices, which had been undertaken by women reformers with the cooperation of some judges. It also represented, on the part of the judicial system, a new attitude toward children that reflected changing perceptions of the nature of childhood. The new act placed on a legal footing the belief that children should be treated as children by the system rather than as criminals, but it also embodied middle-class conceptions of the "proper" behavior of children.

The passing of the law was greeted with considerable enthusiasm by those who had agitated for its adoption.[3] It was seen as a great step forward in helping to deal with problem children, but many reformers recognized it had serious deficiencies that would make its implementation difficult.[4] Some features of the bill had been lost in its journey through the legislature; other provisions that would have eased implementation had been deliberately omitted to ensure the bill's passage. Thus, although the law mandated the appointment of probation officers, it did not provide for their payment; similarly, while the law forbade the holding of children under twelve in a jail or police station, it did not supply an alternative place of detention. Neither deficiency had been addressed in the original bill, probably because reformers were concerned that any new financial burdens would prevent it from passing.[5]

The women reformers who had played such a large part in securing the

3. See, for instance, *Hull House Bulletin* (April and May 1899): 10.

4. The *Chicago Tribune,* June 17, 1899, p. 12, remarked that the Juvenile Court Law just passed could only be a first step in caring for delinquent and neglected children. Judge Tuthill, in an address in 1900, noted the difficulties in implementing the law: Richard S. Tuthill, "The Juvenile Court Law in Cook County," *Proceedings of the Illinois Conference of Charities* (1900), 11–12.

5. "An Act to Regulate the Treatment and Control of Dependent, Neglected and Delinquent Children," sections 6 and 11.

Juvenile Court Law were therefore immediately faced with the question of how to administer the law as it had emerged from the legislature. Clearly, having worked so hard for its adoption, they were not prepared to let it fail because of problems with implementation. Thus, in the early days of the juvenile court, women reformers played a central part in ensuring that the new system conformed to their expectations. For instance, although the choice of a judge to preside over the juvenile court was a matter for circuit court judges to decide, it seems likely that the women reformers exerted some pressure in securing their own choice: Judge Richard Tuthill, who had already been running a separate court session for children's cases at the request of the Chicago Woman's Club.[6]

Tuthill proved a fortuitous choice, for not only had he already shown his interest in working with children, but he also proved to be an enthusiastic publicist for the court. He also recognized that the women reformers continued to have an interest in the juvenile court. A few days before the court was to hold its first session, Judge Tuthill called a meeting to consider plans for its organization. To this meeting he invited a committee of judges appointed to assist in preparing plans of procedure, the Judiciary Committee of the County Board, and a representative appointed by the mayor. Of perhaps more significance, since they had no obvious knowledge of judicial procedures, was his invitation to the Chicago Woman's Club to send representatives.[7]

The meeting held by Judge Tuthill had a dual purpose: to discuss arrangements for the new court, and to publicize the aims of the court and the problems it faced in its administration. Tuthill announced that the court would be held in his own courtrooms, though he does not seem to have made any attempt to modify the appearance of the courtroom or its procedure. A more difficult problem was the question of where the children, especially those under twelve, would be held pending trial. Those present at the meeting came to no conclusions but resolved to determine the number of delinquent children in the city who were likely to need such confinement and the kind of place that would be required.[8] On other occasions Judge

6. Letter from Mrs. Lucy Flower, May 1917, vol. 3, Louise deKoven Bowen Papers, Manuscript Division, Chicago Historical Society (hereafter Bowen Papers).

7. "Meet to Organize New Court: Judge Tuthill Sends Out Notices for a Conference in His Rooms This Afternoon," *Chicago Tribune*, June 22, 1899, p. 8.

8. "Judge Tuthill Tells Plans: Juvenile Court Needs Four Detention Rooms and a Man and a Woman as Custodians," *Chicago Tribune*, June 23, 1899, p. 8; "Juvenile Court Lodge," *Chicago Tribune*, June 26, 1899, p. 6.

Tuthill encouraged the cooperation of the various child-saving societies and women's clubs in the efforts to secure the best results from the law governing the juvenile court. In a speech at the opening of the new dormitories of the John Worthy School on June 30, 1899, Tuthill urged each citizen and the police department to aid in this work and asked that boys who might come before him understand that he did not intend to administer punishment alone but was their friend.[9] Thus, Tuthill proved an active publicist for the court.[10]

He was not alone in this. The reformers of the Chicago Woman's Club and the Hull House community were not content to passively watch while the judges and child-saving agencies administered the law. Rather, they were active in many efforts both to publicize the court and to ensure that it fulfilled their aims. For example, members of the Chicago Woman's Club negotiated with the Illinois Industrial Association, a charitable organization with an interest in children, to donate a building to act as a detention home. The club, through donations by its members, paid for many administrative costs of the home, while the city and county reluctantly paid something toward the expense of feeding the children housed there. A committee of the club continued, in cooperation with the Illinois Industrial Association, to run the detention home. Although these women received intermittent help from the city and county, it was effectively the Chicago Woman's Club that ensured the facility was run smoothly.[11]

Of more significance than the administration of the detention home, which merely provided a means to ensure that children were at no point brought into contact with adult offenders, was the involvement of the women reformers in the development of probation for juvenile offenders. Both the Chicago Woman's Club and, more directly, the Hull House community had been involved in the creation of an informal system of probation in some of the police courts, where many child offenders had been taken prior to the passing of the Juvenile Court Law.[12] Although this probation

9. *Chicago Tribune,* July 1, 1899.
10. See, for instance, the *Chicago Tribune,* June 22, 23, 26, and July 1, 1899; *Proceedings of the Illinois Conference of Charities* (1900), 10–16, 28–29; Hon. Richard S. Tuthill, "Chicago Congregational Club: The Delinquent Classes—What Shall We Do with Them: What Will They Do with Us," speech, 1900, pp. 26–32, Papers of David J. Talbot, Manuscript Division, Chicago Historical Society.
11. Mrs. Joseph T. Bowen, "The Early Days of the Juvenile Court," in Jane Addams et al., *The Child, the Clinic and the Court* (New York, 1925), 300; Tuthill, "The Juvenile Court Law in Cook County," 11–12; Harriet S. Farwell, *Lucy Louisa Flower: 1837–1920: Her Contribution to Education and Child Welfare in Chicago* (privately printed, 1924), 33.
12. December 28, 1898, January 25, 1899, and April 29, 1899, box 21, vol. 93, Chicago

work had occurred on an informal basis, it provided a body of expertise on which administrators of the Juvenile Court Law could draw. Women reformers, particularly those centered around Hull House, had been some of the strongest advocates of the inclusion of probation in the bill, for they saw it as a means to ensure that the children of the slums were given the opportunity to behave as children. They hoped that the introduction of a probation officer into the lives of children who appeared to be in danger of becoming criminal would act as a benevolent influence and prevent the child from developing further criminal tendencies. It is unsurprising, therefore, that these women continued to play a large part in the further development and implementation of the probation system once the Juvenile Court Law came into operation.

Though appointed by the court, probation officers continued to be volunteers, for the county was unable to pay them. It therefore became a concern of the women reformers to find the means to pay salaries to probation officers. At the first session of the court, Mrs. Alzina Stevens of Hull House volunteered her services and was appointed the first probation officer, and Mrs. Lucy Flower, representing the Chicago Woman's Club, offered to pay her salary. Other probation officers were supported by other charitable agencies, most notably the Catholic Visitation and Aid Society and the Protestant Children's Home and Aid Society. In addition, the mayor of Chicago contributed the services of several policemen to act as probation officers, and the board of education similarly provided several truant officers. A number of unpaid volunteers assisted the paid probation officers with a small number of cases. Finally, the law department of the city of Chicago aided the court by providing a legal representative who became chief probation officer. This post was filled by Timothy D. Hurley, President of the Visitation and Aid Society.[13] It was, however, the probation officers whose salaries were paid by private agencies, and particularly the Chicago

Woman's Club Papers, Manuscript Division, Chicago Historical Society (hereafter CWC Papers); February 8, 1899, box 3, vol. 20, CWC Papers; Henriette Greenbaume Frank and Amalie Hofer Jerome, *Annals of the Chicago Woman's Club for the First Forty Years of Its Organization, 1876–1916* (Chicago, 1916), 188; Case Studies (Restricted), June 1897–August 1899, supplement 1, folder 1, Juvenile Protective Association Papers, Special Collections, University of Illinois at Chicago (hereafter JPA Papers); *Hull House Bulletin* (December 1897), and following issues.

13. T. D. Hurley, "Juvenile Court Report," *Proceedings of the Illinois Conference of Charities* (1900), 30–33; letter from Mrs. Lucy Flower, May 1917, vol. 2, Bowen Papers; Carl Kelsey, "The Juvenile Court of Chicago and Its Work," *Annals of the American Academy of Political and Social Science* 17 (1901): 298–304. This kind of financial arrangement between the Chicago Woman's Club and settlement house workers was not unusual. See Kathryn Kish

Woman's Club, who seem to have made the greatest contribution to the development of probation, for they were able to devote themselves full time to the cases assigned to them.

The women reformers not only offered to pay the salary of the first probation officer of the juvenile court, they were also invited by Judge Tuthill to sit on the bench with him during the initial sessions. Clearly, Tuthill greatly respected these women, not only because of the important influence they had had on the creation of the court but also because of their value as advisers in the treatment of children before the court. For some time, members of the Probation Committee of the club, along with Julia Lathrop of Hull House, sat on the bench with Judge Tuthill or simply visited the court in order to be of assistance in its work.[14] In this way these women were able to informally influence the sentencing policy of the court and to ensure that their aims were carried out.

Since none of the women reformers involved with the juvenile court had the legal training or experience necessary to become a juvenile court judge, much of their work for the court involved providing support rather then developing judicial policy. They did so informally, through offering advice on the treatment of children before the court, but also formally, by supplying probation officers and by fund-raising to pay the salaries of an increasing number of probation officers, many of whom were women. Thus, while male reformers and judges tended to concentrate on ensuring the smooth administration of the juvenile court in its daily operations and on developing the legal aspects of and rationale for the court, women reformers focused primarily on the development of the probation system. The Joint Committee of the Woman's Club on Probation Work outlined what it considered to be the importance of its work in an annual report made ten months after the opening of the court on April 28, 1900: "The efficiency of the law depends upon the efficiency of the probation officers and at present these officers must be either policemen or unpaid volunteers, or paid volunteers." Clearly, it argued, paid volunteers were the most essential probation officers: "The policemen are strategically and structurally unfit for this work, the unpaid volunteers are excellent strategically, but often fail structurally. (That is they are not always present in the body) and the work in the

---

Sklar, "Who Funded Hull House?" in Kathleen D. McCarthy, ed., *Lady Bountiful Revisited: Women, Philanthropy and Power* (New Brunswick, 1990), 94–115.

14. Frank and Jerome, *Annals of the Chicago Woman's Club,* 190; letter to Mrs. Groves from Judge Tuthill, December 21, 1899, Grace Groves Clement Papers, Manuscript Division, Chicago Historical Society.

long hard run must depend on paid volunteers."[15] This was because paid volunteers could devote all their time to the work, for they had no other duties.

The Chicago Woman's Club Joint Committee on Probation Work, chaired first by Miss Lathrop and later by Mrs. Flower, continued to pay the salaries of several of the female probation officers. Members of the committee also seem to have acted as volunteer probation workers under the direction of paid officers, and the club invited several of these volunteer officers to speak about their experiences at club meetings.[16] In December 1902 the club proposed forming a general committee of delegates, from clubs and other organizations, that would enlist public interest in probation work and secure the necessary funds. As a result, Mrs. Flower formed the Juvenile Court Committee, which, though a separate entity from the Chicago Woman's Club, drew much of its membership from the club. Miss Lathrop was chair of this committee, and many of its officers were members of the club who had campaigned for the Juvenile Court Law. Its main aim was "to aid in the work of child saving, by securing salaries for probation officers, and by such other means as might seem advisable. . . . Feeling that there was no more valuable work for children than that done by the probation officers, which substitutes wise, kindly personal care, for neglect and prison."[17]

By the end of the first year of the juvenile court's existence, its supporters were pronouncing it a success, and probation work was seen both by the judges, who could now formally use it as an alternative sentence, and by the probation officers themselves as an essential part of the juvenile court system. Thus, Judge Tuthill—using terms that echoed the maternalist discourse of "universal motherhood"—pronounced probation to be the keystone that supported the arch of the law, "an arch which shall be as a rainbow of hope to all who love children and who desire that *all* children shall be properly cared for and who would provide such care for those who are, without it, and who else would almost inevitably come to lead vicious and criminal lives, so that they may be saved and develop into good citizens, honest and useful men and women."[18]

A more considered and scientific explanation of probation was given by Alzina Stevens. As part of the Hull House community, Mrs. Stevens had al-

15. April 28, 1900, box 21, vol. 94, CWC Papers; Frank and Jerome, *Annals of the Chicago Woman's Club,* 190.
16. Frank and Jerome, *Annals of the Chicago Woman's Club,* 190–91, 218.
17. Ibid., 228–30.
18. Tuthill, "The Juvenile Court in Cook County," 13.

ready had several years of experience as an informal probation officer before the passing of the law. She, too, believed that probation was the keynote to the law. She explained that the duties of a probation officer were to visit the homes of children before the court, ascertain their school and police record as well as their home environment, and take note of their physical and mental development together with their moral habits. The probation officer would then report to the court the results of her investigations and take charge of any children paroled to her. Mrs. Stevens concluded that it should be the first effort of the probation officer to keep the child in his or her own home for both the child's and the parents' sake. However, the child's best interests should be considered above all, and this might mean that he be surrendered to some institution or home-finding society.[19] In many respects, Mrs. Stevens's view of probation was much more practical than some of its other advocates, since it was based on her experience as a probation officer and her greater awareness of the conditions in which many of these children lived.

Probation was not designed only to offer guidance and protection to the child offender. Both the women of the Chicago Woman's Club and those of Hull House had emphasized the importance of probation to both the child and his family. Thus, Mrs. Louise deKoven Bowen, who had replaced Miss Lathrop as chairman of the Juvenile Court Committee, noted the importance of the probation officer in the "uplift" of the child's home: "The judge, recognizing the results that have led to the child's violation of the law, places him in charge of a probation officer, the officer becomes the friend of the family, the parents try harder to do better for the child because they consider him under the protection of the law, the standard of the home is raised; it gradually assumes a different aspect; the child learns the meaning of right and wrong and grows up to be a self-respecting citizen, and the state is saved the burden and support of a criminal."[20]

Mrs. Bowen elaborated on this idea in a speech made in 1904: "recognizing the principle that if the child can be helped in the home it is the best thing to do, the judge reprimands the child and sends him home." Mrs. Bowen considered it the duty of the probation officer to visit the child regularly and become an adviser and friend to the family, trying to ensure a decent home. Furthermore, she described the emphasis of probation work as

19. Mrs. A. P. Stevens, "The Juvenile Court Bill," *Proceedings of the Illinois Conference of Charities* (1899), 39–40.

20. "Juvenile Court Committee," pamphlet prepared by Mrs. Bowen to be sent to clubs, among statements dated October 1903–May 1904, supplement 1, folder 17, JPA Papers.

formative rather than reformative. It was the preventive character of probation that above all made it worthwhile, she argued, for it hindered children from becoming criminals.[21]

The preventive nature of probation work was stressed by other women involved in the effort. It was especially noted by several female probation officers that much of their work was concerned with keeping children out of court. In this respect, probation officers based at Hull House were particularly anxious to ensure that parents who feared their children were in danger of getting into trouble would seek the help of a probation officer.[22] Thus, reformers stressed that it was the main aim of probation officers to keep families together and to prevent children from developing into criminals. Nevertheless, the best interests of the child and the welfare of the community should be considered *before* the interests and feelings of parents and relatives. In a set of instructions issued to probation officers in 1901, this point above all was emphasized. The instructions noted that although a child usually would not be separated from his parents, in some cases, where it was in the best interests of the child, he should be removed from his natural home. A number of circumstances dictated that this action was desirable: cases where the parents were criminal, vicious and cruel, entirely unable to support the child, or providing a home of such condition as to make it extremely probable the child would grow up vicious and dependent. The instructions concluded that the court should not be used by parents for the purpose of relieving themselves of their parental obligations.[23]

It is difficult to tell, merely from the records of the juvenile court, why some children were sentenced to an institution while others were placed on probation. No doubt such considerations as the "suitability" of the home in the prevention of delinquency in a child were major factors.[24] How to determine the suitability of a home was, in any case, a highly subjective matter. It

21. Mary Humphrey, ed., *Speeches, Addresses and Letters of Louise deKoven Bowen: Reflecting Social Movements in Chicago* (Ann Arbor, Michigan, 1937), 1:64.

22. Sara Nelson Franklin, "A Workshop of a Probation Officer," *Charities* 11 (November 7, 1903): 414–16; Elizabeth McDonald, "Parole Work," *Juvenile Record* 4 (June 1903): 12–13; *Hull House Bulletin* (Autumn 1900): 11; Julia C. Lathrop, "The Development of the Probation System in a Large City," *Charities* 13 (January 7, 1905): 344–49.

23. "Instructions to Probation Officers," *Juvenile Record* 2 (June 1901): 13. On the question of fears about parents ducking their parental obligations, see Barbara Brenzel, *Daughters of the State: A Social Portrait of the First Reform School for Girls in North America, 1856–1905* (Cambridge, Mass., 1983); Linda Gordon, *Heroes of Their Own Lives: The Politics and History of Family Violence* (London, 1989; first published, 1988).

24. As shown, for instance, in Hurley, "Juvenile Court Report," 30–31, and "Annual Report of the Chicago Juvenile Court," *Juvenile Record* 5 (January 1904): 5.

was often up to the probation officer to judge a child's home surroundings. Since probation officers usually came from middle-class backgrounds, their judgments were colored by this perspective, and any parents who appeared unprepared to conform to middle-class standards were in danger of having their child taken away. High moral standards were set, with drunken parents and single mothers most likely to have their children removed to the "higher" moral atmosphere of non-institutional care provided by an approved foster family or child-saving society. Institutional care was considered to be a last resort.[25] Probation officers were therefore able to act as the moral arbiters of the homes of working-class and immigrant children who came before the juvenile court. This ability to interfere in the family lives of these children and ensure that they conformed, at least outwardly, to middle-class values was, in theory, considerable. In practice, however, most probation officers considered it to be in the child's best interests to remain with his natural parents. Moreover, the ability of probation officers to interfere was tempered by both the size of their caseloads and their own understanding of their role.[26] The majority of the early probation officers placed great emphasis on the importance of family life as a preventive to juvenile delinquency.

The considerable emphasis placed on probation by juvenile court judges, reformers, and probation officers clearly reflected the importance they attached to the family and home as the formative influences in a child's life. In this way, the juvenile court marks the triumph of female values in the treatment of juvenile offenders, for maternalist discourse deemed women to be the protectors of the home and the nurturers of children. In seeking to reform the way the judicial system treated children, women reformers had formulated their arguments in terms of socially acceptable feminine concerns. Thus, they argued that the apparent increase in juvenile crime in

25. Hurley, "Juvenile Court Report," 30–31; Mary Odem, "Single Mothers, Delinquent Daughters, and the Juvenile Court in Early Twentieth-Century Los Angeles," *Journal of Social History* 25 (Fall 1991): 27–43; Ann Vandepol, "Dependent Children, Child Custody, and the Mothers' Pensions: The Transformation of State-Family Relations in the Early Twentieth Century," *Social Problems* 29 (February 1982): 221–35; Linda Gordon, "Single Mothers and Child Neglect, 1880–1920," *American Quarterly* 37 (Summer 1985): 173–92. For a contrary view, see Anthony M. Platt, *The Child Savers: The Invention of Delinquency* (Chicago, 1969), 134–41.

26. "The Juvenile Court" [1904], *Speeches, Addresses and Letters of Louise deKoven Bowen,* 62–67; Franklin, "A Workshop of a Probation Officer," 414–16; Henry W. Thurston, "Probation Work and the Settlement," *Charities and the Commons* 18 (June 8, 1907): 298–300.

Chicago was a symptom of the gradual breakdown of family life in the slums. Moreover, it seemed clear to these women that children living in the poorer areas of the city were not being given the nurture and love that would enable them to grow up into useful and upright citizens. Once these values had been embodied in the juvenile justice system in Chicago, women reformers sought to develop them further.

In this respect it is significant that in Chicago, the majority of the paid volunteer probation officers—who did the most important work for the court—were women. In Denver, by contrast, probation was not considered suitable work for women.[27] For the women reformers of Chicago, however, doing the work was one way to ensure the continuing centrality of maternalist values in the juvenile court system. Probation fitted well with the maternalist construction of femininity, which meant that, even though paid work for married women was generally frowned on, many salaried probation officers were married women, and it was even considered desirable that this should be the case.[28] Women's clubs, under the auspices of the juvenile court committee, were paying the salaries of these officers and consequently were influential in the choice of probation officers. These organizations believed that women had the necessary qualities for the work. Probation workers needed to be nurturing and benevolent, and these were exactly the characteristics attributed to women in their role as mothers. Moreover, when viewed in this way, the women's work as probation officers could be seen merely as an extension of their role as mothers and therefore a legitimate activity. The maternalist discourse was thereby used to create a new profession for women. As probation work became more professional and part of the growing occupation of social work, it continued both to appeal to women and to be considered a proper activity for women. Like settlement workers, however, the new professionally trained probation officers often used the maternalist discourse as little more than a strategic device.[29]

27. Letter from Mrs. Izetta George, April 2, 1902, box 82, folder 4, Ben B. Lindsey Papers, Manuscript Division, Library of Congress. In November 1902 the Juvenile Court Committee paid ten women probation officers and two men: proof sheet of "A Statement Concerning Probation Officers in the Juvenile Courts," November 4, 1902, supplement 1, folder 20, JPA Papers. In January 1905, eleven women and four men were serving as probation officers: Julia Lathrop, "The Development of a Probation System in a Large City," 344–49.

28. Memorandum by Julia Lathrop, May 3, 1917, vol. 2, Bowen Papers. See also various references in Frank and Jerome, *Annals of the Chicago Woman's Club*.

29. See, for instance, Carl N. Degler, *At Odds: Women and the Family in America from the Revolution to the Present* (New York, 1980); Sheila M. Rothman, *Woman's Proper Place: A History of Changing Ideals and Practices, 1870 to the Present* (New York, 1978), 114; Molly

In fact, these probation workers were closely associated with the settlements, often living in and working from them.

Probation work, besides easily being justified in terms of women's proper
role, was also closely associated with the tradition of female social science.
The mainly female probation officers went into the homes of children who
got into trouble and sought to find the cause. This investigative work was
an important part of the probation officer's role, for it determined whether
the child would be allowed to remain in his natural home or removed to another one. It also encouraged some of the officers who were trained in the
social sciences to investigate social conditions and seek remedies for some
of the problems of slum life. Initially, however, the probation officer's main
function was to act as a benevolent influence in the life of the child, ensuring that he receive the nurture necessary to make him a good citizen and
that he attend school regularly or, if beyond school age, secure a steady job.
Probation thus sought to reaffirm the values of home and family life and
thereby prevent the apparent breakdown of families in the slums. Whereas
it operated from prevailing middle-class ideas about childhood and child
nature and sought to apply these to poor and largely immigrant families, it
recognized the importance of ties within these families.[30]

Since the aims and administration of the Chicago probation system were
dominated by women reformers, feminine values continued to be influential
in its development. The working of the juvenile court itself, however, was
much less a female preserve. It relied on the enthusiasm and goodwill of the
juvenile court judges; indeed, in its daily workings, the juvenile court was
heavily dependent on the personality of the judge. The Juvenile Court Law
had embodied the three principles that had been of the greatest concern to
advocates of reform: the state's responsibility for the welfare of all children
in the state; the insistence that children be kept apart from adult offenders
at all stages of the judicial process; and the idea that children be treated not
as criminals but as erring children. All reflected the influence of the women
reformers. But since the law left so much to the discretion of the judge in his
dealings with dependent and delinquent children, the choice of judge was
very important. In this, the Chicago Juvenile Court was fortunate. The post
of juvenile court judge was considered an unattractive one and could even

Ladd-Taylor, *Mother-Work: Women, Child Welfare, and the State, 1890–1930* (Urbana,
1994), 74–76.

30. The importance of family life in the slums is discussed by Jane Addams in *The Spirit of
Youth and the City Streets* (Urbana, 1972; first published, 1909), chap. 2, and *Twenty Years at
Hull House* (reprint, New York, 1961; first published, 1910), chap. 11.

prove a bar to political advancement. As a result the post was not in great demand and was left open to those judges committed to helping children.[31] It also seems that the women reformers, especially once they had formed themselves into the Juvenile Court Committee and were playing a large role in promoting the work of the court, had considerable influence on the choice of a judge. Despite the unpopularity of the post among judges, however, political considerations did at times intrude on the choice.[32]

The earliest juvenile court judges in Chicago proved to be highly committed to the new court and essential to the early development of the institution and its methods. Given the deficiencies in the legislation establishing the juvenile court system, judges less committed to working with children might well have prevented the fulfillment of the juvenile court idea in Chicago. However, the first three juvenile court judges—Richard Tuthill, Julian Mack, and Merritt Pinckney—worked closely with the women reformers and continued to promote the feminine values that lay behind the court. In particular, the judges emphasized the importance of the family in the nurturing of children and often echoed maternalist arguments in their pronouncements.

Tuthill, the first juvenile court judge, had worked closely with the women reformers before the juvenile court legislation was secured and continued to do so during his term as juvenile court judge. He was a keen exponent of the juvenile court ideal both in his work as a judge and in his attempts to publicize that work. He was happy to acknowledge the court's indebtedness to the work of the women reformers and was clearly influenced by them in his treatment of the children who came before him. Tuthill transposed the women's emphasis on the parenthood of the state and the importance of maternal values in the treatment of wayward children into a declaration that the juvenile court should act in a fatherly manner: "I have always felt and endeavoured to act in each case as I would were it my own son that was before me in my library at home charged with some misconduct. I know of no more helpful principle to be guided by in dealing with this class of cases than that embodied in the Golden Rule, modified so as to read, 'Do unto this child as you would wish to have another in your place do unto yours.' "[33]

31. Letter from Mrs. Lucy Flower, May 1917, vol. 2, Bowen Papers; Frank and Jerome, *Annals of the Chicago Woman's Club*, 181.

32. Bowen, "The Early Days of the Juvenile Court," 307–8; minute book, Friday, May 3, 1903, supplement 1, folder 20, JPA Papers; "The Juvenile Court Loses Judge Mack," *Charities and the Commons* 18 (July 13, 1907): 416–17.

33. Richard S. Tuthill, "History of the Children's Court in Chicago," in Samuel J. Barrows,

Tuthill's approach was not, however, the kind of activist fatherhood and masculinity Judge Lindsey of Denver proposed. Judge Tuthill seems to been influenced more by the prevailing attitudes toward childhood, which suggested that children be protected and nurtured, than by ideas about boyhood suggesting that juvenile delinquency was the result of weakness in character and a lack of strong male role models. Tuthill stressed that children before the court should be treated as children and not as adults or criminals. Thus, no child under sixteen should be considered a criminal nor be arrested, indicted, convicted, imprisoned, or punished as one. Although he recognized that some children may commit acts that in an adult would be criminal, the Juvenile Court Law provided that a child in his early life should not be branded as such nor brought into contact with vicious or criminal adults. The object of the court was consequently to exercise the parental care that all parents should give to their own children.[34] Like many of the women reformers, Judge Tuthill saw the children who appeared in the juvenile court as victims of city life and parental neglect. He was not as enthusiastic as the women of Hull House in believing that probation could do much toward improving a child's environment and thus his chances in life, for he felt in many cases that the child should be taken out of a detrimental situation. Yet he was a firm believer in probation for first offenders.[35]

Judge Tuthill was replaced as juvenile court judge in the spring of 1904 by Julian Mack. Judge Mack came from a Jewish background, had been educated at Harvard Law School, and had later spent time at universities in Germany. In 1890 he joined the Chicago firm of Julius Rosenwald, which was made up of well-respected Jewish lawyers. He was not prominently involved in working with children until he became juvenile court judge in 1904, but he had been closely associated with the women of Hull House for some time.[36] Once appointed juvenile court judge, he promoted its cause with enthusiasm. He was, moreover, a noted legal scholar and one of the

---

ed., *Children's Courts in the United States: Their Origin, Development and Results* (Washington, D.C., 1904), 1–6.

34. Tuthill, "History of the Children's Court in Chicago," 1–6; Tuthill, "The Juvenile Court in Cook County," 10–16; Richard S. Tuthill, "Discussion," *Proceedings of the Illinois Conference of Charities* (1900), 28–29.

35. Richard S. Tuthill, "Chicago Juvenile Court," *Juvenile Court Record* 4 (August 1903): 6–7; Richard S. Tuthill, "Address," *Proceedings of the Annual Congress of the National Prison Association* (1902), 115–24.

36. Harry Barnard, *The Forging of an American Jew: The Life and Times of Judge Julian W. Mack* (New York, 1974).

founding editors of the *Harvard Law Review*. In fact, it was Mack who particularly emphasized the legal antecedents of the juvenile court by tracing its origins to the chancery procedure of English courts and the doctrine of *parens patriae*, which recognized the state as the ultimate parent of all children and therefore as responsible for their welfare.[37]

In many respects the doctrine of *parens patriae* was very similar to the idea of universal motherhood espoused by the women reformers. It was, though, framed in legal language, as befitted a male lawyer, rather than in gendered language. Nevertheless, in arguing that the state should be concerned with the welfare of the child, Mack used terms very reminiscent of maternalist discourse: "the state, as the greater parent of all of the children within its border, must deal with the child as the wise, the kind, the just but the merciful parent would deal with his own child, must abandon the idea that for every petty offense the great authority of the state must be vindicated, and its punishment visited upon the minor."[38] In arguing that the court should look into the background of the child, Mack was very clearly echoing the women reformers: "Why isn't it the duty of the state instead of asking merely whether a boy or girl has committed a specific offense, to find out what he is, physically, mentally, morally and then, if it learns that he is treading the path that leads to criminality, to take him in charge, not so much to punish as to reform, not to degrade but to uplift, not to crush but to develop, not to make him a criminal but a worthy citizen."[39] He also noted that some acts for which children were brought before the court were little more than childish pranks and should be treated as such: "Don't let's forget that boys will be boys and don't let's term them delinquents because of mere mischief."[40]

Judge Mack was also concerned with developing the procedures of the juvenile court itself, which he believed should be much less formal than those of adult courts. Moreover, he felt that though the child should be impressed by the authority of the court, he should also feel the state's friendly interest in him. Similarly, the child's parents needed to be shown that the object of the court was to help them train the child to do right and, wherever possi-

---

37. Julian W. Mack, "The Juvenile Court," *Harvard Law Review* 23 (1909): 104–22; Julian W. Mack, "The Law and the Child," *Survey* 23 (February 5, 1910): 638–43.

38. Julian W. Mack, "The Juvenile Court, the Judge and the Probation Officer," *Proceedings of the National Conference of Charities and Correction* (1906), 123; Julian W. Mack, "The Juvenile Court as a Legal Institution," in Hastings H. Hart, ed., *Preventive Treatment of Neglected Children* (New York, 1910), 297; Mack, "The Law and the Child," 638–40.

39. Mack, "The Juvenile Court as a Legal Institution," 297.

40. Mack, "The Juvenile Court, the Judge and the Probation Officer," 131.

ble, to keep the family together, if necessary with the aid of public or private assistance. Mack recognized that, because of this approach, the success of the treatment of delinquent children was very much dependent on the personalities of both the judge and the probation officers.[41]

What concerned him most, however, was that the court investigate closely the circumstances of each child brought before it and consider not only the offense with which he was charged but also the reasons behind the offense. Furthermore, he noted that the court should not be seen as a panacea for all the evils of childhood; its function was purely curative, and judges and reformers should therefore look beyond the court to preventive measures and to efforts that would alleviate the conditions leading to delinquency. The court could only deal with the child once he had gone wrong, but efforts should be made to prevent him from going wrong in the first place. It was not, therefore, merely an instrument of social control; its function was more complex, for the main purpose was to keep working-class families together by improving the conditions in which they lived—not to split them up. Yet the court also aimed, if necessary through the interference of a probation officer, to ensure that these families conformed to middle-class ideas about the family. As Mack noted "we are not doing our duty to the children of today, the men and women of tomorrow, when we neglect to destroy the evils that are leading to careers of delinquency, when we fail not merely to uproot the wrong, but to implant in place of it the positive good."[42]

Julian Mack, in his three years as juvenile court judge of Chicago, had a profound impact on the institution. He helped to develop many procedures of the court and to ensure its aims were carried out. He worked closely with the women reformers on the Juvenile Court Committee, especially Miss Lathrop, to make sure that the court and its probation system ran smoothly and fulfilled their functions. The relationship between Judge Mack and the women reformers seems to have been a symbiotic one. As judge of the juvenile court, Mack clearly was in a position to exercise considerable power over the direction in which the court developed. Nonetheless, he was dependent on the supporters of the court, especially the women reformers, to

41. Mack, "The Juvenile Court as a Legal Institution," 297–312; Julian W. Mack, "Juvenile Courts as Part of the School System of the Country," *Proceedings of the National Conference of Charities and Correction* (1908), 372–80.

42. Mack, "The Law and the Child," 642; Julian W. Mack, "The Juvenile Court," *Juvenile Court Record* 9 (February 1908): 8–9. On social control and the juvenile courts, see Platt, *The Child Savers.*

provide and fund the probation service, which he recognized as an essential part of the juvenile justice system. He absorbed the ideas of the women reformers, incorporating their emphasis on the family as an important bulwark of society, the need to treat children as children, and the judge's responsibility to do all in his power to enable them to grow up to be good citizens. Similarly, the women reformers continued to play an important role in supporting the administration of the court and its probation service, although they were dependent on a juvenile court judge sympathetic to their views to ensure that the court continued to reflect their concerns.[43] Thus, the Chicago court, like the wider juvenile court movement, was an area where male and female reformers cooperated to achieve common aims.

Judge Mack was succeeded, after a brief period in which Richard Tuthill again served as juvenile court judge, by Merritt W. Pinckney. Judge Pinckney, like his predecessors, was a committed supporter of the juvenile court, though he does not appear to have been involved before he became juvenile court judge. He noted the importance of both the court and probation in their role as a benevolent parent toward the child in trouble. The juvenile court, he observed, "stands in relation to the children not as a power, demanding vindication or reparation, but as a sorrowing parent anxious to find out and remove all the causes of delinquency and to reform the child."[44] Like Judge Mack and a number of the women reformers, Judge Pinckney began to look beyond the juvenile court to the causes of delinquency. In many cases he believed that the relationship between the children and their parents was to blame, and he argued that the respect felt by children for their parents had decayed. Yet he also pointed out that in 70 percent of the cases of delinquent children in Chicago, the direct cause of their delinquency was parental neglect and incompetence. Moreover, he noted, many of these children were physically unhealthy and mentally weak. He concluded that it was necessary to study and eradicate the influences leading to delinquency and dependency, and that preventive work

43. Such a relationship between male and female reformers is suggested in Kathryn Kish Sklar, "Hull House in the 1890s: A Community of Women Reformers," *Signs* 10 (Summer 1985): 658–77, and to an extent in Linda Gordon, "Social Insurance and Public Assistance: The Influence of Gender in Welfare Thought in the United States, 1890–1935," *American Historical Review* 97 (February 1992): 19–54. Maureen A. Flanagan, "Gender and Urban Political Reform: The City Club and the Woman's City Club of Chicago in the Progressive Era," *American Historical Review* 95 (October 1990): 1032–50, suggests a less cooperative relationship between male and female reformers.

44. Merritt W. Pinckney, "Testimony of Judge Merritt W. Pinckney," in Sophonisba Breckinridge and Edith Abbott, *The Delinquent Child and the Home* (New York, 1912), 205.

should go hand in hand with curative efforts, with the stress always on prevention.[45]

During its first decade, the judges of the Chicago Juvenile Court acted within the spirit of the Juvenile Court Law as advocated by women reformers during the 1890s. They absorbed and made their own those attitudes toward childhood that had prompted the women of Chicago to advocate a change in the justice system's treatment of children. As the juvenile court developed, the judges emphasized less its curative aspects and the idea that the court was a panacea for childhood evils and began to stress the need for more preventive work. Whereas they believed that the court itself was a preventive agency insofar as it kept children from slipping further into a life of crime and pauperism, Judge Mack and later Judge Pinckney began to realize that the court itself could only act on children who were already in trouble. What was needed were measures to prevent them from ever getting there.

The women of the Juvenile Court Committee had reached this conclusion already and had begun working—both individually (through probation) and on a more general basis—to improve the environment of the children who were coming before the juvenile court. To this end several women, most based at Hull House, had begun extensive surveys of the causes of juvenile delinquency. Drawing on their training in the social sciences and their experience living in a slum neighborhood, these surveys were much more scientific than earlier observations and reflected the growth of the social work profession in Chicago and the continuing participation of the settlements in juvenile court work. The surveys had a practical purpose beyond analyzing the causes of juvenile delinquency, for they demanded action on the findings.[46] They also indicated the emergence of a new discourse among these women—one based on science rather than gender. Their college educations had taught them that science could be used to both explain and im-

45. Merritt W. Pinckney, "The Juvenile Court," in Sophonisba Breckinridge, ed., *The Child in the City: A Series of Papers Presented at the Conference Held During the Chicago Child Welfare Exhibit* (Chicago, 1912), 315–26; Merritt W. Pinckney, "The Funds to Parents Act and How to Prevent Delinquency," *The Welfare of Children* (Chicago, 1912), 35–37, pamphlet, folder 299, Hull House Association Papers, Special Collections, University of Illinois at Chicago.

46. See, for instance, Breckinridge and Abbott, *The Delinquent Child and the Home*. Kathryn Kish Sklar, "*Hull House Maps and Papers*: Social Science as Women's Work in the 1890s," in Martin Bulmer, Kevin Bales, and Kathryn Kish Sklar, eds., *The Social Survey in Historical Perspective, 1880–1940* (Cambridge, Eng., 1991), 111–47, discusses the purpose of an earlier social survey centered on Hull House. Ladd-Taylor, *Mother-Work*, 74–103, discusses the social science tradition among women reformers.

prove their world. The use of a scientific discourse could therefore justify their involvement in reform in still more powerful terms than the maternalist discourse.

The organization that undertook much of the work aimed at preventing juvenile delinquency was the Juvenile Protective Association. It was formed in 1907 from the Juvenile Court Committee, which had existed primarily to raise funds for probation officers and the detention home. This was no longer necessary after 1907, with the passing of both a law providing for the payment by the county of probation officers' salaries and a county merit law. Women reformers had long been concerned that until a merit law providing for the civil service examination of all probation officers was secured, the payment of a salary to holders of these positions would place them in danger of becoming political appointments. The county's subsequent assumption of the salaries of probation officers, the building of a new juvenile court building, which included a detention home within it, and the provision of funds to run the home made the Juvenile Court Committee's role as a fund raiser for the juvenile court redundant. The members of the committee had agitated for the passing of the merit law and the assumption by the county of the costs of the juvenile court, so it was with a sense of major achievement that they turned their attention to other matters.[47]

The chairman of the Juvenile Court Committee and later of the Juvenile Protective Association was Louise Hadduck deKoven Bowen. Mrs. Bowen played a large part in promoting the aims of the association to protect Chicago's youth and prevent them from becoming delinquent. Louise Hadduck deKoven was born on February 26, 1859, in Chicago, the daughter and only child of Helen and John deKoven. Her father was a successful banker, and her grandfather, Edward Hiram Hadduck, had built a large fortune through investments in land. She grew up conscious of her family's great wealth and was taught from an early age the responsibilities that came with it. As a girl she enjoyed the privileges of Chicago's elite and attended the prestigious Dearborn Seminary. In June 1886, Louise deKoven married Joseph Bowen, a banker, and between 1887 and 1893 the couple had four children, whom Mrs. Bowen spent much of her early married life raising. In 1893, Jane Addams asked Louise Bowen to help with the fledgling Hull

47. Louise deKoven Bowen, "Talk to Probation Officers, Cook County Juvenile Court," (1908), in *Speeches, Addresses and Letters of Louise deKoven Bowen*, 117–18; Louise deKoven Bowen, *Growing Up with a City* (New York, 1926), 106–15. Despite the merit law, the probation service did not entirely escape the problems of political influence, "Probation and Politics," *Survey* 27 (March 30, 1912): 2003–14.

House Women's Club, which she agreed to do. From that time onward, she maintained close connections with Hull House, becoming in 1903 a trustee of the settlement and in 1907 its treasurer. She was also an important benefactor.[48] As a prominent member of the Chicago Woman's Club, she had served as its president and later became chairman of its committee on probation work in the juvenile court, which later was formalized as the Juvenile Court Committee. She was involved in many reform activities in both Chicago and the national arena, often in close association with members of the Hull House community. Interestingly, she had not been involved in the agitation for the Juvenile Court Law in 1899, despite her close connection with both Hull House and the Chicago Woman's Club and her later association with the court. This was probably because she was busy with family matters.[49]

The Juvenile Protective Association was formed out of the Juvenile Court Committee and a smaller agency, the Juvenile Protective League. The Juvenile Protective League had been formed in 1905 by Judge Mack, Hastings H. Hart, and Miss Minnie Low. Its aims (which became essentially those of the Juvenile Protective Association) were largely to protect children and to prevent delinquency in congested areas of the city. It sought to do so through an educational campaign informing parents and other adults of their responsibilities toward children and of the laws regarding minors. It also investigated and sometimes prosecuted persons who demoralized children and who encouraged or permitted unwholesome conditions to exist.[50]

Both the Juvenile Court Committee and the Juvenile Protective League had been important support agencies of the juvenile court: the former had been involved in fund-raising to pay the salaries of probation officers, and the latter was formed and staffed by officials of the juvenile court. Although it worked in close association with the court, the Juvenile Protective Association was an independent body. Its was dominated by women and had close associations with Hull House, with the two groups often sharing personnel and cooperating on projects. The association was composed mainly of volunteers, though it did have several paid staff, and it aimed to support the ju-

48. Sklar, "Who Funded Hull House?" 94–115.
49. Biographical details are from Edward T. James, Janet Wilson James, and Paul S. Boyer, *Notable American Women, 1607–1950: A Biographical Dictionary,* 4 vols. (Cambridge, Mass., 1971), 4:99–101, and Louise deKoven Bowen, *Growing Up with a City.*
50. Bowen, "The Early Days of the Juvenile Court," 308; Minnie F. Low, "The Juvenile Protective League," *Juvenile Court Record* 7 (March 1906): 3–4; Minnie F. Low, "Chicago Juvenile Protective League," *Charities and the Commons* 18 (June 8, 1907): 300–302.

venile court by investigating the causes of delinquency and by pursuing various measures to prevent children from getting into trouble.

The Juvenile Protective Association was a less overtly maternalist agency than the Chicago Woman's Club or the Juvenile Court Committee. Indeed, it marks a shift away from the dominance of the traditional maternalist construction of their role by the women involved in establishing and developing the juvenile court. This was in large part because many of the women involved with the Juvenile Protective Association came out of the social science tradition of the settlement houses, which stressed a more scientific approach and rejected the more sentimental view of motherhood held by the traditional maternalists. The Juvenile Protective Association utilized social science methods to investigate the factors that led to juvenile delinquency, looking not just at the child's home but also at the wider social environment in which he lived. The language they used to demand the reforms their investigations convinced them were necessary was, though still gendered, now framed in the discourse of social science rather than that of –maternalism.[51]

Through close observation of the children who came before the juvenile court, Mrs. Bowen and her colleagues concluded that although the court could do much to help the child before it, the more important work lay in preventing the child from ever getting into trouble. They feared that as long as the city offered temptations, children would continue to appear before the court. For while reformers had been busy agitating for and establishing institutions to care for the delinquent child, little attention had been paid to the process by which the delinquents were produced. This was the work the Juvenile Protective Association took on, gearing their efforts toward "endeavoring to get at the child before he goes down, to influence his parents, to raise the standards of the home, to do away with demoralizing conditions, and to try and keep the child away from committing the crimes and misdemeanors which take him into the courts."[52]

For this purpose, the Juvenile Protective Association divided the city into fourteen districts and assigned each a paid officer whose duties were to prevent, among other things, cocaine dealing; to keep children out of disreputable dance halls and houses; and to try in every possible way to safeguard and protect the children. Each of these districts also had a local league of

51. See, for instance, Breckinridge and Abbott, *The Delinquent Child and the Home,* and Louise deKoven Bowen, "How to Prevent Delinquency," *The Welfare of Children,* 3–20.
52. Bowen, "How to Prevent Delinquency," 3–4.

concerned citizens who were expected to get to know their neighborhood, identify the problem areas, and determine what constructive work could be done. The association also sought to persuade dance hall managers not to sell liquor to children and to have chaperons present to safeguard the morals of the young people who attended their establishments.

The Juvenile Protective Association had another function apart from this protective work: it sought to understand the reasons for delinquency. Mrs. Bowen noted that most children go wrong because they are in search of pleasure, as was shown by the records of the juvenile court. The reasons behind this depended on the sex of the child. The average boy offender went onto the street because his home was small and he wanted action. He stood on the street corner and eventually joined a gang. Then, just for fun, he got into trouble with the police. The average girl, on the other hand, went out because the home was uncomfortable and she did not want to see her boyfriends in the presence of her family. Business enterprise had taken advantage of this desire for pleasure on the part of young people, and commercial undertakings had sprung up everywhere, often endangering the morals of children. The association therefore urged the city to establish a recreation commission to supervise all commercial amusements, since recreation, if properly organized, could act as an antidote to delinquency. Association members believed the city should provide more parks, playgrounds, swimming pools, athletic fields, and gymnasiums to draw children away from the streets and the temptations they offered. The Juvenile Protective Association sought to prevent juvenile misbehavior through the provision of sport and other recreational facilities; like the various boys' clubs, the Boy Scouts, and the Young Men's Christian Association, the Juvenile Protective Association sought to direct children's energies into what were considered to be constructive rather than harmful activities.[53] The association thus spent much of its time lobbying for the provision of recreational outlets and providing the funds for these facilities. It also conducted surveys to test the efficacy of its solutions.[54]

Mrs. Bowen made other observations about the children who came before the juvenile court. Her comments reflected her own middle-class atti-

53. See, for instance, David I. Macleod, *Building Character in the American Boy: The Boy Scouts, YMCA and Their Forerunners, 1870–1920* (Madison, Wis., 1983); Joseph F. Kett, *Rites of Passage: Adolescence in America, 1790 to the Present* (New York, 1977); David Nasaw, *Children of the City: At Work and at Play* (New York, 1985).
54. Bowen, "How to Prevent Delinquency," 4, 17–20; Louise deKoven Bowen, *Safeguards for City Youth at Work and at Play* (New York, 1914), 4–12.

tudes toward the nature of childhood and the notion that working-class and immigrant families were failing to guide their children toward responsible citizenship. Thus, she expressed her concern that a large number of delinquent children had foreign-born parents, many of whom did not speak English. She was not entirely unsympathetic to their plight. As she explained, the tendency to crime among such children was almost wholly the result of city life, for immigrants tended to live in the most crowded and insanitary parts of the city, where the conditions taught a disregard for the laws and where the family was under constant pecuniary pressure. Children felt separated from their parents because the children could more easily adapt to American life and learn English. As a result, they began to feel superior to their parents, and parental discipline broke down. Furthermore, many immigrant parents were ignorant of the law and so flouted such measures as the compulsory education law and the child labor laws. The association saw it as a duty to work with these immigrant families to prevent this perceived breakdown in family life and make immigrant parents aware of American laws to protect their children.[55]

Like many of the other juvenile court reformers, both in Chicago and the rest of the United States, Mrs. Bowen reflected a degree of ambivalence in her motives for undertaking this work. Although her analysis of what prompted juvenile delinquency was more sophisticated than that of the early juvenile court reformers, she too seems to have been prompted by a fear that family life in the slums of Chicago was in danger of breaking down. Consequently, she believed that if nothing were done to improve the conditions of life for the children in the poorer sections of the city, society would suffer from an increase in the number of hardened criminals when these children became adults. Nevertheless, the work of the Juvenile Protective Association shows a considerable degree of understanding of what life was like for children in the slums of Chicago and an optimistic belief that given the chance, these children would grow up to be good citizens. Reformers thus sought to introduce more adult supervision into the lives of children who seemed to lack it, just as they would provide supervision for their own children.[56] The work of the Juvenile Protective Association

55. Bowen, *Safeguards for City Youth*, 160–65.
56. Barbara Finkelstein, "Casting Networks of Good Influence: The Reconstruction of Childhood in the United States, 1790–1870," in Joseph M. Hawes and N. Ray Hiner, eds., *American Childhood: A Research Guide and Historical Handbook* (Westport, Conn., 1985), 111–52; Macleod, *Building Character in the American Boy;* Kathy Peiss, *Cheap Amusements: Working Women and Leisure in Turn-of-the-Century New York* (Philadelphia, 1986), 163–84.

should, in consequence, be seen as a continuation and development of those concerns that had prompted the women reformers who had lobbied for the Juvenile Court Law—a desire to protect family life in the slums and ensure that children grow up according to prevailing ideas about childhood.

The Juvenile Protective Association worked closely with the Hull House community, cooperating on projects and sharing personnel. Indeed, the work the two agencies performed in connection with juvenile delinquency was often indistinguishable. Much of this work was of an immediate, practical nature, but some was more academic and analytical. Drawing on the female social science tradition of the settlement houses, and clearly influenced by earlier work on the social survey *Hull House Maps and Papers* (1894), a number of these reformers produced books and reports attempting to analyze the causes of juvenile delinquency. Louise Bowen's work, *Safeguards for City Youth at Work and at Play* (1914), should be included among these, but the writings of some of the settlement house workers reveal a greater depth of analysis and understanding than that shown by Mrs. Bowen, who had neither college training in social science methods nor experience living and working in a slum neighborhood. Her analysis therefore lacked the experience and sophistication of the professional maternalists. The study that most clearly illustrates this higher level of understanding is that by Edith Abbott and Sophonisba Breckinridge, *The Delinquent Child and the Home* (1912), but Jane Addams's *The Spirit of Youth and the City Streets* (1909) also reveals a sympathetic insight into the reasons many children appeared before the juvenile court.[57]

Like Mrs. Bowen, Jane Addams argued that many of the problems of youth could be traced to the failure by the city to provide any legitimate outlets for their desire for recreation and adventure. Instead, commercial entertainments had been allowed to supply this need. They provided little more than lures into vice and degradation, offered by men and women who had no thought for youths apart from what money could be made out of them. Moreover, the city seemed totally blind to the needs of young people and constantly failed in its duty toward them. The result was that sometimes a mere spirit of adventure or a desire to escape the confines of city life could lead a young person into crime. As she wrote, "The young people are overborne by their own undirected and misguided energies. A mere temperamental outbreak in a brief period of obstreperousness exposes a promising boy to arrest and imprisonment, an accidental combination of

57. Bowen, *Safeguards for City Youth*. On earlier social surveys, see Sklar, "*Hull House Maps and Papers*," 111–47.

circumstances too complicated and overwhelming to be coped with by an immature mind, condemns a growing lad to a criminal career."[58] Many of the offenses for which children were brought before the court could be attributed to this desire for excitement.

Jane Addams also suggested that juvenile delinquency could result from the difficulties experienced by immigrant families adjusting to city life and American ways. One symptom of this was a growing generation gap between foreign-born parents and their Americanized children. Addams observed, too, the breakdown of traditional family practices under the pressure of city life—for example, the chaperonage of daughters, which often became merely restrictive in the American city. Whereas she recognized that there was much worth preserving in immigrant culture, the restrictive codes of behavior imposed by some immigrant parents on their children could lead these young people into crime. In some cases, the parents were degenerate and, especially in families where the mother was dissolute, the children never had the opportunities of an innocent childhood.[59]

Jane Addams revealed an understanding and sympathy for young people and a realization of why so many of them came to grief that was lacking among some of the other reformers, but she too was influenced by her middle-class background and the attitudes this produced. For, although she professed to understand the youth of the slums, she was at times less sympathetic toward their parents and other adults in the slums. While offering few concrete solutions to the problem of youth in the city, she concluded that it was the responsibility of the city and of all adults to recognize the special nature of youth and to provide legitimate outlets for their need for excitement and idealism.[60] If this were not done, the misdirected energies of youth would result in crime. As she concluded, "We may either smother the divine fire of youth or we may feed it. We may either stand stupidly staring as it sinks into a murky fire of crime and flares into the intermittent blaze of

58. Addams, *The Spirit of Youth*, 51–52.

59. On family life in the congested areas of Chicago, see Addams, *The Spirit of Youth*, chap. 2, and *Twenty Years at Hull House*, 169–85.

60. Much of this also reflects the ideas of the psychologist G. Stanley Hall on the nature of childhood and adolescence and his theory that adolescence could be a criminal age. As Hall noted, "As the social demand for a larger mutual helpfulness increases, prohibitions multiply. Hence the increase of juvenile crime, so deplored, is not entirely due to city life or growing youthful depravity, but also to the increasing ethical demands of society." G. Stanley Hall, *Adolescence: Its Psychology and Its Relations to Physiology, Anthropology, Sociology, Sex, Crime, Religion and Education*, 2 vols. (reprint, 1922; first published, 1904), 1:405.

folly or we may tend it into a lambent flame with power to make clean and bright our dingy city streets."[61]

Where Jane Addams's panegyric to city youth was often highly romanticized and offered no concrete plan of action, two of her associates at Hull House, Sophonisba Breckinridge and Edith Abbott, produced a more prosaic, but also more scientific, study of the causes of delinquency.[62] While a number of settlement workers explored the reasons for the large numbers of offenses committed by young people, Breckinridge and Abbott concentrated on the home influences on children in their first study, *The Delinquent Child and the Home.*[63] This focus on the home clearly maintained the expectation that women's sphere was the home—an expectation women social scientists continued to recognize.

Breckinridge and Abbott concluded that the delinquent child was the victim of his environment—whether this be a poor, degraded, crowded, or immigrant home—and also the victim of neglect: "we believe that the delinquent child appears in this study as likewise a neglected child—neglected by the home, by the school, and by the community."[64] It was up to the community to lift the child out of the neglect that left him open to the dangers of crime. The juvenile court was the instrument through which the community attempted to direct and supervise the care of the delinquent child, and this largely depended on the conditions in the child's home and neighborhood. Thus, competent parents should be given all possible aid to help in the efficient performance of their parental duties, and inefficient parents should be supervised, though in the case of degraded parents, no concessions should be made. The study finally concluded that the only way of curing delinquency was to prevent it, and the only way to do this was to remove the conditions in which delinquency arose.

These studies and the work of the juvenile court reflect the belief by those

61. Addams, *The Spirit of Youth,* 161–62.

62. Both Sophonisba Breckinridge and Edith Abbott were, at various times, residents of Hull House, and when not actually living there, maintained close contact. They also had close contacts with the Chicago School of Civics and Philanthropy—a training school for social workers that later became part of the University of Chicago. Both women had academic careers in the social sciences and were employed at various times on the faculty of the University of Chicago. Lela Costin, *Two Sisters for Social Justice: A Biography of Grace and Edith Abbott* (Urbana, 1983); Ellen Fitzpatrick, *Endless Crusade: Women Social Scientists and Progressive Reform* (New York, 1990).

63. They also collaborated on another study focused on problem children in Chicago: *Truancy and Non-Attendance in the Chicago Schools* (Chicago, 1917).

64. Breckinridge and Abbott, *The Delinquent Child and the Home,* 170.

concerned with the problem of child life in Chicago that the child could not be held responsible for his actions. Rather, he was the victim of his environment and circumstances and often of poor parenting as well. An expression of the prevailing ideas about childhood that had prompted agitation for the Juvenile Court Law, these theories went beyond those earlier ideas to the belief that not only should the child not be punished for offenses that in an adult would be crimes, but it was the positive duty of the state to prevent the circumstances that led a child to commit these offenses.

By 1911, the year an exhibition was held in Chicago to show what had been accomplished for children in that city and what still needed to be done, the juvenile court of Chicago had been operating formally for twelve years. It had succeeded in achieving much more than its creators had hoped when it first opened and had become one of several institutions helping with the problems of children growing up in the city. These institutions were the outgrowth both of the desire to make the state responsible for the welfare of wayward children and of the realization that the juvenile court was not a panacea for the ills of childhood. The new institutions included a municipal court that dealt with matters concerning domestic relations; a well-developed probation system with paid probation officers; a juvenile court building, which included a detention home; and a clinic where children could be examined for any physical defects that might have contributed to their delinquency.

In 1909 the Juvenile Psychopathic Institute had been established, after considerable agitation by Julia Lathrop. Miss Lathrop became its president and the psychologist William A. Healy, its director. The institution aimed to look at every aspect of the children who were referred to it by the juvenile court—particularly the influences on the formation of their character and conduct—and took these influences into consideration in establishing what treatment was required. It marked a move away from the belief that environment alone was responsible for a child's behavior and undertook a more scientific study of the physical and mental makeup of the individual child.[65] It also suggested that some of those reformers involved with the juvenile

65. Folder, Juvenile Psychopathic Institute, 1910–12, Julia Lathrop Papers, Rockford College Archives, Rockford, Illinois; Jane Addams, *My Friend Julia Lathrop* (New York, 1935), 140–41; draft of *My Friend Julia Lathrop*, 130–31, reel 30, Jane Addams Papers, microfilm; Joseph M. Hawes, *Children in Urban Society: Juvenile Delinquency in Nineteenth-Century America* (New York, 1971), 249–58. William A. Healy produced a study from his work at the Juvenile Psychopathic Institute: Healy, *The Individual Delinquent: A Textbook of Diagnosis and Prognosis for All Concerned in Understanding Offenders* (Boston, 1915).

court were placing more emphasis on a scientific study of the causes of delinquency rather than assuming that family breakdown and an inability to adapt to city life were the only causes.

In many senses, 1911 marked a watershed in the history of the juvenile court in Chicago. It not only saw the holding of an exhibition on the welfare of the child that celebrated the work of the court, but it was also the first year in which the court came under severe attack from its critics. Perhaps the more serious assault was one that sought to replace the chief probation officer with a political appointee by overriding civil service procedures. This threatened the independence of the probation service and its ability to appoint suitably qualified people rather than political placeman as probation officers—a fear that had exercised juvenile court reformers from the early stages of the court. This attack suggested that even the implementation of civil service procedures for the appointment of probation officers had not prevented misuse of the positions. Although the situation was eventually resolved, it highlighted the problems of political interference in an institution like the juvenile court.[66]

In 1911 the juvenile court was under concerted attack by its critics, for not only did it become the target of political place seekers, but it was also condemned for not doing its job properly. Such assaults were contradictory. On the one hand, the probation service was criticized for not maintaining close enough supervision over those children placed in institutions—a matter that was actually not part of the probation service's jurisdiction. On the other hand, its critics charged that children were taken from their parents without regard to due processes and, moreover, that probation officers snooped around families and waited for mothers to neglect their children so they could be removed from their homes.[67] These criticisms were to recur constantly over the next few decades, but it was not until the 1967 Supreme Court decision *In Re Gault,* in which the juvenile court system was deemed to violate constitutional guarantees of due process, that the court's critics achieved any notable success.

By 1911, however, the Chicago Juvenile Court was well able to withstand attacks from its critics. Defenders from the wider reform community both

66. "Probation and Politics," 2003–14; "Social Forces," *Survey* 27 (March 30, 1912): 1989–90.

67. "Probation and Politics," 2003–14; typescript of address entitled "Crimes Against Children Under the Juvenile Law," report of speech given by W. H. Dunn; address given in Champaign, Illinois, by W. H. Dunn, October [1911?] and various newspaper clippings, box 29, folder 9, Illinois Children's Home and Aid Society Papers, Special Collections, University of Illinois at Chicago.

within Chicago and across the United States rallied to its defense, and the attack was repulsed. The Chicago court still remained one of the pioneers in developing a means of addressing the question of how to deal with problem children. The juvenile court judges and a number of other juvenile court reformers had also become interested in discovering the causes of delinquency, and increasingly they were concerned with finding means of preventing children from ever coming before the court, rather than focusing on treating those children already in trouble. This aim was reflected in the work of the support agencies. By 1911, for instance, the interests of the Juvenile Protective Association had switched to preventive work and to fundraising for the Juvenile Psychopathic Institute. Similarly, Juvenile Court Judge Merritt Pinckney was actively lobbying for a mothers' pension law, which many regarded as a preventive measure. This emphasis was reproduced in the wider community of juvenile court reformers, where preventive work, particularly by the schools and local communities, and campaigns for mothers' pensions became the new focus of attention.[68]

The Chicago Juvenile Court had resulted largely from agitation by women reformers who had framed their demands in the discourse of maternalism. Considerations regarded by society as predominantly female had therefore shaped the court, and continued to do so during the first decade of its existence. As the juvenile court and probation system became more firmly established, however, women acting as reformers became less visible in the development of these institutions. Nonetheless, as court officials and experts, they continued to be involved in court operations. These tended to be professional maternalists based in settlement houses or possessing a background in the social sciences, rather than traditional maternalists. Still, women acting first as probation officers and later as juvenile court judges justified this in terms of women's special qualities. A decade after the establishment of the juvenile court, there was a growing insistence, undoubtedly reinforced by the crisis over political appointees in the probation service, that probation officers be college-trained professionals. The discourse of professionalism and expertise gradually came to dominate in the juvenile court and to replace that of traditional maternalism. It was articulated as

68. See, for instance, Thomas D. Eliot, "The Trend of the Juvenile Court," *Annals of the American Academy of Political and Social Science* 52 (1914): 149–58; Thomas D. Eliot, *The Juvenile Court and the Community* (New York, 1914); Herbert W. Baker, "The Court and the Delinquent Child," *American Journal of Sociology* 26 (September 1920): 176–86; Theda Skocpol, *Protecting Soldiers and Mothers: The Political Origins of Social Policy in the United States* (Cambridge, Mass., 1992); Linda Gordon, *Pitied But Not Entitled: Single Mothers and the History of Welfare, 1890–1935* (Cambridge, Mass., 1994).

often by women as by men. Moreover, many of these female professionals continued to maintain a close association with the settlements, often using settlement houses as a base for their work.[69]

If women as reformers were no longer as visible in the operation of the juvenile court by the end of the first decade of the twentieth century, they continued to be prominent in promoting the idea of the juvenile court and in suggesting that the court was not a panacea for all childhood evils but only a beginning solution. A number of women reformers undertook surveys to ascertain the causes of juvenile delinquency, and this led them to demand further reforms: the protection of young people in places of entertainment, mothers' pension laws, and child labor laws. Thus, although by the end of its first ten years the Chicago Juvenile Court was starting to move away from some of the considerations that had motivated its initiators, it remained an embodiment of the belief that the family was the bulwark of society and therefore should be protected and aided in its functions—an idea that, although accepted by the male juvenile court judges, was essentially a female ideal.

69. On this question, see Paula Baker, "The Domestication of Politics: Women and American Political Society, 1780–1920," *American Historical Review* 89 (1984): 620–47; Robyn Muncy, *Creating a Female Dominion in American Reform, 1890–1935* (New York, 1991); Judith A. Trolander, *Professionalism and Social Change: From the Settlement House Movement to Neighborhood Centers, 1866 to the Present* (New York, 1987); Roy Lubove, *The Professional Altruist: The Emergence of Social Work as a Career, 1880–1930* (Cambridge, Mass., 1965).

Conclusion

If the success of a movement may be judged by the extent to which its legislative aims were adopted, then the juvenile court movement was highly successful. By 1920 juvenile court laws had been secured in all but a few states, and the idea had spread beyond the boundaries of the United States to Canada, Japan, and Europe. The juvenile court movement was concerned with more than simply the establishment of juvenile courts and a probation system in every state. It also worked to develop the juvenile court idea and its institutions, both locally and nationally. Moreover, a significant number of the reformers, both male and female, who had been involved in the juvenile court movement at its beginnings maintained their interest. Most also participated in related reform movements during the Progressive Era, helping to establish a rudimentary welfare state in the United States. Many of the same concerns that had prompted them to seek new ways of dealing with dependent and delinquent children also persuaded them of the necessity for other social welfare reforms, especially those relating to women and children. Here, as elsewhere, gender was a central consideration. On a number of levels, therefore, the juvenile court movement maintained its dynamism throughout the Progressive Era.

Yet the movement in its wider sense was not quite as successful as it first appeared. Whereas it was able to secure legislation to establish juvenile courts and probation in virtually every state, its efforts to change fundamentally the way the law dealt with dependent and delinquent children were less impressive. A number of juvenile courts were such in name only, never really shedding the methods or attitudes of the criminal courts. In addition, the juvenile court movement was not able to attain uniformity among juvenile court systems, despite its best efforts to do so. Even where it had succeeded in securing legislation that reflected the principles of the movement, the administration of the law did not always live up to its standards. Local circumstances and the priorities of individual juvenile court judges and administrators were the most important influence on how juvenile court laws operated in practice. This was just as true for the juvenile courts that attracted a great deal of public attention as for those that operated in obscurity. Similarly, it applied as much to courts pioneering new developments as it did to those that never developed beyond separate hearings for children's cases.

Since its creation, the Chicago court often led in the development of innovative methods for treating the children who came before it, but others also inaugurated new ways of dealing with wayward children. For instance, although Judge Ben Lindsey was generally not as concerned with developing institutions and ideas that addressed the causes of juvenile delinquency as, for instance, the women and judges of the Chicago Juvenile Court, he and his supporters did establish various institutions and support agencies around the juvenile court in Denver that sought to deal with juvenile offenders and to prevent juvenile delinquency. Lindsey remained concerned with the individual child and how best to overcome his weaknesses in character, which the judge believed had caused him to commit the offense. Unlike the women of Chicago, who focused on the role of the probation officer in propping up the child's home and saw in this the best way to prevent juvenile delinquency, Lindsey believed that the home was often most at fault in causing a child to err, and through the use of an Adult Contributory Delinquency Law he sought to make parents face up to their child-rearing responsibilities. Indeed, the Adult Contributory Delinquency Law was possibly Lindsey's most significant contribution to the development of the juvenile court, and the law was adopted in a number of other states. It placed responsibility for the delinquency of children firmly on their parents but also allowed juvenile courts to prosecute other adults, such as wine-room operators, saloon keepers, and employers who contributed to delinquency.[1] Lindsey's insistence on parental, especially paternal, responsibility for chil-

---

1. As outlined in a draft bill in "Report to the State Association of County Judges of Colorado," undated, box 284, folder 6, Ben B. Lindsey Papers, Manuscript Division, Library of Congress (hereafter BBL Papers). Also, "Preparing a New Code of Laws: County Judges Will Meet in Denver December Six," *Denver Republican,* clipping, December 1, 1902, box 260, folder 5, BBL Papers.

dren's behavior reflected his continuing belief in the central importance of a father's influence in child rearing.[2]

Lindsey continued to be an important publicist for the movement, both in Denver and on the national stage. He drew on his experiences in the Denver Juvenile Court to illustrate the effectiveness of his methods. Yet, though these stories captured the public imagination, his methods were not copied in other juvenile courts. Indeed, as one commentator noted in 1914, Lindsey's promotion of his own methods may have been detrimental to the wider development of the juvenile courts:

> The reform of gangs, the honor system, "snitching bees," and recreation features, though not the real heart and secret of the success of the Denver court, were made prominent in the public eye because of their possibilities of picturesqueness; and such things, rather than the sober considerations of social economy influenced the early ideals of some courts. Thinking people have grown somewhat tired of this sort of explanation. All credit is due to Judge Lindsey, however, for really valuable service in spreading ideas of the court faster than any one else did, and for his real accomplishments in Colorado.[3]

Lindsey's emphasis on the "personal touch" and the centrality of his own role in the Denver Juvenile Court obscured the fact that the court was able to function smoothly during his frequent absences from Denver. It seems likely that, as in other juvenile courts, probation officers played a much more important role in the day-to-day functioning of the Denver court than Lindsey was willing to admit.[4] Nevertheless, Lindsey does seem to have had a sympathetic understanding for the children who came before him and an ability to persuade them to overcome their weakness of character and to do right. This, however, emphasizes the uniqueness of the Denver Juvenile Court and its judge's methods.[5] In many other respects the Denver Juvenile

2. Judge Ben B. Lindsey, "The Child, the Parent and the Law," *Juvenile Court Record* 5 (May 1904): 9–10; Ben B. Lindsey, "My Experience with Boys," *Ladies Home Journal* (December 1906), box 260, folder 4, BBL Papers.

3. Thomas D. Eliot, *The Juvenile Court and the Community* (New York, 1914), 2.

4. See, for instance, letter to Charles Libby, November 8, 1903, box 86, folder 1, BBL Papers; several letters in box 3, folder 5, BBL Papers.

5. Ben B. Lindsey and Rube Borough, *The Dangerous Life* (reprint, New York, 1974; first published, 1931), 218–25; Ben B. Lindsey and Wainwright Evans, *The Revolt of Modern Youth* (New York, 1925). Some of Lindsey's critics cast doubt on the efficacy of his methods. See, for instance, *Eel Martin's Record*, republished from *Clay's Review* (June 18, 1910).

Court developed in a similar fashion to the Chicago court and was often directly influenced by it. It created a detention home, a Juvenile Improvement Association, and a probation service. Although the Denver Juvenile Improvement Association did not carry out investigations into the causes of juvenile delinquency, it did make some attempts to lobby for recreational facilities to counteract the influence of commercial amusements.[6]

Even after a decade as juvenile court judge in Denver, Lindsey had not developed a sophisticated explanation for juvenile delinquency. He still believed that weakness in character was responsible for many youthful misdemeanors, but increasingly he also blamed corrupt interests for producing the conditions in which weak children were tempted to do wrong. This new emphasis on the power of the "interests" reflected Lindsey's own entanglement in politics and his fight against political corruption in Denver. It led him to conclude that the juvenile court could only be a palliative against the problems of child life in the slums and that these problems would continue until the corrupt interests of business and politics, which debauched the homes of the city, were overcome. Lindsey's endeavors to expose corruption in Denver and to fight against what he saw as the evil grip of the interests almost cost him his position as judge. Indeed, so virulent were the attacks on Lindsey that there were occasions when the juvenile court itself was in danger of becoming a victim of the fight. For a while, Lindsey's ability to maintain the support of women voters and reform elements in Denver, as well as the endorsement of the wider reform community, ensured that both he and the Denver Juvenile Court survived.[7] In 1928, however, having alienated the churches and many of his supporters through his public support for the sexual revolution and his advocacy of what he called "companionate marriage," and having provoked the opposition of the Ku Klux Klan, Lindsey was no longer able to rally sufficient support and was ousted.[8]

6. Certificate of Association of the Juvenile Improvement Association, March 1905, box 226, folder 1, BBL Papers; "Statement About Juvenile Improvement Association," undated, box 284, folder 5, BBL Papers; Lilburn Merrill, "The Juvenile Improvement Association," *Juvenile Court Record* 6 (December 1905): 6; clipping from *American Primary Teacher* (June 1905), box 312, folder 6, BBL Papers.

7. Lindsey documents this fight in Ben B. Lindsey and Harvey J. O'Higgins, *The Beast* (reprint, Seattle, 1970; first published, 1910). W. M. Raine, "How Denver Saved Her Juvenile Court," *Arena* 41 (July 1909): 403–14; Lincoln Steffens, *The Autobiography of Lincoln Steffens,* 2 vols. (London, 1931), 2:516–20; Lincoln Steffens, *Upbuilders* (Seattle, 1968; first published, 1909), 92–243; Ben B. Lindsey, "My Lesson from the Juvenile Court," *Survey* 23 (February 5, 1910): 652–56.

8. Marjorie Hornbein, "The Story of Judge Ben Lindsey," *Southern California Quarterly* 55 (1973): 469–82. The books which outlined Lindsey's position on the sexual revolution and

By this time, however, the juvenile court movement had long since lost its momentum, and Lindsey's association with it was greatly diminished.

Many juvenile courts seem to have undergone challenges to their existence during the first decade of the twentieth century. In Denver, this was due to Lindsey's confrontation with political interests. In Chicago, attempts were made to appoint political placemen or sinecurists as probation officers as well as to challenge the authority of the juvenile courts. Other juvenile courts had their constitutionality challenged, and some of those states that established juvenile courts in the years that followed had to frame their legislation in such a way as to avoid these pitfalls.[9] It was not until 1967, however, with the Supreme Court case *In Re Gault,* that the procedures of the juvenile courts were seriously tested.[10] During much of the Progressive Era, juvenile courts and probation were widely seen by both reformers and the media as the solution to the problem of juvenile delinquency, despite continuing problems with enforcing the basic principles of the juvenile court idea in some areas.[11]

By the end of its first decade, many reformers were beginning to move beyond the development of the institutions of the juvenile court, no longer seeing it as a panacea for all the evils of childhood. Instead they had begun to look for means to prevent juvenile delinquency and thus obviate the necessity for children ever to come before the juvenile court. Studies were undertaken to discover the causes of juvenile delinquency and, while some concluded that social factors were the root cause, others deduced that physical and mental deficiencies in the individual delinquent were at fault. Consequently, many reformers, though still maintaining an interest in the juvenile court itself, began to consider how the educational system, the child's

companionate marriage were, respectively, Ben B. Lindsey and Wainwright Evans, *The Revolt of Modern Youth* (New York, 1925); and Ben B. Lindsey and Wainwright Evans, *The Companionate Marriage* (New York, 1927).

9. "Pennsylvania Law Again in Working Order," *Juvenile Record* 4 (May 1903): 5; letter to T. D. Hurley, September 20, 1902, box 84, folder 1, BBL Papers; letter from T. D. Hurley, January 3, 1903, box 1, folder 3, BBL Papers.

10. Lawrence M. Friedman, *Crime and Punishment in American History* (New York, 1993), 416–17; David J. Rothman, *Conscience and Convenience: The Asylum and Its Alternatives in Progressive America* (Boston, 1980), 205.

11. Edward Lindsey, "The Juvenile Court from a Lawyer's Standpoint," *Annals of the American Academy of Political and Social Science* 52 (1914): 140–48; Herbert W. Baker, "The Court and the Delinquent Child," *American Journal of Sociology* 26 (September 1920): 176–86; Bernard Flexner and Roger N. Baldwin, *Juvenile Courts and Probation* (New York, 1914).

environment, and the family could be reformed in order to prevent juvenile delinquency.[12]

The second decade of the juvenile court saw the proliferation of a number of auxiliary institutions. Among these were detention homes, family relations courts, clinics, and reformatory institutions, as well as paid probation services staffed by trained probation officers. Also during this period, the way in which many juvenile courts were administered was the subject of considerable criticism. A survey undertaken by the Federal Children's Bureau concluded that there were indeed many deficiencies in administration and that these should be rectified.[13] Reformers were not just concerned with the development of further institutions to help the juvenile court in its work, or to ensure its efficient administration. Experience had taught many of them that juvenile delinquency needed to be prevented at its source.

Solutions to the problem of how to prevent delinquency were numerous and varied. They also highlighted the extent to which any child who did not conform to middle-class perceptions of "proper" childhood behavior could be regarded as a potential juvenile offender. Experts of various kinds pressed their own area of expertise as the solution to the creation of incipient offenders. Thus, educationalists argued that the answer lay in the schools, medical experts believed the problem to be a physical one, and the newly formed profession of psychology saw juvenile delinquency as the result of mental deficiency.[14] Although education was widely seen by juvenile court reformers and administrators as a means of preventing delinquency by teaching children middle-class values and codes of behavior, many also began to recognize that the child's environment was often at fault.[15]

Organizations such as the Juvenile Protective Association of Chicago

12. See, for instance, Flexner and Baldwin, *Juvenile Courts and Probation;* Sophonisba Breckinridge and Edith Abbott, *The Delinquent Child and the Home* (New York, 1912); Eliot, *The Juvenile Court and the Community.*

13. Evelina Belden, *Courts in the United States Hearing Children's Cases: U.S. Children's Bureau Publication 65* (Washington, D.C., 1920).

14. See, for instance, the essays in Jane Addams et al., *The Child, the Clinic and the Court* (New York, 1925); Isidor H. Coriat, "The Mental Condition of Juvenile Delinquents," *Juvenile Court Record* 8 (December 1907): 17–23; Thomas D. Eliot, "The Trend of the Juvenile Court," *Annals of the American Academy of Political and Social Science* 52 (1914): 149–58; Bernard Flexner, "The Juvenile Court as a Social Institution," *Survey* 23 (February 5, 1910): 607–38. See also, Mary E. Odem, *Delinquent Daughters: Protecting and Policing Adolescent Female Sexuality in the United States, 1885–1920* (Chapel Hill, 1995).

15. Ben B. Lindsey, "Four Questions and Juvenile Crime," *Charities* 20 (August 15, 1908): 590–92; Julian W. Mack, "Juvenile Courts as Part of the School System of the Country," *Proceedings of the National Conference of Charities and Correction* (1908), 369–83; Hannah Kent Schoff, *The Wayward Child: A Study of the Causes of Crime* (Indianapolis, 1915); Breck-

were actively involved in efforts to manipulate the urban environment in order to prevent juvenile delinquency. Other groups of reformers sought more
fundamental reforms that involved using the state to protect the welfare of
its children, not only to prevent juvenile delinquency but also to improve
the lives of children in general. Thus, the juvenile court became just one of
a number of other Progressive Era reforms concerned with the welfare of
the child. Campaigns to secure mothers' pensions, restrict child labor, and
to provide minimum medical services for mothers and their children,
though not always directly related to the prevention of juvenile delinquency,
were often advocated by those who had participated in the juvenile court
movement. The campaign for a Federal Children's Bureau, to collect information related to the welfare of children, was waged by many reformers
with experience in the juvenile court movement.[16] Significantly, like the juvenile court, many other child welfare reforms were initiated by women reformers, often acting from a gendered consciousness.

As this book has shown, gender consciousness played a central role in
shaping the legislation that created the juvenile courts. It also played a significant part in shaping the policy of these courts toward the children who
came before them, for boys and girls were often treated differently. The vast
majority of delinquent children brought before the juvenile courts were
boys. They were most often charged with such offenses as incorrigibility,
truancy, burglary, robbery, and disorderly behavior. Girls were arraigned
for similar offenses, but they also often found themselves charged with the
offense of "immorality"—a charge not levied against boys. Similarly, boys
were much more likely to be placed on probation than were girls, who were
most frequently placed in some kind of institution for female offenders.[17]

---

inridge and Abbott, *The Delinquent Child and the Home;* Russell Sage Foundation, *West Side
Stories: Boyhood and Lawlessness* (New York, 1914).

16. On these other campaigns, see Theda Skocpol, *Protecting Soldiers and Mothers: The
Political Origins of Social Policy in the United States* (Cambridge, Mass., 1992); Molly Ladd-
Taylor, *Mother-Work: Women, Child Welfare, and the State, 1890–1930* (Urbana, 1994); Seth
Koven and Sonya Michel, eds., *Mothers of a New World: Maternalist Politics and the Origins
of Welfare States* (New York, 1993); Linda Gordon, *Pitied But Not Entitled: Single Mothers
and the History of Welfare, 1890–1935* (Cambridge, Mass., 1994); Robyn Muncy, *Creating a
Female Dominion in American Reform, 1890–1935* (New York, 1991).

17. "Annual Report of the Chicago Juvenile Court," *Juvenile Court Record* 5 (January
1904): 5–6; "New York Parole Report," *Juvenile Court Record* 5 (January 1904): 6–7; Ben B.
Lindsey, "Additional Report on Methods and Results," in Samuel J. Barrows, ed., *Children's
Courts in the United States: Their Origin, Development and Results* (Washington, D.C.,
1904), 125–32. See also Steven Schlossman and Stephanie Wallach, "The Crime of Precocious
Sexuality: Female Juvenile Delinquency in the Progressive Era," *Harvard Educational Review*
48 (February 1978): 65–94; Odem, *Delinquent Daughters.*

This difference in the charges and treatment of boys and girls who came before the juvenile courts can be explained by the prevalence of socially constructed ideals of the proper behavior of boys and girls. Judge Lindsey's belief that boys got into trouble because of a weakness in character was not widely held among juvenile court judges; instead, boys' offenses were often assumed to spring from a mere excess of energy, or a sense of adventure, combined with a failure in their upbringing.[18] Girls, on the other hand, were expected to behave in a ladylike manner and to remain virtuous. The charge of immorality was a euphemism for what Steven Schlossman and Stephanie Wallach have called "the crime of precocious sexuality." At a time when girls were expected to remain chaste until they married, those who did not do so were regarded as deviant and probably mentally deficient.[19] It was not only Lindsey who had an ambivalent attitude toward such girls. Many other male juvenile court judges found it much easier to delegate such cases to a female assistant on the grounds of delicacy. Since these girls were regarded as morally and mentally deficient and likely to contaminate those with whom they came into contact, custodial sentences were considered the best way to deal with them.[20] Although middle-class values regarding female sexuality and proper female behavior permeated the sentencing policy of the juvenile courts, there is considerable evidence to suggest that working-class and immigrant parents also commonly brought their daughters before the juvenile court for incorrigibility or immorality in order to try to control their behavior.[21]

Most frequently, however, it was middle-class officials—social workers, judges, and probation officers—who brought working-class and immigrant

18. See, for instance, Julian W. Mack, "The Juvenile Court, the Judge and the Probation Officer," *Proceedings of the National Conference of Charities and Correction* (1906), 131; Myron E. Adams, "The Causes of Juvenile Crime," *Outlook* 83 (August 4, 1906): 796–801; Jane Addams, *The Spirit of Youth and the City Streets* (Urbana, 1972; first published, 1909).

19. Schlossman and Wallach, "The Crime of Precocious Sexuality," 65–94; Ruth S. True, *The Neglected Girl* (New York, 1914); Olga Bridgeman, "Delinquency and Mental Deficiency," *Survey* 32 (June 13, 1914): 302. On adult women, see Estelle B. Freedman, *Their Sisters' Keepers: Women's Prison Reform in America, 1830–1930* (Ann Arbor, 1981).

20. Schlossman and Wallach, "The Crime of Precocious Sexuality," 65–94; Bridgeman, "Delinquency and Mental Deficiency," 302; Mary M. Dewson, "Probation and the Institutional Care of Girls," in Sophonisba Breckinridge, ed., *The Child in the City: A Series of Papers Presented at the Conferences Held During the Chicago Child Welfare Exhibit* (Chicago, 1912), 355–70.

21. Mary Odem, "Single Mothers, Delinquent Daughters, and the Juvenile Court in Early Twentieth-Century Los Angeles," *Journal of Social History* 25 (Fall 1991): 27–43; Kathy Peiss, *Cheap Amusements: Working Women and Leisure in Turn-of-the-Century New York* (Philadelphia, 1986).

children before the juvenile courts. This question of how deeply middle-class values permeated the creation and policy of the juvenile courts has interested a number of historians.[22] This book has suggested that the juvenile court ideal grew out of middle-class perceptions about the proper behavior of children. These perceptions in turn influenced reformers to define as delinquent certain behavior—on the part of working-class and immigrant children living in the slums of America's cities—that both in the countryside and in the immigrants' homelands would have been perfectly acceptable. To characterize the juvenile courts as instruments of class or social control is, however, too simplistic and assumes that juvenile courts were used only by the middle classes to impose their own values on working-class and immigrant children. The evidence suggests that the reality was more complex, for some parents in the slums used the juvenile courts as a means to assert parental control over difficult children. Moreover, Judge Lindsey frequently narrated stories of children who would "come alone" to his court when they had problems.[23] Although such encounters could be fraught with danger, clearly not all working-class parents and their children regarded the juvenile court and probation officers as an alien presence in their neighborhoods.[24] Yet many middle-class reformers saw the juvenile courts, and more particularly probation, as a means by which working-class and immigrant children and their parents could be taught proper, middle-class methods of child rearing. Although reformers generally saw this as a humanitarian act, underlying many of their efforts was the fear that if something were not done about the unruly behavior of slum children, social order might be undermined.

The forces of industrialization, urbanization, and mass immigration in the late nineteenth- and early twentieth-centuries created a rapidly changing world and prompted a good deal of anxiety among the middle classes. Many of the social reforms in the United States during this period may be seen as part of a wider process by which the middle classes sought to estab-

22. The clearest example of this is Anthony M. Platt, *The Child Savers: The Invention of Delinquency* (Chicago, 1969).

23. Case Studies (Restricted), supplement 1, folder 7, Juvenile Protective Association Papers, Special Collections, University of Illinois at Chicago; Lindsey and Borough, *The Dangerous Life*, 219–25; Lindsey and Evans, *The Revolt of Modern Youth*; Odem, "Single Mothers and Delinquent Daughters," 27–43. Linda Gordon suggests other ways clients shaped the policy of a welfare agency in *Heroes of Their Own Lives: The Politics and History of Family Violence* (London, 1989; first published, 1988).

24. T. J. Jackson Lears, "The Concept of Cultural Hegemony: Problems and Possibilities," *American Historical Review* 90 (1985): 567–93; Gordon, *Heroes of Their Own Lives*.

lish their cultural hegemony. As they had done earlier in the nineteenth century, middle-class women reformers became involved in this process through their own organizations, and by the end of the 1800s, they had established a tradition of constructing ideological justifications to explain their involvement in activities beyond the confines of their homes. As this book has shown, a new discourse began to emerge in the last years of the nineteenth century that idealized women's role as "educated" or "scientific" mothers, well-versed in new ideas about child rearing. It was this discourse of "maternalism" that both prompted and was used to justify women's involvement in campaigns for child welfare reform.

The establishment of juvenile courts is, in many senses, illustrative of a number of other maternal and child welfare reforms during the Progressive Era. However, it does differ in one important respect in that it was not directly concerned with the family wage system, as were so many other Progressive Era social welfare reforms. It focused specifically on the child and was heavily influenced by new ideas about the nature of childhood and new theories of child rearing that became prevalent among the middle classes during the late nineteenth century, thus shaping the maternalist discourse. Nonetheless, like many other Progressive Era child welfare initiatives, its central concern was the role of women as mothers. This focus provided both the justification for women to become involved as reformers and the rationale behind the reform itself. Like many other social welfare proposals of this period, culturally determined female values—that is, maternalism—shaped the juvenile court movement.

Although most female reformers espoused a maternalist discourse, they did not all share the same concerns and perspectives. The members of some groups, such as the Chicago Woman's Club and the National Congress of Mothers, were traditional maternalists, for most were mothers clearly committed to the ideals of motherhood and domesticity that late nineteenth-century society mandated for middle-class women. At the same time, they believed their ideals laid a responsibility on them to extend these principles beyond their own homes by working in the public sphere of reform to improve the lot of society's dependents—especially women and children.

To these traditional maternalists, the cause of children who got into trouble with the law was a natural source of concern, and their interference on behalf of these children could be easily justified using the discourse of maternalism. Other groups of women reformers, such as those connected with Hull House, were professional maternalists and utilized the discourse of maternalism in a different way. Many had a college education and a background in the social sciences that, together with their experience of living and working in slum neighborhoods, influenced their pursuit of reform. Their identification as women and the social expectation that they would be mothers were usually secondary to these other factors in prompting their social activism. Nonetheless, the discourse of maternalism proved useful to them in pursuing children's reforms.

These different uses of the maternalist discourse had a distinct effect on the priorities of the women reformers in their pursuit of reform. Ultimately, though, women reformers were much more willing to use the state to create new institutions to deal with the problem of dependent and delinquent children than were their male counterparts. Although male reformers were involved in the juvenile court movement, it was most often as supporters of the women reformers' initiatives rather than as initiators of reform themselves, and so male reformers often adopted the discourse of maternalism. Judge Lindsey, who operated within the boundaries of an older masculine tradition of reform, was far from typical among juvenile court reformers, yet he himself acknowledged that the support of sympathetic women was essential to the successful operation of his juvenile court. Nevertheless, his construction of masculinity dictated a different perspective on the treatment of juvenile delinquents—one not in tune with new ideas about child rearing or the nature of childhood and that differed markedly from that of the women reformers.

As this book has shown, gender consciousness played a central role in shaping legislation that dealt with the problem of dependent and delinquent children in the United States. Additionally, reformers utilizing a gendered discourse disseminated the juvenile court idea and tried to ensure that their values remained to the fore in the operation of the juvenile courts and the probation system. As the juvenile courts developed, however, the discourse of professionalism and expertise gradually came to dominate. Nonetheless, women reformers, though not always very visible, continued to be an important element both in the operation of the juvenile courts and in further reform efforts aimed at preventing juvenile delinquency before it occurred. They did so as professionals and experts—and as maternalist reformers. Their involvement in the juvenile court movement made many of these women reformers realize the need for further welfare reforms to help poor families adjust to the problems of city life. The women reformers hoped thereby to prevent the breakdown of traditional family life and thus protect the existing social order.

The history of the juvenile court movement raises some important issues for historians of women's social welfare reform, for the kind of female values evident in the juvenile court movement may be found in other social welfare reforms of the Progressive Era. The provision of mothers' pensions and the foundation of the Federal Children's Bureau may also be explained in terms of women reformers' initiatives to preserve the traditional American family and ensure that children were properly nurtured and protected. The juvenile courts were one of the earliest Progressive Era social welfare reforms, and the willingness of women juvenile court reformers to use the state to achieve their aims foreshadowed later efforts by women reformers to establish the rudiments of a welfare state in the United States. The history of the juvenile court movement also demonstrates that gender consciousness was an important element in shaping social welfare legislation during this period and explains why measures aiding women and children were some of the earliest social welfare policies to be implemented in the United States.

Much of the current scholarship on the origins of the welfare state in the United States has concentrated on the issue of gender and its role in shaping welfare legislation. Some of this scholarship has been concerned only with writing women back into the history of the welfare state, both as clients and as reformers. The most recent work, however, has suggested that women played a pivotal role in this process, often taking the initiative in reform. Also beginning to emerge is the fact that men and women had considerably different visions of welfare and that this influenced their perceptions of the problems they faced and their solutions to these problems.[25] This book has discussed the essential role gender consciousness played in shaping social welfare reform. But the discussion has also demonstrated that historians of gender and welfare need to look beyond the different welfare visions of men and women and examine the differences among middle-class women reformers. For there were distinct versions of maternalism, and this had an effect on the women reformers involved, influencing their priorities in reform.

25. A review of this literature appears in Elizabeth J. Clapp, "Welfare and the Role of Women: The Juvenile Court Movement," *Journal of American Studies* 28 (December 1994): 359–83.

Index